City of Shadows

Alongside debates over rising inequalities, the stubborn persistence of urban poverty, globally, has emerged as a major academic and policy concern, typically framed by the paradigms of basic services and welfare. In the backdrop of Bangalore's evolution into India's Silicon Valley, *City of Shadows* presents research spanning old, inner-city slums, new migrant settlements in urban peripheries, slum development projects, and garment export and construction workers. This research highlights that, inter-generationally, the urban poor remain tied to traditional, low-income occupations, or get incorporated into new urban growth channels, such as export industries and low-end services, under highly unfavourable terms and conditions. Debates on the developmental state, democracy and the urban poor's political agency are used to problematise the complex relationship of informal work to contemporary theories of class. Using the concepts of the old poor and the new poor to explore channels of urban inclusion and exclusion, *City of Shadows* demonstrates that the poor's vulnerabilities vary profoundly under different regimes of informal economies actively constructed by both the state and the market.

Supriya RoyChowdhury is currently Visiting Professor with the Urban and Mobility Studies Program at the National Institute of Advanced Studies, Bengaluru. She was earlier Professor of Political Science at the Institute for Social and Economic Change, Bengaluru.

City of Shadows

Slums and Informal Work in Bangalore

Supriya RoyChowdhury

CAMBRIDGE
UNIVERSITY PRESS

CAMBRIDGE
UNIVERSITY PRESS

University Printing House, Cambridge CB2 8BS, United Kingdom

One Liberty Plaza, 20th Floor, New York, NY 10006, USA

477 Williamstown Road, Port Melbourne, VIC 3207, Australia

314–321, 3rd Floor, Plot No.3, Splendor Forum, Jasola District Centre, New Delhi – 110025, India

103 Penang Road, #05–06/07, Visioncrest Commercial, Singapore 238467

Cambridge University Press is part of the University of Cambridge.

It furthers the University's mission by disseminating knowledge in the pursuit of education, learning and research at the highest international levels of excellence.

www.cambridge.org
Information on this title: www.cambridge.org/9781108839365

© Supriya RoyChowdhury 2021

First published 2021
Reprint 2023

Printed in India by Avantika Printers Pvt. Ltd.

A catalogue record for this publication is available from the British Library

Library of Congress Cataloging-in-Publication Data

Names: Roychowdhury, Supriya, author.
Title: City of shadows : slums and informal work in Bangalore / Supriya RoyChowdhury.
Description: Cambridge, United Kingdom ; New York, NY: Cambridge University Press, 2021. | Includes bibliographical references and index.
Identifiers: LCCN 2021017217 (print) | LCCN 2021017218 (ebook) | ISBN 9781108839365 (hardback) | ISBN 9781108989930 (ebook)
Subjects: LCSH: Urban poor--India--Bangalore. | Slums--India--Bangalore. | Informal sector (Economics)--India--Bangalore. | Bangalore (India)--Social condtions--21st century. | Bangalore (India) | Economic conditions--21st century. | BISAC: POLITICAL SCIENCE / Political Economy | POLITICAL SCIENCE / Political Economy
Classification: LCC HV4140.B36 R69 2021 (print) | LCC HV4140.B36 (ebook) | DDC 362.509173/2095487--dc23
LC record available at https://lccn.loc.gov/2021017217
LC ebook record available at https://lccn.loc.gov/2021017218

ISBN 978-1-108-83936-5 Hardback

Contents

Tables

Acknowledgements

This book is based on the findings of research projects that were carried out at the Institute for Social and Economic Change (ISEC), Bangalore, over several years. A grant from the 'Globalization and the Indian State' project, led by Neera Chandok and Pratap Bhanu Mehta, had enabled me to make the first survey of 16 slums in Bangalore. Between 2009 and 2013, the Planning Department of the Government of Karnataka supported a research project on 'Migration, Informal Work and Welfare: A Policy Perspective on Karnataka's Cities'. This project made it possible for me to do a study of peripheral as well as inner-city slums in Bangalore. Finally, a research grant from the Indian Council of Social Sciences on a project entitled 'India's Changing City Scapes: Work, Migration and Livelihoods' during 2017–19, which was collaboratively undertaken by ISEC and the National Institute of Advanced Studies (NIAS), Bangalore, enabled me to revisit the slums, update the information and hold a fresh set of qualitative discussions. Research on the ready-made garment industry in Bangalore has been supported through seed money grants by ISEC. A small grant by the Centre for Women's Development Studies, New Delhi, during 2017–18 in collaboration with the International Labour Organization's 'Work in Freedom Project' made it possible to update the information on this sector and hold a set of interviews with migrant women workers. I am grateful to each of these agencies for supporting my research.

The research in various phases was conducted with the help of several city non-governmental organisations and trade unions. I would like to thank Mr Lakshapati of APSA, M. Nagraj of Pragati Charitable Trust, Ms Kathyayini Chamraj of CIVIC, Mr Pakri Sami of the National Centre for Labour, Mr Jayram and Pratibha of the Garments and Textile Workers Union (GATWU) and Mohan Mani of the New Trade Union Initiative for their help in carrying out the field research as well as for sharing their valuable insights. A special word of thanks to Mr Gopinath of Civil Initiatives for Development, as over the years we became fellow travellers in the journey to understand women's work in global supply chains. Several corporators, legislators and bureaucrats gave generously of their time, and I am grateful to them all. There are no appropriate words to thank the many men and women in low-income and under-serviced neighborhoods across the city and in construction work sites who shared their time and provided a window to a universe hitherto unknown to me.

At ISEC, my colleagues Professor K. S. James, who is currently Director of the International Institute for Population Sciences (IIPS), Mumbai, B. P. Vani and Dr N. Sivanna were my collaborators in the 'Migration' project, and I would like to thank them as well as the current Director, Professor S. Madheswaran, Professor Krishnaraj and Professor G. Karanth for their friendship and collegiality through the many years. I am grateful to former Director of ISEC, Professor R. S. Deshpande, who provided a great deal of support to the 'Migration' project and remained interested in my work. ISEC's large and awe-inspiring library is one of the best places in Bangalore to spend time in, and I am grateful to the library staff, particularly to the current Librarian, Dr B. B. Chand, for his ready help in providing me with some of the material used in this book, especially during the dark days of the Covid-19-related lockdown. Thanks also to the Research Associates who worked in my projects at different times, particularly Archana Raj, Dr K. C. Smitha, Anitha and, most recently, Visakha Warrier and Pragati Tiwari. I am grateful to my former student Dr Neil Tannon, who helped with the analysis of the secondary data on Bangalore. Some of the chapters in this book have been presented in seminars and conferences, at the South Asia Centre, Oxford University; the Centre for Political Studies, Jawaharlal Nehru University, New Delhi; NIAS, Bangalore; the Indira Gandhi Institute of Development Research (IGIDR), Mumbai and the Centre for Women's Development Studies, New Delhi. I am grateful to my hosts on these occasions, where I had received very useful comments and suggestions.

Aparna Sundar, Ramachandra Guha and Smriti Srinivas never lost faith in this book, even though it took so long that they lost track of what it was about. Many thanks to them. Carol Upadhya of NIAS has been a valued collaborator on recent projects. I am grateful to Professor Barbara Harriss-White of Oxford University for her interest in my work. I would like to thank Dwaipayan Bhattacharjee of JNU, Michael Goldman of the University of Minnesota, A. R. Vasavi, formerly of NIAS, and Chandan Gowda of Azim Premji University for their interest in my research, as also for many years of friendship and support. A special word of thanks to Atul Kohli of Princeton University for remaining a very valued mentor and friend over the past many years.

A chance meeting at the annual Labour Conference in Mumbai in 2018 with Anwesha Rana of Cambridge University Press, New Delhi, led me to restart thinking about this book. I am very grateful to Anwesha for her interest in my work and for enabling the journey of the manuscript through different phases. Two anonymous referees for Cambridge University Press provided very constructive criticism which helped strengthen the theoretical frame of the work. I am particularly grateful to Aniruddha De of the Cambridge University Press for his meticulous and excellent editing of the manuscript.

My daughter, Lavanya, maintained a strict vigil; her gloomily voiced question from across the seas every other day, 'So are you finishing it or not?' kept me going. This book is for her, as she now embarks on her own journey as a researcher in the social sciences.

Supriya RoyChowdhury

1

Introduction

The debate on urban theories

In the late 20th and early 21st centuries, socio-economic exclusions, deeply encrusted in cities of both the Global North and the South, not only contradict earlier understandings of the urban as homogeneous and uniform, but also pose serious challenges to the modernisation theory – entrapped understanding of the urban as a process and promise of development which will engulf all. Emerging debates are linked by two fundamental dilemmas: First, how does the specificity of the regional/local and the diverse trajectories thereof call for a distinct theory of the city in the Global South? Second, what could be an appropriate conceptual framework for imagining urban marginalities?

The argument for specificity, in post-colonial theorisations of cities of the Global South, rests largely on the deep and stubborn pockets of poverty and social marginalisation in which many disadvantaged urban communities continue to live. Moving away from overarching theories of Southern exclusion, drawn from dependency and world-systems theories, recent scholarship on cities in the Global South has understood urban exclusion primarily in terms of space, broadly defined.[1] Scholars have critiqued typical policy frameworks which see slums in Third World cities as only material spaces to be measured and reconstructed. Instead, and drawing closely on David Harvey's (2009 [1973]) conceptual distinction of space as material and relative,[2] they have pointed to the need to see urban marginality, slums in particular, in terms of the context in which they evolved as spaces for living and livelihood (a process which is negotiated and incremental), their porous and fluid character (in contrast to the exclusivity of the residential space of upper-class urban citizens) (Bhan 2019), and their often seemingly contradictory opposition to state-sponsored housing projects. These features – more or less ubiquitous in cities of the Global South – of urban exclusion have led scholars to new ways of thinking about urbanisation, rooted in the Southern context. Theresa Caldeira's (2017) conception of peripheral urbanisation sees the space in which the urban poor live as one marked by a particular kind of temporality and agency, with a set of relations to law and property that are very different from those that characterise the formal domain, which generate a distinct kind of politics and therefore necessarily lead to highly unequal and diverse cities. This genre of thinking has seen spatial exclusion in terms of communities of chronically poor people who are institutionally excluded from the government support structures that are necessary for their well-being (Pernell and Pietrrse 2010). What frames this kind of analyses is a broad understanding of post-colonial states, where recently formed governance structures are inadequately equipped to bring civic infrastructure and human resources to the urban marginalised. Thus, space as the context of urban exclusion is an understanding of history and institutions as they shape the way in which the urban poor have lived and worked, in contrast to a typically ahistorical and one-size-fits-all policy intrusions into their lives through housing or other similar schemes.

Increasingly, scholars writing in this genre have converged on the idea that cities of the Global South must generate not only a new, Southern paradigm of the urban and of urbanisation, but also a new epistemology, where knowledge and theory must begin and be located in the specific context of the Global South. This critique itself has been critiqued as particularistic and essentialist in terms of its understanding of the Global South as unique and different. Without going into the details of these arguments (Scott and Storper 2015; Roy 2016), one might point out, briefly, that there is a certain irony to this debate: the argument for a theory of the urban, anchored in the Global South, is opposed in fact to essentialising and othering (for example, to seeing the Third World city as the less developed counterpart of the First World city). And it is in fact linked to larger questions, for example, of modernity and democracy. The Southern city is increasingly seen as a centre point of modernity – and in fact of multiple modernities, that are not necessarily only western – and democratic agency and resistance as shaped by and shaping the post-colonial city, in ways that challenge the understandings of modernity and democracy from the western perspective. What frames these understandings, at the broadest level, are epistemological questions critiquing the process of production of knowledge in the social sciences which remain tied to western theorisations. Thus, the argument that 'it is necessary to view all cities from this particular place on the map' (Roy 2016) may appear to be essentialising the Southern city, but in fact could be read as a plea for reversing the location from where we do urban studies.

An important theme in this context has been the broader question: would the issue of specificity not lead us then to abandon the pursuit of more general urban theories and succumb instead to what has been termed 'provincial' theories (Scott and Storper 2015)? At the same time, there is very little clarity on what could be the basis of a comparative framework for a general urban theory that would make sense empirically and conceptually. Cities of the western world also have poverty, ghettoisation, rising informality and persistent exclusion. Urban inequities are reflected in extremes of wealth and marginalities (Nutalle and Mbembe 2005; Sheppard, Leitner, and Maringanti 2013).[3] How do we confront the question of overarching theories that could bind the urban poor of vastly different contexts of the Global North and South? The concept of the unity of the worker, defined as the industrial proletariat, cutting across nations, is now all but obsolete. In cities across the world, the urban poor may be employed in occupations that look similar: petty shop owners, street sellers, sweatshop workers, illegal immigrants working as domestic helpers, and so on. These spaces of economic marginality are marked by diverse social identities, race, ethnicity, gender, community, caste, and so on, making the task of factoring these into a unifying theoretical framework vastly challenging.

And it is in this sense that the second dilemma of urban studies is possibly posed – the question of informality. While informality is universal to contemporary capitalism, competing interpretations of informality – from flexible efficiency to dependency-inspired understandings as structured exclusion – sharpen the question: can informality be the overarching conceptual framework that broadly defines the urban in our times? Does informality indeed provide the lens through which we can view urban inequalities and marginalisation across the world? And if so, what is the theoretical lens through which we should view informality?

As is well known, economic downturns have periodically affected western economies, cutting down jobs and social benefits. Globalisation's more lasting impact in terms of creation of work and income insecurities and inequalities in developed economies has been widely chronicled. One thinks of Saskia Sassen's analysis of global cities – New York, London and Tokyo – which are densely networked nodal structures representing the transformation of economic dynamics from industrial to finance capital, powered by a rapidly developing information technology (IT) that binds global financial networks together. Finance capital is global, hyper-mobile and invisible. Sassen's contribution was to show that while the hyper-mobility of capital has been highlighted in the literature, it is important to understand that the work process still occurs in the space of the city, and which, according to her, brings with it an emphasis on economic and spatial polarisation because of the disproportionate concentration of very high and very low income jobs in these major global city sectors. 'Emphasizing place, infrastructure, and non-expert jobs matters precisely because so much of the focus has been on the neutralisation of geography and place made possible by the new technologies' (Sassen 2005). Sassen thus lays out also the possibility of a new politics of resistance that might emerge from these cities, given the inequalities inherent in the technology- and finance-driven economic model.

A more specific view from the ground on the same theme was provided by Guy Standing's concept of the precariat. With the consolidation of finance capital, whereby the nature of capital is transformed from productive to rentier capital, its other, the precariat replaces the declining proletariat. For the precariat, a life of unstable labour is marked by temporary, flexible, contractual work, characteristic of financial and IT services, but also increasingly found in other professions, such as teaching, law and administration (Standing 2016, 2018).

Cities of the Global South, too, are increasingly globally connected, technology-driven, powered by the financial and information services sectors and manned by highly skilled and high income technical personnel, but resting on a non-formal, unregulated, voiceless and unskilled or partially skilled workforce which constitutes the base or the support system of the new economy. In Global South cities, an informal professional class is increasingly seen in domains such as teachers in schools as well as higher education institutions, in lower rungs of administration, both in government and non-governmental organisations. Insecure work, the relentless threat of downsizing and dismissals, individually negotiated rather than norm-based compensation packages, and contractualisation translate into precariousness in middle and lower levels of employment in private and state sectors across developed and developing countries. In this sense, informality in the age of globalisation possibly provides a broad frame within which urban vulnerabilities could be seen across the Global North and the South. Despite these emerging commonalities, to date, however, there are no substantive theories that link the impact of globalisation on categories of marginalised citizens in advanced industrialised and low-income countries.

In the Global North, precarity, although increasingly a cause of concern, is cushioned to some extent by universal school education, still existing robust welfare systems in western Europe, a living minimum wage and regulated working conditions. These features are all but absent in cities of developing or so-called low-income countries. What further makes the question of comparison almost impossibly tricky is the fact that in cities of the Global South, vulnerable communities are not only those who are attached to the new economy, albeit on unfavourable conditions (workers in call centres, or in emerging lower rungs of services, or migrant labour in global supply chains), but also the much larger numbers who remain confined to traditional unskilled work (construction, head-load bearing, road cleaning, domestic work, and so on). These urban livelihoods, discussed in detail in the chapters that follow, highlight not only irregular and unprotected incomes, but also highly inadequate access to civic infrastructure, health and education. Informality, then, while a common frame in the broadest possible sense, nevertheless reproduces itself in very different ways in different parts of the world.

An important strand of scholarship has looked at the complex ways in which the urban space is defined by property as capital.[4] In the context of cities of the Global North, redevelopment/gentrification projects have redefined land value and reshaped urban space. Broadly the same processes may be at work in developing country cities, but with vastly different features. In Indian cities, as both state and the private sector, the latter frequently involving large multinational companies (MNCs), increasingly engage in the business of land appropriation, not only are agricultural lives and livelihoods deeply affected, but the merging of the semi-rural and the peri-urban produce spaces which defy understanding in terms of received theories of the urban and urbanisation. The same processes can be seen when urban poor communities, with deeply divided interests in urban land, respond in conflicting ways to housing projects for the urban poor, in which governments are also increasingly attempting to involve large private builders. The political economy of urban real estate in developing countries like India must be understood primarily in the context of city and regional politics, the character of the local land mafia, the complex networks that bind local politicians to real estate developers, urban poor communities split along linguistic and ethnic divides, and their diverse and often conflicting interests in urban land.

Drawing this section to a close, one could say that there are features of the urban in cities of the North and of the South which point towards the possibility of broad theorisations. However, until substantive justifications of comparison and robust methods of doing comparisons can be found, the idea of a generalised urban theory must remain an academic one, while we stay with the broadly shared view that the specificities of urban development in the Global South merit an altogether different paradigm of studying cities that received theories, drawn from the western experience – which see the urban as uniform and urbanisation as unilinear – do not offer.

What the book is about

Urban poverty is of increasing concern in policy and scholarly circles in India. While there was a recorded decline in percentage terms of urban households in the below poverty line (BPL) category (from 31.8 per cent in 1993–94 to 25.7 per cent in 2004–05 to 13.7 per cent in 2011–12), absolute numbers of the urban poor rose by 4.4 million persons between 1993–94 and 2004–05, and in 2011–12, the absolute number of the poor in Indian cities was 76 million persons (GOI 2018). As the gains of economic growth post liberalisation can be seen more prominently in cities, the intransigence of urban poverty has raised obvious questions about the appropriateness or otherwise of the growth model being pursued and its impact on disadvantaged urban communities. Larger debates on urbanisation of poverty have anchored discussions in India on whether urban poverty is a carry-over of rural poverty, the impact of migration on poverty, and to what extent have economic policies and democratic politics provided bridges between hitherto marginalised slum communities, on the one hand, and the technology- and services-led dynamic growth channels of modern cities, on the other. These themes are covered in Chapters 2 and 3 of this book.

Bangalore (also known as Bengaluru), the capital city of Karnataka in southern India, provides an appropriate entry point into these debates. As India's Silicon Valley, the core of the city's economic dynamism is the export of IT and IT enable services (ITES), surrounded by multinational banking, finance, venture capital, start-ups, real estate and the concomitant appearance of luxury concepts in services. An expanding middle class has gained from, as well as contributed to, these channels of economic dynamism. Spill-over effects have resulted in some expansion of opportunities of employment and earnings, particularly in the lower rungs of services, for hitherto disadvantaged groups, but there is also a growing presence of an urban underclass, excluded from the city's growth channels. The anchoring question that runs through the chapters is: what happens to the poor in a city that is rapidly growing rich? The present work looks at channels of both exclusion and inclusion. The field research that supports this work was conducted over several years, spanning the study of slums in inner city neighbourhoods, peripheral slums, garment workers' settlements and new housing projects for slum rehabilitation.

Conceptual/theoretical framework

Theorisations on urban space, briefly discussed earlier, have greatly taken forward our understanding of urban marginality, particularly where caste and community as social markers of identity are closely and historically identified with spatial exclusions. Recent work on Bangalore has particularly emphasised the issue of urban land speculation and land as a means of dispossession of those working and living in rural peripheries (Goldman 2011). Other recent work on Bangalore has underlined the transformation of urban space, as a transnational capitalist class has come into its own via the IT revolution in India's post-liberalisation phase, even as older forms of inequalities and accumulation persist (Upadhya 2004, 2016). In each of these works, urban land has been seen as a space which has reconfigured class-based inequities. The concept of space deeply informs understandings of urban marginality in Bangalore. The Janaagraha-Brown Citizenship Index report (2014), based on a survey of more than 4,000 respondents across Bangalore city, defines citizenship in terms of access to basic amenities. The study, acknowledging that access to basic amenities is unevenly distributed across different parts of the city, and class drives this effect, nevertheless underlined that the space occupied by people in the city as citizens emerges as a universal category of entitlement. 'Citizenship significantly abates class in Bengaluru' (Janaagraha-Brown Citizenship Index 2014). This could be interpreted as: while space-as-class divides entitlements, space-as-citizenship offers an umbrella-like universalising effect.

Finally, the narratives around urban deprivation are caught in competing perspectives on land: claims of slum residents to right to property on slum land; governments regularly conduct evictions and razing down exercises, presenting slum residents as illegal encroachers; while large corporations/ real estate developers make a stake for the same land for the purpose of construction of housing, malls, hospitals. On the other hand, arguments for the urban poor's right to slum land, most often made in the context of housing, becomes more complex when slum land is seen also as a means of livelihood. Benjamin (Benjamin and Bhubaneswari 2006, 2011), studying local markets in Bangalore's Azadnagar, KR Market and Yashwantpur slum areas, raises the point that far from being the static and marginalised survival strategy with which the informal sector is associated in the popular mind, these markets represent dense networks of wholesale and retail trade, and are marked by a complex web of finance, with capital flowing between real estate, trade, manufacturing, and so on. According to Benjamin, these localised markets provide vast employment multiplier effects as well as produce numerous and relatively easy entry points for poor groups in the form of openings as head-load bearers, manual workers and street hawkers. Although governments and non-governmental organizations (NGOs) are attracted by housing schemes, housing interventions inevitably disrupt these local markets, which need to be encouraged because of their employment generation as well as their dynamic nature.

As is known, slum land serves the poor both as a space for living and frequently also as a space for setting up small enterprises, in both manufacturing and trade. Benjamin's plea for preservation of land for its existing purposes has a practical as well as a normative component, and strongly echoes the typical slum dwellers' desperate efforts to cling to their land, whatever its size, and however precarious their claim to it might be. Our research on inner city slums in south central Bangalore revealed that slum residents have differential interests in land. Those who have relatively larger and/or more than one plot, have built vertically, are otherwise economically resourceful or are politically networked, versus those who have little or nothing. The former groups define slum resistance to new housing projects and layouts (which may threaten not only their livelihoods, but also, importantly, their rentier interests in the land which they occupy) while the latter group may aspire for new layouts and buildings but may not be vocal articulators of such aspirations (discussed further in Chapter 7). There is thus no uniformity of interests of slum residents in slum land.

In any case, looking beyond these, the defence of slum-based local economies may point to a situation where the urban poor's economic opportunities would remain permanently tied to low levels of economic activities, predicated on low investments and subsistence incomes. Benjamin's own examples (Benjamin and Bhubaneswari 2006, 2011) are of head-load bearers, manual workers and street hawkers, who may live in slums and use these spaces as well as neighbouring low-end local markets for their economic activities. It should be remembered that, representing the lowest end of the urban informal workforce, these groups are marginalised, socially and spatially, and earn low and precarious incomes, with limited access to social security, education and health. The domain of self-employment has been seen by some as a possible panacea for the urban poor, and by others as a domain of permanent structural exclusion. Without going into the details of these debates, it is perhaps possible to point out that Benjamin's defence of local slum-based livelihoods may provide very little scope to imagine the typical slum dweller's exit and mobility from the limiting framework of petty self-employment and low-wage work.

While deeply enriched by the insights emerging from this genre of literature, the present work, however, locates urban marginality primarily in terms of work and incomes of the urban poor, and traces the structure of work to the broader political economy that determines the character of industrial development, employment and incomes of the urban underclass. The centrality of wage, specifically, and income, more broadly, which the book uses as the primary anchor for looking at the lives and livelihoods of the urban underclass, connects this research to a broadly Marxist framework of analysis. Dependency theories have long shaped our understanding of post-colonial development, while at the same time the limitations of dependency have increasingly come to prevail on our understanding of the dynamics of development in the Global South. The original theorisations of the North and South as core and periphery have been challenged with the rise of new economic powers in Asia and Latin America; overall, the effort within the structuralist imagination of dependency has been to emphasise the space of autonomy of dependent states and the distinctiveness of national politics; thus, specific and contextualised class configurations, coalitions and conflicts may lead to different policies and constraints, generating varying developmental trajectories. Structuralist theory thus assumes that outcomes are not just inscribed by existing economic structures; there is a space for political strategies and interactions to make a difference.[5]

The discussions about whether the state is autonomous or determined by capital (taken up in more detail in Chapter 2) are interesting only up to a point, and the pendulum could swing continuously, as in the real world one could find illustrations of both, in varying degrees and within the same context. Overarching ideas of macro determinations – as given in the world-systems theory, an important variant of dependency, that the global system shapes the conditions of each country's development at the national level – remain useful reminders of the broad limits of development in the Global South. But, as is well known, in pitching class conflict at the global level, dependency theory provides no conceptual tools with which to imagine the nitty-gritty of class relations underpinning the interrelated process of domestic and global accumulation at the national level. More germane to the present work is the fact that neither classical Marxist theory nor dependency theory provides us with tools to examine conflicts that involve large numbers of the urban working class who are not proletariats in the Marxist sense. The central questions then are: who are the urban poor, and what is the locus of urban power which defines and maintains the structure of urban economic inequalities in cities of the global south? To these questions, there are no easy answers to be drawn from existing theoretical frameworks.

Given these limitations of existing theoretical frameworks, in this book I use an eclectic combination of concepts drawn from each of these. Bangalore's economy, tightly networked into the global IT/financial sectors, approaching that of other global cities, may represent a shift from production to finance/ services as the locus of capital's power. As technology and finance capital spin wealth but no jobs, large numbers of jobless or small-time self-employed may be seen to be at the sharp edge of the contradictions of globalised capitalism. However, in practical terms, the contestation between global capital and petty producers/traders remain in the abstract. Kalyan Sanyal, in his acclaimed book (2007), saw this class as the outside of capital, and petty self-employment as the sponge that absorbs all who cannot be absorbed within the circuit of capital and cannot even be considered the reserve army of capital, as they are the permanent outcasts of modern industrial capitalism, but which help sustain the latter by providing a subsistence base to all who remain outside. While this is a powerful conceptualisation of urban exclusion, in practical terms it is difficult to imagine the petty self-employed workforce in any kind of relational context, particularly in terms of conflicts related to economic interests, although of course economic hardships may get articulated through political mobilisations of their diverse social identities.

Indeed, the reality on the ground in Third World cities is that a large supply of unskilled (often migrant) labour is available, and there is in fact an increasing significance of wage work in informalised, contractual or casual work, both in manufacturing and in services, and in the public as well as private sectors. Thus, while the monistic theory of the capital–labour conflict needs to be modified in the context of the multiple forms and domains of wage labour, the present work makes an argument for reiterating the centrality of wage as it defines urban vulnerabilities. Self-employed petty producers/ service providers are in fact inextricably linked to the world of informal wage and work, and may move between the two domains. This conceptual framework, then, building on informalised wage as the primary domain of urban vulnerabilities, allows us to view both the capital–labour relationship as it is played out in different domains and the state as both employer and regulator of wage labour. The price of labour force is distributed in a much more unequal way than are the productivities of social labour. Or, in other words, the differences in productivity are far less than the differences in social value. With free trade and relatively open borders allowing MNCs to move to where they can find the cheapest labour, the law of value operates at the global level to allow extraction of the value produced in the peripheries to the benefit of the monopoly capital of the centres (Amin 2017). This extraction, however, happens with the direct and indirect collaboration of the state, as has been pointed out with regard to female garment workers in global supply chains. The role of the state in extraction, structured by informality, is further elaborated later.

I see informality as the key concept that links different aspects of the reality of urban poor lives and livelihoods. Defined minimally as absence of regulation, informality presents itself in reality in complex ways where varying degrees of regulation are intertwined and where, remarkably, the state, which is the regulator, shows itself to be a major factor in the structuration of informality.

There are indeed three axes through which informality cuts into the material presented in this book. First, as the empirical chapters show, across different livelihoods, it is informality which constitutes the edge of vulnerability in the lives of the urban poor. Low and unprotected wages and incomes constitute a central point in the understanding of urban marginalisation. This is seen in different domains: in casual wage earning, in self-employment, or in unregulated or inadequately regulated salaried work in manufacturing or services. Head-load bearers and unskilled construction workers, as casual wage earners who may get work two or three days of the week and can claim no social insurance, possibly constitute the bottom of the heap. However, the diversities in the domain of informal work also demonstrate its complex character, which must be understood in terms of different degrees of organisation and regulation. Security personnel – a rapidly expanding domain of service workers – who work through registered agencies, typically for large organisations (companies, malls, hospitals), are entitled to government-regulated salaries and social insurance, although they have no security of tenure; those employed through unregistered contractors may receive a salary but no other entitlements, while those employed directly, by residents or small commercial complexes, may receive a much lower wage and no entitlement to social security. Similarly, waste pickers engaged by the city corporation as direct employees or those who work for large companies or five-star hotels earn a regular salary/income, while those employed by the corporation through contractors earn much less and do not even get paid regularly. While most women workers in the apparel export industry suffer long and coercive working hours and conditions, many now receive at least the minimum wage and some social insurance (provident fund, medical insurance). However, at least a quarter fail to get even the stipulated minimum wage or any social security. Amongst self-employed street sellers, groups who are organised around sourcing from wholesale markets and selling at fixed points earn higher than those who buy from local markets and may sell at isolated street corners or at traffic lights. This empirical diversity indicates that within the broad framework of informal work, one finds degrees of regulation and organised activities, which bring a modicum of security to low-income workers, while the complete absence of regulation greatly worsens their exposure to multiple vulnerabilities.

Second, this complexity draws attention to the fact that informal work is not only a domain marked by the absence or lack of regulation (although that is an important dimension of it), as though the informal somehow lies outside the boundaries of the state, but rather that the state plays a central role in the structuring of informality in the Indian context. This happens not only through the state's role as an employer of informal workers (contract workers in public sector enterprises, in city corporations), but also through its tacit endorsement of the failure of the regulatory mechanisms. In the case of women workers in the apparel export industry, the state-appointed wage board itself fails to revise the minimum wage according to accepted norms; the state sets up a Construction Workers Welfare Board, but ignores the need to put in place appropriate governance mechanisms that could reach welfare to a migrant, cyclical workforce, who drift between the city and the country and do not have continuous employment; the state itself is an employer of informal, contract workers, whether in public sector companies or in city corporations. The role of the state in directly and indirectly maintaining and perpetuating a large informal workforce that works on highly disadvantageous terms and conditions is important to highlight. Recent work on developmental states has converged on the understanding that in the context of globalisation, as regular work and permanent workers increasingly disappear, worker-citizens must look to the state, rather than to private employers, for social insurance (Chatterjee 2008; Agarwala 2012). The present work, to the contrary, highlights the state's complicity in the creation of informal workforces and their continuing exclusion from claims to regulated incomes and social insurance.

Third, in mainstream development literature, urban poverty has been seen primarily as a result of the migration of the poor from rural areas, and policy focus has been on basic amenities/services, with scant attention to questions of income and livelihood. My research led to the location of poverty in second- or third-generation slum households – the old poor – as well as in migrant settlements, the new poor. Migration and civic deficiencies are therefore only of second-order importance in explaining, or addressing, urban poverty. Thus, the most critical issues which define urban deprivation are the flouting of minimum wage stipulations, irregular and insecure work, absence of work-related social insurance, and vulnerabilities relating to contract work, across the public and private sectors, in production or in services. The informal structure of work and earnings – stemming from the character of the city's political economy – holds the key to understanding the issue of urban vulnerabilities. The present work therefore raises questions, grounded in field-based findings, about mainstream understandings of urban poverty.

There is of course a close relationship between social identity and the lower rungs of informal work that this research has examined. In the surveys we conducted in slums, among construction and garment sector workers, households belonged predominantly to the Scheduled Castes (SCs) and Scheduled Tribes (STs) or were Muslims. This inevitable correlation between lower-caste/minority communities and absence of economic opportunities needs to be underlined, as also that social identity is constitutive of people's relationship to the means of production and reproduction. Intersectionality possibly remains the most useful method to examine poverty and exclusion. However, given the limitations of a single work, the conceptual framework here has mainly used the multiple forms of economic exclusion, manifested in different domains of informality and anchored in national- and state-level economic policies, as a window to understand urban marginality.

The analysis

A changing economic institutional structure, increasingly marked by globalisation, supported by state policies aligned with the national and international paradigms of liberalisation/privatisation, provide the broad framework within which the ground-level realities of the lives and livelihoods of the urban poor are contextualised here. More specifically, the larger political economy of India and the state of Karnataka, and that of Bangalore as a high growth, services-led city, provides the context in which urban lower-class livelihoods are sought to be understood. While Karnataka is one of India's more advanced states, where the gross state domestic product (GSDP) has consistently remained above the national growth rate, the state has steadily fallen behind on social sector expenditure and in its record on human development, compared, particularly, to other states in south India. More germane to the present enquiry, and in contrast to the image of the state as a leader of India's IT revolution and growing financial and other high-growth sectors, a large number of people remain tied to agriculture, even as agriculture's share in the state's GSDP steadily declines. This is a feature of the national economy as well, and it is a widely shared concern that agriculture, despite declining productivity and profits, remains the largest employer in a context where the pattern of urban and industrial growth has seen only stunted growth of jobs in urban areas. In the case of Karnataka, this anomaly highlights the narrowness of both the process of urbanisation – confined to large metropolitan cities, while smaller cities and towns have stagnated – and of the nature of urban growth, which have made cities like Bangalore exclusivist epicentres of technology and consumption. While Bangalore's growth as an IT hub has brought it an iconic status as India's Silicon Valley, attracting a technical/professional class of globally connected citizens, there is a clearly discernible wasteland outside, perhaps which can be imagined in terms of three ribbons: those who work in low incomes and harsh working conditions in the city, somehow eking out a living from wages in export manufacturing (garments), low-end services, self-employment as petty traders, and so on; migrant labour in the peripheries, whose only relation to the city is their daily journey to construction sites; and, in the background, a vast army of rural dwellers who remain tied to low incomes in agriculture, but who would not find a foothold in the city.

The policy and institutional history of Karnataka and Bangalore in the last four decades[6] provides clues to this exclusivist trajectory. At the onset of independence, Karnataka's political economy was possibly an iconic representation of the vision of development shared by India's political leaders: a large number of public sector industries, both state and central level, dominated the industrial scene in Karnataka, supported by a sprawling small-scale industries sector. The labour-intensive textile industry had a significant presence in Karnataka, symbolised by large mills situated in the heart of Bangalore, while the power-loom industry developed in its suburbs. These sectors provided the backbone of a robust industrial working class as well as a growing and upwardly mobile lower administrative class employed in a large number of office/clerical jobs both in the public and private sectors. Chapter 4 traces the eventual decline of the public sector and of small-scale industries in the state, particularly in Bangalore. In the emerging industrial scenario, both state-owned and small-scale industries declined, and the private corporate sector moved increasingly towards globally competitive, high-technology domains, in electronics and telecommunications, pharmaceuticals, biotechnology, food processing and automobiles. The question of employment of unskilled and semi-skilled labour became the blind spot of public policy. This was indeed the background in which the city's economic profile shifted to the IT-led, high-growth space of wealth generation and consumption, but where the boundaries of exclusion – represented by the three ribbons mentioned earlier – were clearly demarcated. This book thus uses this broadly political economy framework within which the transition is traced from a quietly prosperous city – defined by a large state sector and labour-intensive industries – which had an inclusive flavour, to a technology- and competition-driven, market- and private-capital-led space, which generated the exclusion of large sections of the urban lower classes from the city's strident wealth and materiality.

The chapters

Following this introductory chapter, the second chapter locates the study in the context of contemporary debates on the developmental state, particularly around the ideas of the effectiveness of state autonomy and of democracy in ensuring broad-based development. The chapter traces the turning of scholarly and policy discourse from questions of employment, work and income to a preoccupation with welfare, broadly defined. Two thematic questions are pursued in this chapter. First, the issue of a meagre and uncertain income that stalks the average unskilled worker provides a somewhat ironical twist to the question of welfare: can one talk about welfare without at the same time talking about work? Second, much of the discourse on statist welfare is woven around the idea that the interests and aspirations of the poor, for social insurance, are articulated to the state in a variety of forms of collective representation, which may range from the slum association to the caste group. To what extent does informal work, marked by a scattered and fragmented workforce, structure and limit the voice and political agency of the poor?

Poverty of cities and the phrase 'urbanisation of poverty' has drawn much recent scholarly and policy attention.[7] The third chapter touches on the debates around the relationship between migration and poverty. While the World Bank and other international policy institutions have held the spillover thesis (urban poverty is a result of the carry-over of rural poverty by poor migrants), and that cities provide opportunities for mobility for all, in India there is a serious and ongoing debate on who migrates, and what is the impact of migration on the poverty of migrants? This question in fact turns on the nature of the urban political economy, and the opportunities available to the poor, both migrant and non-migrant. The chapter points to three key features of India's urban policies and political economy: first, the stagnation of small towns and cities, which renders urban opportunities narrowly available only in large metropolitan cities; second, the halting nature of the economy's structural transformation, as agriculture remains the biggest employer; and, third, even as there are emerging signs that large numbers are leaving agriculture, and there is a rise in regular salaried work in urban areas, such work is mainly in construction and lower rungs of services, framed by absence of state regulation of wages and working conditions. The chapter provides information on the structure of urban employment, drawing attention particularly to the relationship between urban informality (in self-employment, casual and salaried wage work) and poverty. These arguments are then set in the context of competing views on the nature of informality, and its impact on different sections of the urban poor.

The themes of the third chapter echo in Chapter 4 in the context of the political economy of the state of Karnataka and the city of Bangalore. I highlight some obvious dualities in the state's developmental trajectory: Karnataka's growth rate has remained consistently above the national average, but combined with higher poverty rates and lower human-development performance compared to other southern states. Three main features are discussed that have a specific bearing on the issue of urban poverty: first, regional imbalance in development between the northern and southern parts of the state and relatively low levels of public expenditure on social sectors; second, continuing dependence on agricultural employment that directs our attention to the narrowness of urban growth; and, third, the structure of urban employment highlights the crowding of large numbers of the urban workforce in low-paying, casual work.

These broad features of the state's developmental trajectory provide the context for a more specific discussion on Bangalore's political economy in the next section. This section traces Bangalore's growing profile as a technology city, driven by the private-capital-led IT industry. The parallel rise of biotechnology is greatly supported through state funding and facilitation of scientific and technical innovation as a key ingredient of growth. The state's offering of superior facilities to these and other globally competitive industries, such as automobiles, as incentives, credit, infrastructure and land demonstrate that a technology-led model of development drives the imagination of the state's leaders, supported by the presence of a large and expanding middle and upper class of scientific and technical personnel, new generation entrepreneurs who drive the city's start-up culture, and framing all this, a services-led economy. As state-owned manufacturing, the small-scale industries sector, and labour-intensive industries like textiles declined, these domains were no longer available for unskilled and semi-skilled labour. The share of manufacturing employment is much lower in Bangalore (21.3 per cent) as compared to urban India (24.3 per cent) and to million-plus cities (28.4 per cent). The highest rise in employment within the secondary sector in Bangalore has taken place in the construction and ready-made apparel industries, where wages and employment conditions remain largely unregulated. As the service sector constitutes 73 per cent of employment in Bangalore, one would assume that much of what is described as regular or salaried employment is to be found in the service sector. In the lower rungs of services, salaries remain low and service conditions and tenure are unregulated.

The empirical chapters (Chapters 5 to 8) provide the lens through which the trends, described here, are seen in the lives and livelihoods of the city's underclass located in diverse sites: old, inner-city slums, new migrant peripheral settlements, redeveloped slums, construction sites, and garment factories.

The newer set of slums in the city's periphery house recent migrants in unstable, self- constructed tenements, and the majority crowd into the city's construction industry via contracting agencies. The fifth chapter provides information on low wages and uncertain incomes, and highlights the continuing exclusion and marginalisation of these migrant communities as their children flit between the city and the village of origin, lack opportunities for systematic and continuous schooling, have high drop-out rates, and many eventually join the construction industry or other sectors as unskilled workers.

The sixth chapter looks at old, inner-city settlements of migrants who came to the city 60–70 years ago, where second and third generations of dwellers now live alongside a continuous stream of new entrants. Older slums demonstrate a complex set of relations of slum residents to the city's economy: while a relatively small number of households have crossed the bridge and found a foothold in the city's newly emergent services sector, a large number remain tied to traditional, low-paying work – construction workers, head-load bearers in the city's central markets, domestic workers, rag pickers, pushcart vendors, sellers at traffic lights, and so on. The narrative highlights that slums remain spaces of exclusion as, inter-generationally, slum households are unable to access the dynamic channels of the city's economy. Service jobs have brought some social prestige, but with unregulated and variable pay, and little scope for mobility, the sector produces a vulnerable, footloose and unstable workforce.[8] Therefore, whether one is looking at traditional low-paying occupations or more modern occupations such as retail seller or driver, informality provides the broad framework that defines the vulnerabilities of urban lower-class lives and livelihoods.

The seventh chapter examines an important policy intervention in the lives of slum households: new housing projects introduced by the Jawaharlal Nehru National Urban Renewal Mission (JNNURM), the Rajeev Awas Yojana (RAY), both introduced by the Congress-led United Progressive Alliance (UPA) government over 2004–13, and the more recent Pradhan Mantri Awas Yojana (PMAY) introduced by the Bharatiya Janata Party (BJP)–led National Democratic Alliance (NDA) government in 2014. The chapter examines the impact of JNNURM and RAY through housing-related relocation and resettlement programmes. Housing projects provide freedom from rent and eviction, but fall short of the urban poor's long-standing demand for right to own the land on which they have lived in slums. State-constructed one-size-fits-all apartments ignore slum dwellers' use of habitation as livelihood, and at the same time bring little qualitative improvement in terms of civic and infrastructural services or human resources. Importantly, the process of slum redevelopment highlights the multilayered and complex structure of interests of slum households in urban land and their frequently incompatible and conflicting responses to state policies.

The eighth chapter is on the export-oriented ready-made garment (RMG) industry in Bangalore, connected to the multibillion-dollar global supply chain in apparel retail. Driven by large global corporate houses, the labour-intensive apparel industry relocated in successive stages from advanced industrialised economies to Japan and the newly industrialising countries (NICs) in South East Asia and, finally, to South Asia and the Middle East (India, Bangladesh, Sri Lanka, Indonesia), primarily in search of cheaper labour markets.[9] In India, Bangalore emerged as a major hub in apparel export, providing employment to large numbers of unskilled workers, mainly migrant women. Although in principle governed by a wage board which periodically sets a minimum wage, apparel manufacture in Bangalore is marked by the classic features of informal work, where at least a quarter of the workforce does not receive the minimum wage, working hours are unregulated and working conditions are coercive. For Bangalore's political economy, the garment sector typifies the many contradictions of a rapidly globalising urban scenario, which brings global connectedness and wealth generation along with structured exclusion.

The conclusion (Chapter 9) brings together the major findings to reflect on questions of conflict and power, underpinned by the inequalities inscribed in the structure of the urban political economy. In mainstream development literature, the future of the urban underclass is imagined as driven by the agency of the local community, in collaboration with NGOs, governments and donors. In contrast, woven through the empirical chapters in this book is the story of a faltering domain of activism – whether of slum-based associations, caste associations or trade unions struggling with informal workers – and the indifference of local- and state-level politicians to urban poor issues, whether of employment, income or land. The diversity of the structure of informal work eludes theorisation, and the disparateness of workers is hugely challenging for activists. Both domains – theory and movements – have struggled, explicitly or implicitly, with the concept of 'class'. Is the informal sector a domain of 'classlessness'? Does class remain a theoretically relevant concept, or should we abandon it?

Notes

1. This literature is wide ranging. For a sampling, see Bhan (2017, 2019), Roy (2005), Shepherd, Leitner, and Maringanti (2013), Parnell and Pieterse (2010) and Caldeira (2013). The present work does not engage directly with these debates. The brief discussion on this literature is indicative; the purpose is more to delineate the conceptual framework that is used in this book.

2. Material space is that which can be measured, surveyed, demarcated and calculated. In contrast, relative space must be understood in the context in which it is situated, both temporally and spatially, while relational space refers to when space is seen in objects.

3. See also Picketty (2013) and Saez and Zucman (2019).

4. See Ghertner (2014) and Bhide (2019).

5. This literature, again, is vast. For a sampling of the early statements, see Fernando and Cardoso (1979) and Evans (1979, 1995). For more detailed references to this literature, see Chapter 2.

6. For a nuanced presentation of this history, see Nair (2005).

7. According to the World Bank, currently an estimated one-third of all urban residents are poor, which represents one quarter of the world's total poor. Approximately 750 million people living in urban areas in developing countries were below the poverty line of $2/day, and 290 million people were below the $1/day in 2002. Forty-six per cent of the world's urban poor were in South Asia. The literature on urbanisation of poverty is fairly voluminous. See, for example, UN (2007), World Bank (2008), Ravallion, Chen and Sangrula (2007), Ravallion and Chen (2008) and Lucci et al. (2016). Of these, Ravallion and Chen provide broad conclusions based on household surveys across a large number of countries. In this view, although the rural share of poverty is higher, at 75 per cent, the rate of decline of rural poverty is faster than the rate of decline of urban poverty, and the absolute numbers of the urban poor are rising while the absolute numbers of the rural poor are falling. I do not enter into greater details of these discussions, as the purpose here is only to highlight the salience of urban poverty as seen in the development literature.

8. For detailed surveys and analyses of the services sector employment, see RoyChowdhury and Upadhya (2020).

9. China is the only industrially advanced economy, currently, to have a large ready-made apparel export sector.

References

Amin, S. 2017. Interview by Ingras H. Kvangraven. In *Dialogues on Development, Volume 1: On Dependency*. New York: Young Scholars Initiative, Institute for New Economic Thinking.

Agarwala, Rina. 2012. *Informal Labor, Formal Politics and Dignified Discontent*. New York: Cambridge University Press.

Benjamin, S., and R. Bhubaneswari. 2006. 'Urban Futures and Poor Groups in Chennai and Bangalore: How These Are Shaped by the Relationship between Parastatal and Local Bodies.' In *Local Governance in India: Decentralization and Beyond*, ed. N. Jayal, A. Prakash and P. Sharma, 221–67. New Delhi: Oxford University Press.

———. 2011. 'Illegible Claims, Legal Titles and the Worlding of Bangalore.' *Revue Tiers-Monde* 206 (2): 37–54.

Bhide, A. 2019. 'Urbanization Unbound: Indian Urbanization through the Lens of Real Estate and Housing'. *Urban India* 39 (11): 9–20.

Bhan, Gautam. 2017. 'From the Basti to the "House": Socio-Spatial Readings of Housing Policy in India'. *Current Sociology* 65 (4): 587–602.

———. 2019. 'Notes on a Southern Urban Practice'. *Environment and Urbanization* 31 (2): 639–54.

Caldeira, T. 2017. 'Peripheral Urbanization, Auto Construction, Transversal Logics and Politics in Cities of the Global South'. *Environment and Planning* 35 (1): 3–20.

Chatterjee, Partha. 2008. 'Democracy and Economic Transformation in India'. *Economic and Political Weekly* 43 (16): 53–62.

Evans, Peter. 1979. *Dependent Development: The Alliance of Multinationals, State and Capital in Brazil*. Princeton: Princeton University Press.

———. 1995. *Embedded Autonomy: State and Industrial Transformation*. Princeton: Princeton University Press.

Fernando, H., and E. Cardoso. 1979. *Dependency and Development in Latin America*. Berkeley: University of California Press.

Ghertner, D. A. 2014. 'India's Urban Revolution: Geographies of Displacement beyond Gentrification'. *Environment and Planning* 46 (7): 1554–71.

Goldman, M. 2011. 'Speculative Urbanism and the Shaping of the Next World City.' *International Journal of Urban and Regional Research* 35 (3): 555–81.

Harvey, David. 2009 [1973]. *Social Justice and the City*. Athens: University of Georgia Press.

Janaagraha–Brown Citizenship Index. 2014. *Citizenship in Urban India: Evidence from Bangalore*. Bangalore: Janaagraha Centre for Citizenship and Democracy and Watson Institute of Contemporary South Asia, Brown University.

Nair, J. 2005. *The Promise of the Metropolis: Bangalore's 20th Century*. Delhi: Oxford University Press.

Nuttall, S., and A. Mbembe. 2005. 'A Blase Attitude: A Response to Michael Watts'. *Pubic Culture* 17: 193–201.

Parnell, S., and E. Pieterse. 2010. 'The Right to the City: Institutional Imperatives of a Developmental State'. *International Journal of Urban and Regional Research* 34 (1): 146–62.

Piketty, T. 2013. *Capital in the 21st Century.* Paris and Cambridge, MA: Editions du Seuil and Harvard University Press.

Ravallion, M., and S. Chen. 2008. 'The Developing World Is Poorer Than We Thought, but No Less Successful in the Fight Against Poverty'. *Quarterly Journal of Economics* 125 (4): 1577–625.

Ravallion, M., S. Chen and P. Sangrula. 2007. 'New Evidence on the Globalisation of Urban Poverty'. *Population and Development Review* 33 (4): 667–701.

Roy, A. 2016. 'Who's Afraid of Post-Colonial Theory'. *International Journal of Urban and Regional Theory* 40 (1): 200–09.

RoyChowdhury, S., and C. Upadhya. 2019. 'India's Changing City Scapes: Work, Migration and Livelihoods'. Unpublished report, ISEC and NIAS, Bangalore.

Saez, E., and G. Zucman. 2019. *The Triumph of Injustice: How the Rich Dodge Taxes and How to Make Them Pay.* New York: WW Norton & Company.

Sanyal, K. 2007. *Rethinking Capitalist Development: Primitive Accumulation, Governmentality and Post-colonial Capitalism.* London: Routledge.

Sassen, Saskia. 2005. 'The Global City: Introducing a Concept'. *The Brown Journal of World Affairs* 11 (2): 27–43.

Scott, A. J., and M. Storper. 2015. 'The Nature of Cities: The Scope and Limits of Urban Theory'. *International Journal of Urban and Regional Research* 39 (1): 1–15.

Sheppard, E., H. Leitner, and A. Maringanti. 2013. 'Provincializing Global Urbanism: A Manifesto'. *Urban Geography* 34 (7): 893–900.

Standing, G. 2016. *The Precariat: The New Dangerous Class.* London: Bloomsbury Academic.

———. 2018. 'The Precariat: Today's Transformative Class'. *Development* 61: 115–21.

UNFPA. 2007. *State of World Population 2007: Unleashing the Potential of Urban Growth.* Geneva: United Nations. Upadhya, C. 2004. 'A New Transnational Capitalist Class? Capitalist Flows, Business Networks and Entrepreneurs in the Indian Software Industry.' *Economic and Political Weekly* 39 (48): 5141–51.

———. 2016. *Reengineering India: Work, Capital and Class in an Offshore Economy.* New Delhi: Oxford University Press.

World Bank. 2008. *World Development Indicators 2008: Poverty Data.* Washington, DC: World Bank.

2

Welfare and Work

State Autonomy Revisited*

The troubled relationship between economic growth and redistribution/welfare is a long-standing concern in the social sciences. Globalisation, associated increasingly with the duality of rising wealth and continuing deprivations, has brought an added sharpness to this concern. Two principal genres of a critical discourse can be located. Marxist critiques of globalisation and market-led economic growth – anchored in the dependency perspective, and infused with class analysis – are theoretically rich but marked by a deep, brooding pessimism and lacking in robust alternatives. On the other side, strands of liberal, mainstream social science are rooted in a pragmatic world view: that alongside a capitalist and market-based economic model, an appropriate degree of state responsibility should be restored and maintained. Marked by a nostalgia for the post-war social-democracy-inspired welfare state, and an anxiety to restore some dimensions of it, this genre of scholarship remains at the same time strongly committed to retaining the gains of the new economic model of globalisation and privatisation.

Partly a reincarnation of post-war Keynesian statist welfarism, this genre of writings can also be looked at as a narrative attempting to re-theorise the developmental state. Emerging at a time when the market had gained legitimacy of hegemonic proportions, reiterations of the state's centrality, which have emerged from global institutions and from leading scholars, are critical interventions that shape a new political normativity of justice and public responsibility. Do they do more? Does a substantively new theory of the state emerge from contemporary writings on the capitalist developmental state?

As a generalised critique of the inequitable nature of globalisation/market-led development began to emerge in both academic and public discourses, the expansion of social rights became part of the defined political agenda of

---

* This chapter is a revised version of my article 'Welfare without Work or Wages: A Contradiction?' *Economic and Political Weekly* 53, no. 35 (1 September 2018): 53–60.

democratic governments as well as of scholars striving to provide a humane face to a market-driven model of development. Critical of the inequitable impact of global capitalism, these writings have nevertheless stayed away from a determinist interpretation of the capitalist state as inevitably exclusivist and moved towards a more eclectic theorisation, which leaves open the possibility of inclusive social policies. Within this broad conceptual framework, scholars have reiterated the need for state attention to employment-generating economic policies as well as state-sponsored social insurance targeting poorer sections of the population.

The recorded diversities in policy and performance with regard to welfare are such that the task of drawing systematic interrelations between variables, or making meaningful comparisons, is indeed challenging. Despite these challenges, much of the literature has maintained a lively discourse on the possibility of a negotiated balance between the inherent narrowness of a globalisation/market-led growth model, on the one hand, and the developmental state's capacity to sustain a more welfarist, inclusive pattern of growth, on the other.

This theorisation of possibilities rests on two important, albeit old and now refurbished, concepts in Comparative Politics. The concept of state autonomy, which had been widely used in Comparative Politics in the mid-1980s and informed the work of a whole generation of Weberian scholars writing on developmental states, has in fact been brought back with a renewed emphasis on studying welfare and redistribution. Briefly, on this view, developmental states have the choice, more precisely a space of political autonomy, to be more, rather than less, inclusive. Particularly in the context of liberalisation and globalisation, when developmental states have been seen as increasingly closely aligned to capital, both domestic and foreign, state autonomy has emerged as a central conceptual pillar to reassert the state's redistributive and welfarist profile. The next section provides a broad outline of this literature.

The second important pillar is provided by a re-reading of democracy. It is through democracy that states are nudged towards more inclusive policies. Particular aspects of democratic governance have been highlighted – role of NGOs, judicial activism, rise of popular movements, associational expressions of lower-class demands through the formation of political society, and so on – which can successfully steer states towards more redistributive/welfare policies. This reading rests on the widely shared view that the capital–labour contestation is no longer central to our understanding of lower-class demands, and that organised labour, the key traditional constituency of welfare, has been replaced by a multitude of groups, variously defined. State autonomy and democracy, understood as broadly based popular empowerment, thus provide the two pillars on which theorisations of a rights-based capitalist developmental state stand.

The critical question here, and one that is insufficiently theorised in the literature, is indeed the relationship between welfare and labour. Does the decline in numbers and political salience of organised industrial labour need to be factored in our understanding of emerging welfare theories? How indeed does the changing face of labour, from organised to informal, from industrial to services, impact on welfare? I make a brief diversion here by referring to contemporary debates on how this question looks in the context of developed countries. Mature industrialised democracies feature a small, highly skilled industrial workforce, a large service sector, state-sponsored access to universal education, and a long history of social democracy and statist welfarism. In such contexts, while organised industrial labour has declined in political salience, a plurality of organised groups have emerged as powerful claimants and defenders of welfare (Pierson 1995). Recent literature on western welfare states has acknowledged this new politics, while at the same time reiterating that the relationship of labour and welfare possibly requires deeper probing (Mettler 2015). The re-emergence of industrial sweatshops in cities like New York, the growing incidence of irregular and part-time work, particularly after the economic crisis of 2008, and the many challenges posed by a large body of unauthorised immigrant workforce point to a situation where the question of labour must re-emerge in the debates around western welfare.

This implicit question mark becomes even more significant in the case of the NICs. In the NICs, with globalisation, the decline of organised industrial employment and the advent of a largely service-led economy saw the growth of a dualistic labour market, with increasing numbers of workers now in irregular work. Social insurance, hitherto tied to employment, increasingly became redefined as state-sponsored universalised insurance; however, insofar as contributions remained an important part of insurance, large numbers of irregular workers fell outside the scope of insurance. The debate on NICs, as it is closer to the Indian experience, is taken up in a longer discussion in the third section.

In the case of India, and possibly other countries in similar stages of development, the question of the relationship between work/employment, labour and welfare is much sharper. Vast numbers of unskilled workers – who may be daily-wage earners or in petty self-employment in trade, production or services – are situated in an economic structure which may provide a small subsistence, but little else. The issue of a meagre and uncertain income that stalks the average unskilled worker provides a somewhat ironical twist to the question of welfare: can one talk about welfare without at the same time talking about work? Second, much of the discourse on statist welfare is woven around the idea that the interests and aspirations of the poor, for social insurance, are articulated to the state in a variety of forms of collective representation, which may range from the slum association to the caste group (discussed later in the third section). To what extent does informal work, marked by a scattered and fragmented workforce, structure and limit the voice and political agency of the poor?

These questions bring the issue of welfare to the rough edge of questions relating to economic structure, employment, regulation and security of work and wages, broadly to the domain of political economy. In talking about welfare, many have consciously stayed away from these questions. In an important recent contribution to the literature on the comparative politics of welfare in Indian states, the authors state that they do not subscribe to reductionist political economy arguments about the limits of welfare (Tillin, Deshpande, and Kailash 2015). While not stated so explicitly, recent writings on the capitalist developmental state as a whole seem to share this view that questions relating to the economic structure/labour market and the state's welfarist policies are somehow in two different domains. Reductionism (by which is possibly meant essentialist interpretations of the capitalist state as necessarily and only working for the capitalist class) is indeed passé, and in this context would close off the possibilities of considering what the capitalist state might actually achieve by way of welfare. On the other side, universalist reiterations of state capacity to promote welfare within a capitalist developmental framework possibly lack a historically specific understanding of the state–class relationship within the context created by globalisation – liberalisation – in developing countries. Therefore, steering away from either/or, or zero-sum, frames of reasoning, this chapter explores the directions in which the literature on welfare appears to move, and poses the question: does the informal sector constitute a blind spot in theorisations of welfare in the Indian context?

The next section provides in broad outline the central premises of contemporary writings on the capitalist developmental state, including a discussion on the NICs, frequently cited as examples of successful developmental states. The following section highlights what has been called India's new architecture of welfare and India's democracy as the touchstone of the supposedly revitalised state welfarism. On the other side, the structure of the economy, marked by vast, unorganised and irregularly employed workforce, points to the limits of organised claims on welfare and redistribution.

The capitalist developmental state re-theorised?

Around the mid-1980s, the impact of structural adjustment programmes (SAPs), pursued by a large number of developing countries as part of loan conditionalities and liberalisation/privatisation policies imposed by the International Monetary Fund (IMF) and the World Bank, began to be widely perceived as having generated economic hardships in much of South Asia and sub-Saharan Africa. The early critical literature on SAPs had emerged in fact from multilateral institutions. The well-known 1987 report of the United Nations Children's Fund (UNICEF), 'Adjustment with a Human Face', highlighted that the strict budgetary adjustments and deflationary measures advocated by SAPs had resulted in reducing demand, depressed employment and real incomes. In 1999, the Poverty Reduction Strategy Papers (PRSPs) of the IMF reiterated the importance of state engagement with poverty.

Among others, the work of two iconic economists who also emerged as public critics of unfettered globalisation – Joseph Stiglitz and Amartya Sen – represented the discomfiture of an important section of academics with the exclusionary impact of globalisation-led growth, and a shared concern amongst the scholarly community to recreate a blueprint for statist welfarism.[1] Stiglitz echoed 'Adjustment with a Human Face' in his 2002 book where he stated that in many countries of South Asia and sub-Saharan Africa, SAP-induced deflationary measures – cutting deficits, raising taxes – led to declining public expenditures, loss of investment, reduced demand and lowered spending on social sectors. Rapid trade liberalisation, at a time when many of these countries were unprepared for global competition, led to huge economic dislocation in terms of closures, declining employment, and so on. On the other hand, citing the examples of pre-crisis East Asia and post-reform China, Stiglitz (2002) pointed out that in each of these cases, the states had the autonomy to liberalise their economies, both externally and internally, at their own pace, taking care to create jobs and to protect industries until such time as there was readiness for greater integration into the global economy. The developmental state, then, must play a crucial balancing role in chalking out a context-specific trajectory that combines the role of state and market. According to Stiglitz, many of the countries that took a more gradualist policy eventually succeeded in making deeper inroads into the market.[2]

Amartya Sen, in successive important interventions, has underlined the need for balancing the role of the government – and of other political and social institutions – with the functioning of markets. In the context of India, there is, according to him, a 'deep complementarity between reducing, on the one hand, the over-activity of the state in running a 'license raj,' and on the other, removing the under-activity of the state in the continuing neglect of elementary education and other social opportunities' (Sen 2000). Sen recommends combining extensive use of markets with the development of social opportunities as part of a broader comprehensive approach to development (Sen 1994).

Sen and Stiglitz can be seen to have provided the first building blocks of a refurbished theory of the developmental state, firmly ensconced in the logic of market- and globalisation-led development, but where a space of state autonomy is retained, vis-à-vis the market and other forces, to ensure job creation, social opportunities and welfare. A new sensibility of state action emerged, with globalisation/liberalisation as the backdrop, with a renewed commitment to take care of groups who may be disadvantaged vis-à-vis the market. These views are echoed in much of recent political economy research on developmental states, which has maintained a lively discourse on the possibility of this negotiated, creative balance that can be constructed by states between markets, globalisation and private profit, on the one hand, and state-guided social welfare, on the other. In the following I briefly outline the literature on the NICs, pertaining particularly to the relationship between welfare and the emerging formal–informal duality in the labour market.

It is now widely acknowledged that the Asian NICs' dramatic development in the post-war years was largely state-guided, although private-sector-led and market-driven.[3] Stiglitz (2002) points out that East Asian countries took advantage of globalisation to expand their exports and grow faster as a result, but they dropped their protective barriers carefully, systematically phasing them out when new jobs were created. They ensured that there was capital available for new jobs.

The NICs' more decisive turn towards economic liberalisation from the 1980s onwards led to questions about the specific future trajectory of capitalism in this region. This period would see the increasing pre-eminence of foreign capital and the greater integration of these economies into global markets. This was also the period when the NICs made the transition from authoritarian military regimes towards democratisation. And, finally, the period following the economic crisis of the late 1990s highlighted the emerging role of the IMF, via loan conditionalities. Amongst scholars of this region, a dominant view seems to be that, post economic liberalisation and political democratisation, purposive state action in these countries made it possible for political regimes to balance the competing pulls of marketisation and distributive justice.

During the pre-1980s phase of development, in both South Korea and Taiwan, social security was tied to occupations. From the mid-1980s onwards, and particularly after the financial crisis situation of the late 1990s, deeper integration into globally competitive markets meant that in South Korea and Taiwan there was a shift from manufacturing-based economies to service-oriented and knowledge-based economies, calling for greater labour market flexibility and a corresponding increase in demand for flexible and skilled labour. With the onset of democratisation in both countries in the 1980s and early 1990s, more broad-based political regimes created universalised social insurance, and self-employed workers and family dependents were included in these programmes.[4] According to some scholars of the region, neoliberal reforms and the strengthening of social security went hand in hand, and this model represents a vision of economic pluralism in which competitive markets and social objectives could be reconciled.[5]

On the other hand, critics have pointed to serious limits to state-sponsored welfare in South East Asian capitalism, and that these have been reinforced in the post-liberalisation, post-economic crisis periods.[6] First, universalised social security came about in a context where the structure of the industrial workforce was being irreversibly changed. Thus, in 1996 a new labour law was passed in South Korea, which facilitated the introduction of a flexible work week, easy dismissals and the recruitment of a temporary workforce. Reforms also included the liquidation of state-owned enterprises and privatisation of loss-making enterprises to foreign buyers. In Taiwan, the Koumintang (KMT), which was elected in 1996, began the process of privatisation of state-owned enterprises (SOEs) in the face of labour resistance. In 1996 the government introduced bans on strikes in key industries, removed compulsory arbitration, and so on. Second, the welfare system that was put in place had significant limitations. It has been pointed out that although social insurance was extended to the informal sector workforce, it remains tied to contributions, and non-regular workers suffered from lower coverage. In the South Korean context, scholars have pointed out that large, powerful trade unions remained within the large chaebol (family-owned business conglomerate)-dominated corporate sector, and a strong tradition of enterprise-based union economism led to corporate benefits being extended only to regular workers. This, and the weak presence of left-oriented political parties, prevented a more robust welfare system that could have included the increasing numbers of informal sector workers. Thus, the emerging dualism in the structure of the labour market precluded a more genuinely universal social security system.

There are, then, two central points that emerge from this discussion. First, while expanding the role of the market, NIC states were simultaneously promoting social security measures. Second, and on the other side of the debate, scholars have drawn attention to the decline of formal sector manufacturing and the increasing narrowness of contributions-related social security as a dualistic labour market began to emerge. How one views the political economy of NICs would depend on the relative emphasis placed on these different features of development in this region.

What is perhaps equally important is that the East Asian situation is marked by an initial condition of economic growth and development which cushioned the dynamics of markets and welfare. Research on economic liberalisation reforms in both South Korea and Taiwan rightly points out that the macroeconomic context right up to the economic crisis was one of robust growth with tight labour markets (Kong 2005). This background of growth meant that South Korea and Taiwan were not faced with absolute economic choices about economic policy reform. Universal education and a highly skilled workforce facilitated the transition to a knowledge and capital-intensive economy.

These conditions are largely unavailable in most developing countries. In India, recent economic growth has been rapid, but overall development is caught up in the complex issues posed by a large population, a huge unskilled labour force, and where governance of welfare is fraught with multiple issues of corruption and inefficiency. The argument that the state can balance the dualistic demands of neoliberal reforms and of social justice looks far more complex in such a context. The debates generated around these issues highlight these very complexities.

India: the rational and autonomous state

From the mid-1980s onwards, as is well known, liberalisation of the economy, both internally and externally, has become a key aspect of economic policy. And it is indeed from this point onwards that the characterisation of the Indian state in terms of its developmental (both redistributive and welfare activities) capacities has generated an interesting range of theorisations, which perhaps could be grouped into two categories: the celebratory, and the critical but optimistic.

For the first set of scholars, the Indian state has done well in both growth (by increasingly inviting the market to take its place) and welfare (by taking advantage of increased economic growth to expand the sphere of welfare). This understanding is firmly grounded in the notion of the state's autonomy.

Economic liberalisation was seen as the moment of the state's decisive political action to break away from ideological shackles (socialism) and perceived failures of the past (import substitution).[7] Economic reforms thus provided a context of a shared and rich imagining of the state as an autonomous actor, framed by the rational/technical discourse of neoclassical economics, thus independently undertaking a rational set of policies (Ahluwalia 2004, 2005; Bhagwati 1988, 2004; Bhalla 2002, 2006; Nayar 2009; Panagariya 2008, 2010; Varshney 2000).

On this view, the Indian state continues to be welfarist, as seen in efforts to extend primary education, health care, the National Rural Employment Generation Scheme (NREGS), and so on. Some have written that economic liberalisation ultimately empowered the masses by generating more wealth and making this available to larger numbers (Varshney 2000; Nayar 2009). If at all there is a deficit in distribution, it is because of flawed implementation – inadequate governance – rather than lack of public spending, or any contradiction between liberalising reforms and welfare (Nayar 2009). The state, then, is seen as an agency endowed with a space for rational and autonomous action – where it abrogates its central role in the economy to the market and the private sector, and at the same time retains its welfarist profile.

Others – who can be broadly described as a second genre – are critical of serious welfare deficits as well as the inequitable nature of employment and income in India. At the same time, this genre of scholars adhere to a framework of possibilities. Sen and Drèze (2013) are hugely critical of India's welfare deficit, particularly in comparison to other developing countries – not only the great East Asian performers, but states such as Bangladesh and even Nepal, who did not match India's impressive post-liberalisation growth records, but where steady state action on welfare over time was reflected in higher performance in basic indicators of human development, such as women's health, infant mortality, literacy, and so on. Sen and Drèze also importantly draw attention to variations in the performance of states within India, not only the well-known case of Kerala, but also that of Tamil Nadu and Himachal Pradesh. In each of these three states, welfare policies and their implementation have put their human development indicators much ahead of other states and of India's national average.

Sen and Drèze provide a wide-ranging narrative of the factors that account for better performance; thus, it may be NGOs and women's progress in the case of Bangladesh, effective local governance in the case of Himachal Pradesh, and a socially committed state in the case of Kerala. The outlier success cases within India, as well as the examples of other South Asian countries which score better than India on welfare, affirm the realm of the possible.

On a similar vein, John Harriss (2011) points out that despite flaws in implementation, the UPA government's (which came to power in 2004 and was re-elected in 2008) flagship social programmes represent both civil society and left parties' pressure on the state, and the fact that the state, to the extent it has conceded to these pressures and enacted welfare policies, has moved away from a classical neoliberal model. Other scholars have highlighted what has been called the Indian state's new welfare architecture, a whole new set of rights, enacted by the central government over the last 10 years of the Congress Party–led rule of the UPA.[8] The new rights agenda has been propelled by judicial activism and expanding popular participation. This genre of opinion too has been quick to reaffirm the importance of state–market balance. 'Can the proponents of India's rights agenda realise its ambitions without jeopardising the dynamic economic changes witnessed over the last two decades?' (Ruparelia 2013). After all, it is the enhanced growth rates that have made it possible to even imagine expanded social expenditure.

The vision, then, is all about retaining the best of capitalism and creating the best of welfare. More specifically, while the market and globalisation provide the framework for economic growth, socially committed states, propelled by democratic forces, must attend to welfare and redistribution, as some have indeed done with success.

In the third category are an important group of scholars who have consistently indicated that an exclusionary trajectory appears to be broadly structured by economic policies. For several scholars, such as Frankel (2005), Bardhan (2009), Harriss (2011) and Kohli (2012), the key to this narrowness lies in the nature of industrial/employment policies, which have been knowledge and skill intensive, excluding large numbers of unskilled manpower. The current model of economic growth is predicated on the expansion of services, rather than manufacturing, and in high-skill sectors like IT and ITES. The overwhelming majority of India's poor do not have access to the kind of skills that could incorporate them into the knowledge-based IT services. The potential impact of IT services playing a catalytic role in creating employment and raising incomes thus is problematic in a situation where the initial steps have not been taken in redistributing opportunities and resources (Frankel 2007). In a recent article, John Harriss (2011) has highlighted that throughout the 1990s, India had no employment policy. In the context of the high growth that the economy experienced throughout the 1990s and early 2000s, the absence of an employment policy obviously meant that growth and employment were no longer aligned public policy concerns. Atul Kohli (2012), in a work appropriately entitled *Poverty Amid Plenty in the New India*, underlines that industrial growth has been lacklustre; the growth of services, while dramatic, has not been accompanied by growth of employment in this sector. Although the growth of IT provides the most dramatic face of the growth of the service sector, it in fact constitutes only 2 per cent of the gross domestic product (GDP), and has not led to any significant growth in employment opportunities, particularly for the unskilled workforce.[9]

Scholars in this third genre have written more about employment/labour market policies, and engaged less with welfare; interestingly, however, their overall interpretation of the nature of the capitalist developmental state converges with the theorisation of possibilities that marks the literature on welfare. Thus, these scholars have provided an open-ended reading of what may be possible for the capitalist developmental state. The state has made some policy choices which have an inegalitarian impact, but these are choices (not necessarily determined or inevitable).

> It is increasingly accepted that the relationship of growth to inequality is mediated by policy. Among the important determinants of growing inequality in India is the decline of public investment in agriculture and in India's poor regions. *There is nothing inevitable about such policy choices.* (Kohli 2012, 222, italics mine)

Pranab Bardhan, in a 2009 article, emphasised that a specific trajectory is the result of policy choice, and policies or trajectories are not determined by the logic or structure of capitalism. Poverty in India cannot be extended to be a criticism of the overall trajectory of late capitalist development.

> In the last quarter century, China and Vietnam, and a few other South East Asian countries, had rapid capitalist development with massive labour intensive industrialisation ... If it is thus not inherent in capitalist development, why is India different, with the labour absorption process so sluggish[?] (Bardhan 2009: 36)

In his opinion, too, when there is political action and negotiation, it is possible to get the state to benefit structurally unemployed workers, as has happened in western welfare states. While conceding that European systems are vastly different, Bardhan maintains that his qualitative point remains on similar lines, that it is indeed possible for the state to bring some benefits to the jobless 'without fundamentally altering the basic nature of capitalist relations' (2009: 33).

Bardhan and Kohli, particularly, share the view that policy remains a matter of choice, more so for democratic states, and therefore there is nothing determined, or inevitable, about the inequitable nature of capitalist development. Thus, even as these scholars provide very critical readings of India's exclusionary growth, they assert that states have the choice to make policies that can generate more employment, provide more welfare, and so on.

Interestingly, then, for this genre of scholars, the narrowness of India's development is not theorised in terms of the overall nature of the developmental, capitalist state. While the state–capital relationship is part of the explanation of the exclusivist nature of India's growth trajectory, and this is underscored particularly in Kohli's work (2006, 2012), the analytical framework nevertheless remains open-ended in terms of the state's potential capacity to adopt policies which might have a more pro-people slant.

Welfare, democracy and activism

The theorisation of possibilities of the developmental capitalist state has been taken forward and fine-tuned by scholars writing on democratic politics. Despite the problematic relationship of democracy to poverty/redistribution, democracy indeed remains the touchstone of the domain of possibilities. Within the overall framework of state-centric writings, in recent times, perhaps one of the most imaginative interventions has come from Partha Chatterjee. In a widely discussed article written in 2008, Chatterjee refers to the dispossession that occurs in the process of capitalist accumulation (appropriation of agricultural land, displacement of people from traditional habitats and livelihoods, denial of space to small sellers on city pavements, loss of public sector jobs, loss of small businesses, and so on). The state, according to Chatterjee, can no longer afford to ignore the claims of these sections, made via a democratic electoral system and expressed through various associational activities in political society. While the state may be predominantly pursuing a capitalist growth path which benefits a narrow class, willy-nilly it also brings some welfare to the poorer classes, not because it has good or bad intentions, but because it is forced/persuaded by the democratic imperative to ensure some sharing of the fruits of growth.

Earlier, Chatterjee (2004) had provided the concept of 'political society' – the space for subaltern associational activities. Political society may well frequently be seen in the margins of legality (slum dwellers organising for rights on encroached land, pavement sellers organising for rights to sell on public roads, and so on). The claims of people therefrom are a matter of continuous political negotiation and the results are never secure or permanent. Their entitlements, even when recognised, never become rights.

The value of the idea of political society lies in that it represents one of the first efforts to conceptualise political agency in the informal sector.

> The difficulties of class organisation in the so-called informal sector of labour, where the capitalist and petty modes of production are intertwined in a mutually reinforcing tangle. Despite sincere efforts of many activists, Leninist strategies of working-class organisation have floundered here. The political leaders of the left have instead turned their attention to elsewhere and found much greater success – in political society. (Chatterjee 2004: 64)

The informal sector, then, becomes central in the imagining of the welfare state.

Can we indeed make a substantive set of connections between the political economy of the informal sector, a possible politics of welfare, and the state? Chatterjee himself has looked only, and briefly, at transitory associational expressions of claims of the urban underclass, not at the structure of the informal sector itself. How does the political activism of informal workers, qua workers, look on the ground?

Recent empirical work on informal sector workers' political representation has asserted that informal workers have increasingly and successfully looked to the state for welfare, rather than to private employers for fair wages. This underpins a fundamental mutuality – labour works for unregulated wages, while empowered to bargain for social benefits from the state. Rina Agarwala (2013), in a comparative study of *bidi* (a thin cigarette filled with tobacco flakes wrapped in a leaf) and construction workers across three Indian states, found that early workers' movements in these sectors strove to transform the informal workforce in the mirror of formal workers. More contemporary movements reflect a gradual shift of attention from employer to the state, from work- and wage-related issues to more general social-welfare-related rights. This then leads Agarwala to the conclusion that this alternative model 'incorporates the informal sector as an active participant in capitalist growth'.[10] In this sense, then, her thesis falls squarely within Chatterjee's broader reading of how democracy might bring some benefits to poor groups.

The different genres presented here are a sample of an emerging, fairly hegemonic construction: marking a departure from the neoliberal idea of minimalist governments, the core understanding is that the capitalist developmental state can and must have a serious welfare commitment. The idea of state autonomy – that the state has the space to exercise the choice of being more inclusive – provides a central conceptual ingredient to this framework. And a new imagining of popular empowerment, through political society, new trade unions, and so on, provides the outer ribbon that supports this conceptual framework.

Two related sets of questions could be asked about the welfare- and state-centric framework outlined here. First, in India the fact that both central and state governments have enacted a vast number of welfare measures could hardly be contested. The question raised here is more about the paradigm within which welfare is conceived, that the concern with welfare appears to have argued work and wages out of the framework of redistributive concerns. The second question relates to the thornier question of political agency of informal sector workers: can one assume that democracy works for informal workers, and what are the political resources available to informal workers in a political economy context which defines their fragmentation and powerlessness?

Elsewhere I have presented in detail findings from studies across Bangalore on construction workers' wages and other benefits. Close to half of the workers surveyed earned less than the minimum wage and work availability was insufficient and irregular. State-sponsored social security, through Welfare Boards, is given in terms of accident insurance, pension, scholarships, and so on. The claims recognised by the state and sought to be implemented through the Boards do not speak of wages, income and housing, the three most important points of deprivation in the lives of construction workers. The number of workers registered in the Boards is low, and awareness and implementation of the welfare measures remain partial and inadequate (RoyChowdhury 2017). My findings are confirmed by other studies of construction workers, conducted across the private and public sectors. Overall, the situation speaks of deprivation on both fronts: wages and social security. These findings raise questions about the emerging paradigms in labour studies, discussed earlier, that state-sponsored social security can address the plight of industrial workers whose wages are low and unregulated. Can one indeed talk about industrial worker welfare through state-sponsored social security in a context where the issue of wages remains unaddressed?

Perhaps one could raise a tentative question about the so-called South Asian models as well, taking particularly the case of Bangladesh into account. As mentioned earlier, Sen and Drèze have held up the case of Bangladesh as an example of a small nation which has made impressive gains on welfare even though the rates of economic growth do not match those of India in the post-reform period. Bangladesh's welfare gains are particularly impressive in the areas of overall health, literacy, infant mortality rates, and so on.

Sen and Drèze have provided an analysis of the factors that have made this stellar performance possible in an otherwise poor nation, stating that women's education has made a huge difference to awareness about health issues, and particularly highlighting the role of grassroots women health activists and social workers who undertook sustained door-to-door rural campaigns to raise awareness about health issues. The overall framework of analysis then leads to the conclusion that with a combination of state-supported social policies in health and education and a well-functioning civil society, activated, importantly, through women's education and awareness, welfarist human development becomes a possibility in a developing country context, even in the more poor ones.

On the other hand, both in the public media and in academic research, many questions have been raised about the wages and conditions of women workers in Bangladesh's large export-oriented apparel industry. While this global supply chain has provided employment to large numbers of unskilled young women in Bangladesh's cities, the industry is characterised by widespread violation of minimum wages, denial of social security, imposition of unfair and unpaid over-time work and the use of child labour. These features of exploitation of a female workforce has drawn much international attention to Bangladesh's garment industry, highlighting primarily that women's inequality in a highly traditional society has been used and reproduced in this global supply chain. Thus, while subsistence-level incomes have been generated for women workers, this has not led to economic security or empowerment of the workforce.

The literature on this subject is vast, and I do not go into details of that discussion here. What needs to be highlighted is that the advancements in women's health and education in Bangladesh, as pointed out by Sen and Drèze, must remain commendable; on the other hand, the blind spots constituted by a vast swathe of unregulated manufacturing, marked by the exploitation of unskilled women's labour, raise serious questions about workers' rights in the context of Bangladesh's increasing integration into the global economy through export industries based primarily on cheap labour. To what extent, then, can we theorise the welfare capacities of developmental states, even where there are some recorded and commendable advances in human development, in a context where the structure and practices of economic production underpin the disempowerment of an already vulnerable section, that is, unskilled women workers.

More broadly, these findings throw open central question of collective action and political representation of informal workers. What are the political spaces available to informal workers to press even their social welfare claims on the state? Finally, within a democratic framework, what are the ideologies and institutions that are constitutive of informal workers as a political force, if at all? Theorisations of the state's active role in providing welfare have possibly paid relatively little attention to these questions.

Choice and structure

The different streams of arguments outlined here, when read together, constitute what could be seen as efforts to re-theorise the capitalist developmental state. With the NICs, the argument that states can balance social insurance with market-driven growth is based on these countries' small populations, a longer (compared to South Asian states) history of economic growth, as well as of universal education, which created a foundation for the shift to globally integrated manufacturing and a service-sector–dominated economy. The NIC experience, briefly outlined earlier, highlights that even in the context of these highly favourable conditions, the changing structure of the labour market towards increasingly irregular employment places large numbers of persons beyond the scope of full state-sponsored social insurance, and a dual labour market creates differential access to state-sponsored protection.

In the context of India, several scholars have asserted that heightened economic growth, made possible by liberalisation, can be used to expand social expenditure, and thus to create more inclusive systems. Sharper critiques of India's growth story have highlighted the limited scope of welfare, and the lack of growth of jobs for the unskilled, nevertheless maintaining that developmental states in principle have the choice to make more inclusive industrial policies. The element of choice, emphasised by scholars such as Bardhan and Kohli, and the accommodative capacity of democracy as in Chatterjee's work, constitute the conceptual pillars of this genre of recent theorisations of the capitalist developmental state. Framing this theorisation is the understanding, widely shared, that democratic politics allows for the representation and articulation of lower-class interests.

Are state policies that generate exclusivist growth determined by the choices made by political regimes at given times, or are these determined by the deeper structural logic of capitalism? At one level, these questions may generate a theoretical quicksand. An over-determinist perspective on this closes down the possibilities of a more nuanced and comparative understanding of the different options available within the broadly defined framework of state-supported capitalism. The idea that political regimes indeed have the choice to make more, or less, inclusive policies makes both empirical and common sense.

However, the question of choice leads us back to the issue of the nature of state power and what drives state policies in one direction rather than in another; why is it that democratically elected political regimes fail to make policies that would tilt the scales in favour of those who remain excluded from the benefits of growth? The questions that remain unaddressed are: What could be the possible foundations of such a politics, and, more specifically, its relationship to the political economy? Does the structure of informal work, closely aligned to the dominant growth model, preclude the formation of the political agency of informal workers?

The empirical materials in this book present a somewhat different story, which tells us that the disadvantages of the poor are in fact deeply rooted in the structure of the accumulation system, which prevents the poor from becoming part of the structures that generate economic growth. Informal work not only defines the livelihood of the poor, but also provides the boundaries which limit a possible politics of the poor. These themes with regard to the urban poor in Bangalore city are presented in the empirical chapters (5–8). I turn now to the literature which provides an outline of the debates on urban poverty in India.

Notes

1. See, for example, Rodrik (1997).
2. Stiglitz's analysis of the East Asian crisis is predicated on the same argument that it happened when East Asian states lost their autonomy vis-à-vis foreign banks and multilateral institutions. Thus, briefly, according to him, financial and capital market liberalisation, pressed on these states by the bank fund, made these countries vulnerable to external investment fluctuations, and high interest rates, again an IMF conditionality, forced a large number of companies into bankruptcy.
3. In this earlier phase, these developmental states were built on successful land reforms of the 1950s. Moreover, redistribution and welfare initiatives were consistent with the paternalistic ideologies and security concerns of the ruling KMT in Taiwan and the military in South Korea. See, particularly, Amsden (1989) and Haggard and Moon (1990).
4. In South Korea, scholars have noted a gradual shift towards irregular employment (Kalinowski 2007). However, during two successive progressive, left-leaning regimes (1997–2008), existing insurance schemes such as the National Pension Scheme, the Health Insurance Scheme and the Employment Insurance Scheme were extended and universalised to the entire workforce.

It should be noted that social spending in South Korea remains one of the lowest amongst Organisation for Economic Co-operation and Development (OECD) countries.

5. See, particularly, Kalinowski (2007) and Kong (2005).

6. For a critique of repressive labour policies in the early phase of South Korea's development, see Deyo (1989); for a more recent critical assessment of the impact of globalisation and economic crisis on employment and labour policies in South Korea and Taiwan, see Yang (2013).

7. One of the earliest in this genre was Jagdish Bhagwati's (1988) article in which he spelt out the mistakes of a controlled and closed economy.

8. The more prominent among the UPA's progressive legislation are the Right to Information, the National Rural Employment Generation Act (NREGA), Recognition of Forest Rights, the Right to Education and, finally, the National Food Security Act.

9. Frankel's work provides an analysis that comes close to a classical Marxist position, that the state has aligned itself with propertied classes, the landed elite, followed by the corporate business interests. To that extent, Frankel's analysis falls within a determinist, structuralist framework.

10. See also Tietelbaum (2010), who in a study of industrial disputes in three Indian states, came to similar conclusions. Democracy, according to him, facilitates the peaceful resolution of disputes, and therefore enhances the prospects of industrial and economic growth. Political parties need industrial workers' political support during elections. Therefore, it is to the interest of political parties to facilitate the resolution or prevention of industrial disputes (through trade union activities).

References

Agarwala, Rina. 2013. *Informal Labor, Formal Politics and Dignified Discontent in India.* New York: Cambridge University Press.

Ahluwalia, Montek Singh. 2004. 'Policies for Development in a Globalising World.' Thirty First Foundation Day Lecture at Indian Institute of Management, Bangalore.

———. 2005. 'India's Experience with Globalization.' David Finch Memorial Lecture at Melbourne University, Australia.

Amsden, Alice H. 1989. *Asia's Next Giant: South Korea and Late Industrialization.* New York: Oxford University Press.

Bardhan, Pranab. 1984. *Political Economy of Development in India.* New Delhi: Oxford University Press.

———. 2009. 'Notes on the Political Economy of India's Tortuous Transition.' *Economic and Political Weekly* 44 (49): 31–36.

Bhagwati, Jagdish. 1988. 'Poverty and Public Policy.' *World Development* 16 (5): 539–55.

————. 2004. *In Defence of Globalization*. New York: Oxford University Press.

Bhalla, Surjit S. 2000. *New Economic Policies for a New India*. New Delhi: ICSSR and Har Anand Publications.

————. 2002. *Imagine There's No Country: Poverty, Inequality, and Growth in the Era of Globalization*. Washington, DC: Institute for International Economics.

————. 2006. 'Rethinking Indian Growth 1950–2005: Misunderstood or Misjudged?' NCAER-NBER conference paper at Neemrana, India, January.

Chatterjee, Partha. 2004. *Politics of the Governed: Reflections on Popular Politics in Most of the World*. New York: Columbia University Press.

————. 2008. 'Democracy and Economic Transformation in India.' *Economic and Political Weekly* 43 (16): 53–62.

Cornia, Giovanni A., Richard Jolly and Frances Stewart. 1987. *Adjustment with a Human Face*. Oxford: Oxford University Press.

Deyo, Frederic. 1989. *Beneath the Miracle: Labour Subordination in the New Asian Industrialization*. Berkeley: University of California Press.

Drèze, Jean. 2007. 'NREGA: Dismantling the Contractor Raj.' *The Hindu*, 20 November.

Frankel, Francine. 1978. *India's Political Economy, 1947–1977: The Gradual Revolution*. Princeton: Princeton University Press.

————. 2005. *India's Political Economy, 1947–2004: The Gradual Revolution*. Princeton: Princeton University Press.

Haggard, Stephen, and Chung-In Moon. 1990. 'Institutions and Economic Policy: Theory and a Korean Case Study.' *World Politics* 42 (2): 210–37.

Harriss, John. 2011. 'How Far Have India's Economic Reforms Been Guided by Compassion and Justice: Social Policy in the Neo Liberal Era.' In *Understanding India's New Political Economy: A Great Transformation?* edited by S. Ruparelia, S. Reddy, J. Harriss and S. Corbridge, 66–80. Oxford: Routledge.

John, Mary, and Satish Deshpande. 2008. 'Theorising the Present: Problems and Possibilities.' *Economic and Political Weekly* 43 (46): 83–86.

Kalinowski, Thomas. 2007. 'Democracy, Economic Reforms and Market-Oriented Reforms'. *Comparative Sociology* 6 (3): 344–73.

Kohli, Atul. 2006. 'Politics of Economic Growth in India: 1980–2005'. *Economic and Political Weekly* 41 (13): 1251–59.

————. 2012. *Poverty Amid Plenty in the New India*. Cambridge: Cambridge University Press.

Kong, Tat Yan. 2005. 'Labour and Neo-Liberal Globalization in South Korea and Taiwan.' *Modern Asian Studies* 39 (1): 155–88.

Mettler, S. 2015. 'Twenty Years On: Peter Pierson's Dismantling the Welfare State?' *Political Science and Politics* 48 (2): 270–73.

Nayar, Baldev Raj. 2009. *The Myth of the Shrinking State: Globalization and the State in India*. New Delhi: Oxford University Press.

————. 2010. 'Economic Globalization and State Capacity in South Asia.' In *South Asia's Weak States: Understanding the Regional Insecurity Predicament,* edited by T. V. Paul, 98–121. Stanford: Stanford University Press.

Nayyar, Deepak. 2008. *Liberalisation and Development.* New Delhi: Oxford University Press.

Panagariya, A. 2008. *India: The Emerging Giant.* New Delhi: Oxford University Press.

————. 2010. 'India's Unfinished Business.' *Foreign Policy,* 4 November.

Pierson, P. 1995. *The New Politics of the Welfare State: Reagan, Thatcher and the Politics of Retrenchment.* Cambridge: Cambridge University Press.

Rodrik, D. 1997. *Has Globalization Gone Too Far.* Washington, DC: Institute for International Economics.

Ruparelia, S. 2013. 'India's New Rights Agenda: Genesis, Promises, Risks.' *Pacific Affairs* 86 (3): 569–90.

RoyChowdhury, Supriya. 2017. 'New Paradigms in Labour Studies: How Much Do They Explain'. In *Political Economy of Contemporary India,* edited by R. Nagaraj and S. Motiram, 179–202. New Delhi: Cambridge University Press, 2017.

Sen, A. 1994. *Beyond Liberalization: Social Opportunity and Human Capability.* New Delhi: Institute of Social Sciences.

————. 2000. *Development as Freedom.* New Delhi: Oxford University Press.

Sen, A., and J. Drèze. 2013. *An Uncertain Glory: India and its Contradictions.* Princeton: Princeton University Press.

Stiglitz, Joseph. 2002. *Globalization and Its Discontents.* London: Penguin Press.

Tietelbaum, E. 2010. 'Mobilizing Restraint: Economic Reforms and the Politics of Industrial Protest in South Asia.' *World Politics* 62 (4): 676–713.

Tillin, L., R. Deshpande and K. Kailash, eds. 2015. *Politics of Welfare: Comparisons across Indian States.* New Delhi: Oxford University Press.

Vanaik, Achin. 1990. *The Painful Transition: India's Bourgeois Democracy.* London: Verso.

Varshney, Ashutosh. 2000. 'Why Haven't Poor Democracies Eliminated Poverty? A Suggestion'. *Asian Survey* 40 (5): 718–36.

Yang, Jae-Jin. 2013. 'Parochial Welfare Politics and the Small Welfare State in South Korea.' *Comparative Politics* 45 (4): 457–75.

3

Urban Poverty and Informal Work

Poverty of cities and the phrase 'urbanisation of poverty' has drawn much recent scholarly and policy attention.[1] The overall consensus and a shared concern seem to be that rural poverty is declining significantly, while the pace of reduction of urban poverty is slower. Beyond this broad consensus, however, the literature shows that there are very different approaches to understanding urban poverty. International policy agencies have mostly seen urban poverty as a spillover of rural poverty, caused by the process of migration of the rural poor. On the other hand, particularly in the Indian case, scholars have argued, on the basis of migration data, that the poorest do not migrate, and on this view, the roots of urban poverty lie in the structure of the urban and industrial political economy rather than in the poverty of migrants.

This political economy framework of analysis rests on three important dimensions of the urban context in India: first, the narrowness of urbanisation, as the number of small towns and cities, their developmental trajectories as well as their potential as providers of industrial employment remain stunted due to lack of policy attention; second, the absence of structural transformation in the economy, as large numbers remain tied to agriculture (disproportionate to agriculture's declining share in GDP) primarily because of lack of growth of jobs in the manufacturing sector; and third, work available to the unskilled or semi-skilled urban workforce, whether migrant or non-migrant, is in the informal sectors of manufacturing, construction, lower rungs of the services or in self-employment. Marked by low and irregular wages and income as well as lack of job security and social insurance, informal work underpins the poverty of large numbers of urban workers. In this context, some scholars have emphasised that state-sponsored social insurance can be an instrument of inclusion of poor informal workers into higher levels of access to health, education and other services, thus presenting formality–informality as a continuum, rather than as a binary. Contrarily, others have seen informality as structured exclusion, a result of globally competitive, high-technology production and services, naturally excluding the unskilled and underprivileged. The following sections provide information on some broad features of the Indian economy framed by the debates on migration, employment and informality.

Migration and urban poverty

An important strand of scholarly opinion, associated with the World Bank and other international agencies, appears to hold that despite the growing incidence of poverty, cities remain spaces of dynamic and growing opportunities. There are three important points in this genre of literature: First, in this view, it is the poor who are urbanising faster than others. The gains of urbanisation, however, may not be large enough for all previously poor new urban residents to escape poverty. Thus, it is migration that puts a brake on the decline in urban poverty. Rising urban poverty incidence is thus consistent with falling overall poverty. Second, this literature highlights the opportunities provided by urbanisation to rural–urban migrants, as well as second-round effects of urbanisation such as remittances and tighter rural labour markets (Ravallion, Chen and Sangrula 2007). Third, the urban poor may be at the bottom of the economic ladder, but there is at least a ladder for them to start climbing in cities and towns. Urban areas provide opportunities for the children of migrants through better education and job prospects (United Nations Human Settlements Program 2007). Rising or stagnant urban poverty is 'only the other side of the coin to what is in large part a poverty reducing process of urbanization' (Ravallion, Chen and Sangrula 2007).

In India, as per the 2011 census, migration was predominantly from rural to rural areas (47 per cent), followed by urban to urban areas (22.6 per cent). Migration from rural to urban areas was 22.1 per cent, rising marginally from 21.8 per cent as recorded in the 2001 census. The share of rural–urban migrants in the population rose from 5.06 per cent in 2001 to 6.5 per cent in 2011. Six districts are the largest rural–urban migrant-receiving districts in the country: Mumbai Suburban, Surat, Thane, Pune, Bangalore and Ahmedabad. In 2011, out of the 78 million rural–urban migrants, only 19.6 million were inter-state migrants; the rest moved within the state. The union territories have small local populations, and therefore, in comparison to states, receive larger percentage of inter-state migrants.

The thesis that the poorest migrate, and that urban poverty is a result of migration of those who are unable to take advantage of urban opportunities, put forward by international organisations (outlined earlier), appears to have been challenged in recent years, particularly by scholars in India. Well-known migration scholar Amitabh Kundu's work documents that the poorest in rural India do not migrate. Basing his analysis on the 55th round of the National Sample Survey (NSS) (1999–2000), which combines information on migration with information on consumption expenditure and employment, Kundu shows that the relatively better-off/better-informed among the rural population are those who are able to actually move to cities and towns; economic deprivation is not the most critical factor in migration (Kundu and Sarangi 2007; Kundu 2012). The rise in the share of regular workers among rural–urban migrants at the place of destination suggests, according to Kundu, mobility at the higher stratum of the socio-economic hierarchy (Kundu 2012, 2011).[2] Similarly, Dubey, Jones and Sen (2006) argue on the basis of their analysis of the 1999–2000 round of the NSS that individuals from the SCs and STs and those with little or no education are less likely to migrate to urban areas. Other scholars have, however, critiqued interpretations based on national-level surveys. It has been pointed out, on the basis of case studies of local-level migration processes, that the poorest do migrate, particularly from remote rural areas. Priya Deshingkar (2010), for example, using information from six village-level case studies in Andhra Pradesh and Madhya Pradesh, has shown that migration is higher among chronically poor groups in remote rural areas, the majority of them belonging to SC, ST and Other Backward Classes (OBCs).

The debate on who migrates has obvious implications for understanding the structure of urban opportunities and the impact of migration on migrants. I have outlined earlier that international institutions have taken a uniformly positive view of migration, insisting that even for the poorest, the urban provides a ladder of opportunities which they would eventually start to climb. In contrast, there has been a steady stream of work which has pointed to the highly exploitative dimensions of the poor's migration, as well as to the understanding that migration leads to mere subsistence, rather than to well-being or socio-economic mobility (Breman 1978; Olsen and Ramanamurthy 2000; Reddy 1990). More recent research on migration has taken a more middle-of-the-road position. Deshingkar's work, mentioned earlier, looked at households in six villages across a seven-year time period. Critical of the position that migration worsens urban poverty and destroys families, she records that for many households seasonal migration meant that they could return their loans, their families ate better and healthcare was possible. The history of these households indicated that migration helps them to better cope with poverty, rather than graduating out of poverty. The study revealed that seasonal migrants remain confined to work that is described as dirty, degrading and dangerous. Deshingkar pointed to the need for insuring households against risks and costs of migration.

A largely similar conclusion was reached by another study (Mitra 2010) where slums in four north Indian cities, Ludhiana, Mathura, Jaipur and Ujjain, were studied. Mitra concluded from this study that rural–urban migration has been beneficial to migrants, that is, they may experience some improvement in income. On the other hand, large numbers of long-duration migrants and natives have low levels of well-being and high incidence of poverty. Mitra thus critiqued the spillover thesis, while drawing attention to the persistent nature of urban poverty and the need for policy attention on urban employment programmes. Pattenden's work on seasonal migrants from Raichur in northern Karnataka, who work as construction workers in Bangalore, showed that low skill and otherwise resourceless migrants move from one site of exploitation, that of small agrarian capital, to another, that of large builders in Bangalore. Nevertheless, seasonal urban employment provides migrants with some degree of negotiating power vis-à-vis local landlords (Pattenden 2012). The literature therefore seems to swing – between the uncritical optimism of international organisations about the positive impact of migration, the pessimism of others who narrate the hardships and deprivations of migrant lives, and more cautious middle-of-the-road positions which recognise the benefits of migration while highlighting the risks and costs and continuing marginalisation of the urban poor, both migrants and non-migrants.

An important strand of anthropological scholarship on migration has suggested that the understanding of migration must go beyond its association with economic distress. Alpa Shah's research on workers from Jharkhand working in brick kilns in West Bengal indicated that the newly created tribal state, generating a discourse of migration as a 'problem' and a threat to purity and regulation, had pushed young men to migrate. Such youth may be motivated to migrate to escape problems back home, a vigilante state, explore a new place or the possibilities of amorous relations, and so on (Shah 2006). The idea that migration is a choice, rather than determined by economic distress, echoed in earlier anthropological writing as well. Studying West Bengal's jute industry, De Haan made the interesting point that Bihari workers remain seasonal migrants by choice, preferring to use their urban industrial incomes to enhance their rural resources, rather than to become the urban proletariat. De Haan's (1994, 2002) research on western Bihar's more than a century's history of continuous and cyclical out-migration led him to believe that migration is not a transitory phenomenon, that is, an immediate response to poverty, but must be seen as defined by history, culture and regional identity.

Specific case studies, as shown here, of course lead to more nuanced understandings of migration than given in a mono-causal poverty–migration paradigm. However, a wide range of studies from across the country have shown that cyclical migration remains primarily a response to extreme economic need. In West Bengal's Sunderbans, several scholars and commentators have recorded the impact of climate change and natural disasters forcing young men's migration, particularly to Kerala, as construction workers. Their tragic journeys back and forth – driven by cyclones Alia and Ampha in 2009 and 2020, devastating floods in Kerala in 2018, and the huge dislocations caused by the COVID-19 pandemic (2020) – occur in a context of the region's overall lack of development and successive government's failure to provide rehabilitation and rebuilding of livelihoods (Samling, Das and Hazra 2015; Afroz 2020). On a different plane, Maharashtra's power-loom industry, which contributes 60 per cent of the country's textiles production, runs on the labour of migrants from Bihar and Uttar Pradesh, who returned to their villages of origin in the wake of the pandemic-related lockdown in March 2020. Within a few months of this so-called reverse migration, as power-loom towns like Bhiwandi and Malegaon gradually reopened production, thousands of migrant labourers returned, who had found no means of livelihood in their villages. These cases would suggest the continuing centrality of economic distress and vulnerabilities that mark the lives of large numbers of cyclical migrants in different parts of the country, thus raising questions around the pattern and nature of urbanisation that is actually occurring. What also emerges from these processes of cyclical migration is that a huge and easily replaceable labouring class is continuously produced for the urban industrial and service sectors, while the cyclical nature of this labour force prevents the creation of a robust, urban and inter-generational workforce. I return to this point in the concluding Chapter 9.

Urbanisation and small cities and towns

Recent and emerging work on urban issues in India indicate that poverty of cities may be rooted in the structural features of the urban political economy, rather than in the poverty of migrants, thus challenging the spillover thesis. These structural features have been seen in the nature of industrial development that has failed to produce work for large numbers of the unskilled workforce.

This is indicated, first, by the slow rate of urbanisation. Despite high economic growth, the rate of urbanisation in India – the percentage of the population living in urban areas and the annual growth rate of urban population – has in fact been one of the lowest in the context of developing countries.[3] Second, the lacklustre pace and pattern of growth of small towns and cities show the narrowness of urban opportunities. The *India: Urban Poverty Report 2009* noted that urban growth in smaller towns is significantly below that in other categories. During the 1980s, smaller towns and cities recorded a growth rate of 2.57 per cent compared to 3.25 per cent in metro cities. The 1990s saw a further decline in the growth rate for small towns, coming down to 2.22 per cent only, as compared to the metro cities recording a growth rate of 2.88 per cent. Class 1 cities grew slower than metro cities, and it is noteworthy that there was a decline in the growth of all size classes of cities (Hashim 2009). It has further been shown that it is basically towns having populations between 50,000 and 200,000 that have experienced economic decline and consequently low demographic growth (Kundu and Sarangi 2005).

The pattern of urbanisation in India, as is well known, has been heavily biased towards metro cities. The census of 2011 showed that the number of urban conurbations grew from 5,161 in 2001 to 7,935 in 2011; however, this was mainly because of reclassification of settlements from rural to urban as they start showing higher population density (more than 1,000 persons per square metre) and as non-agricultural work becomes dominant. While transformed into 'cities' in their legal–bureaucratic identities, they are, however, not officially recognised as 'urban', as they continue to lack the institutional and administrative machinery and support provided to urban areas. They suffer from absence of strong institutions of local governance, state-sponsored development schemes, private sector investment, and continuing loss of agricultural and forest land to development and infrastructural projects that do not necessarily benefit their residents (Kundu 2011; Sharma 2012). Scholars have drawn attention to newly created small towns, as they floundered because of lack of focussed industrial and infrastructural development, and their potential as drivers of growth and providers of employment remained unexplored. At the same time, erstwhile prosperous small towns and cities which had earlier been vibrant centres of industrial activity stagnated and declined. On the other side, as the larger metro cities became artificial epicentres of India's technology-led, highly consumerist, globally connected growth, the underbelly of this trajectory was represented by large numbers of unskilled migrant labour crowding into low-paid work in construction and services, their lives confined to under-serviced, informal settlements or labour colonies.[4]

Structural transformation

Third, and relatedly, one of the most widely discussed themes in contemporary Indian political economy is that while agriculture's share in GDP has steadily fallen, currently to about 18 per cent, the percentage of people dependent upon agriculture as a means of livelihood continues to be unusually high at close to 50 per cent.[5] Thus, a widely shared concern is that the structural transformation of the economy, typically represented by the movement of large numbers from agriculture to industry, has not taken place in India on the expected scale.[6]

The wide-ranging debates amongst economists on structural transformation are only indirectly relevant here; as such, I touch upon dimensions of the debates which are of particular significance, from the perspective of the present work, in understanding the nature of urban poverty.[7] According to the *India: Urban Poverty Report 2009*, why agriculture continues to harbour workers beyond its capacity is a complex problem but one obviously related to the nature of industrial and urban growth, and in general this situation underscores the lack of opportunities for relatively low-skilled workers in urban areas (Hashim 2009). Of particular relevance is that the manufacturing sector – historically the employment destination of unskilled workers – has failed to expand its employment share significantly over the last two-and-a-half decades, remaining in the range of 10–13 per cent of the workforce. As Table 3.1 shows, manufacturing employment remained virtually stagnant during the decade 1999–2000 to 2009–10, and during 2004–05 to 2009–10 it showed a decline of more than 5 million jobs. Between 2011 and 2015, the number of jobs in manufacturing remained the same, at 50 million. It should be highlighted, however, that during this period the share of organised sector jobs in manufacturing increased from 18 per cent to 27.5 per cent. While this increase has been widely noted and hailed as a positive development, many have also pointed out that a rise in organised sector jobs has meant a rise in contract work and apprenticeships, wherein employers have a diminished

Table 3.1 Sectoral share (in per cent)/absolute numbers (in lakhs) in employment

	1999–2000	*2004–05*	*2009–10*	*2015–16*
Manufacturing	11.1/44.5	12.2/55.75	11.0/50.74	12/50
Construction	5.3/17.54	6.5/26.02	10.5/44.08	50
Services	23.7/94.20	24.7/112.81	25.3/116.34	30.2/150
Agriculture	59.9/257.77	56.6/258.93	53.2/244.85	42.79

Source: Economic Survey of India, several years.
Note: 1 lakh = 100,000.

and undefined responsibility to ensure minimum or statutory wages, social insurance and security of tenure.

Between 2004–05 and 2011–12, around 35 million workers moved out of agriculture into non-agricultural occupations, and this was the first time in India's post-independence history that there was a decline in the absolute numbers of workers engaged in agriculture. There are several competing interpretations of this movement, and I touch very briefly on the debate here. The change has been hailed by some as indicating that structural transformation is underway. Large numbers leaving agriculture, combined with increasing numbers moving from rural to urban areas (discussed earlier), has been seen as a breakthrough: 'the Lewsian turning point took about half a century to arrive'; the doubling of internal migrants in the 2000s, relative to the 1990s, indicates that the rewards (prospective income and employment opportunities, as in the Harris–Todaro model) have become greater than costs and risks that migration might entail (Mehrotra 2019).

However, the question of where this workforce was absorbed does not lead us to optimistic answers. The increase in the share of employment has been mainly in construction and, to a lesser extent, in services. Employment share of manufacturing has increased only marginally. Thus, we find that from 2004–05 to 2011–12, India's non-agricultural GDP grew by an average of 9.4 per cent annually, but employment grew only at 3.5 per cent (Table 3.2). Services and manufacturing grew the fastest, at 10.1 per cent and 8.9 per cent respectively. However, they added jobs at only 2.5 per cent and 1.5 per cent respectively (Kasturi 2014; Srivastava and Naik 2017).

According to the Working Group on Migration (GOI 2017), a little less than 30 per cent of the manufacturing sector workforce is composed of male migrants (16.80 per cent of these are short-term migrants, 13.10 per cent are long-duration migrants). This has been interpreted as indicating that

Table 3.2 Average annual growth rate from 2004–05 to 2011–12

	Real GDP (%)	Employment (%)
Manufacturing	8.9	1.5
Construction	8.8	10.1
Mining	4.9	4.3
Services	10.0	2.5
Total non-agriculture	9.4	3.5

Source: Economic Survey of India, 2013–14.

migrants are not necessarily confined to activities like street vending, but are actually spread across sectors (Mehrotra 2019). However, as has been pointed out earlier, migrant workers employed in industries are often in informal and unregulated work, receiving barely the minimum wage, lacking security of tenure or access to social services. Research on the automobile industry in the National Capital Region (NCR), the power-loom industry in Maharashtra's power-loom cities and the export-oriented apparel industry in cities of north and south India has revealed that migrant workers are indeed employed in the manufacturing sector, but at highly exploitative terms and conditions.

The jobs available to the unskilled urban workforce are mainly in the construction sector. Between 2004–05 and 2011–12, the share of construction in employment almost doubled (from 6.5 per cent to 10.5 per cent); the rise in absolute numbers was even more dramatic (from 26 million to 44 million between 2004–05 and 2009–10, to 50 million in 2012–13). Between 2000–01 and 2010–11, the compound annual growth rate in construction sector was 9.1 per cent, and between 2010–11 and 2015–16, it went up to 9.5 per cent, much higher than in the manufacturing sector. It is of course well known that low wages and multiple deprivations attend the lives of construction workers, particularly the unskilled, who constitute the vast majority of this workforce. Therefore, it is important to underline that the rise in the number of construction workers may indicate a rise in non-agricultural, and mostly urban, employment, but what this trend also signals is that the only employment avenue open to unskilled workers is this sector, marked by low wages and low security.

Finally, while the contribution of the service sector to GDP has grown exponentially (from 49 per cent in 2004–05 to 57.3 per cent in 2009–10, to 66 per cent in 2015–16), its share in employment has lagged behind, growing from 23 per cent in 1999–2000 to 25 per cent in 2009–10 and thence to 30 per cent in 2015. As of 2016, total employment in the services sector stood at 150 million, and of these only 26 million, that is 20 per cent, were in the organised sector. Fifty-five per cent of the service sector employment is in domains like petty retail, hotel, transport (by which is meant small eateries, drivers of public transport, truck drivers) and domestic work, much of which is in the informal, unregulated sector. The proportion of total employment in organised activities increased from 11.5 per cent in 2011 to 15 per cent in 2015 (Basole and Jayadev 2018: 20). This expansion reflects the professionalisation and corporatisation of services that were earlier provided mainly through informal arrangements, such as hospitality, housekeeping, big retail, transportation and logistics, financial services, beauty and wellness and security services. However, informal employment relations characterise much of the so-called formal employment in services, rising from 50.8 per cent to 60.1 per cent between 2011 and 2015 (Basole and Jayadev 2018: 20), drawing attention to what has been called the growth of the precariat within the corporate sector (Gooptu 2013: 11).

Emerging research in this domain has revealed that the lower rungs of the services sector is an unregulated domain of work, where wages can be as low as INR 7,000–8,000 per month and service conditions are undefined and insecure, thus creating an unstable and footloose urban workforce who may move horizontally between jobs in search of an additional few hundred rupees, have few opportunities of moving up in any occupational ladder, may equate work only with earnings, not with a career trajectory, very often return to the village from where they had come, and despite aspirations for a better life, remain excluded from more dynamic channels of growth.[8]

Debate on policy

The two different views on urban poverty, outlined in the previous section, one emerging from international institutions, the other from scholars in India, have led to contrasting policy prescriptions. A World Bank report (Baker 2008) defined slum upgradation primarily as provision of toilets, water supply, health clinics and electricity. The constraints to such upgradation are seen in weak political institutions, challenges in acquiring land, problems in maintenance and cost recovery. Employment- and income-related issues are presented as institutional, rather than structural: the need for job training, micro-enterprise development and childcare facilities. The report stays away from typical features of urban political economies in developing countries: the decline of jobs in the manufacturing sector, informalisation of work and its relation to urban poverty, and so on. According to a study by the Asian Development Bank (ADB), poverty in urban India is characterised by lack of access to basic amenities, shelter, health care, education, and so on. As such, schemes to reduce urban poverty should be related to human development rather than to employment generation (ADB 2009). These perspectives have continued into recent writings in this genre. In a very recent report, *East Asian and Pacific Cities: Expanding Opportunities for the Urban Poor* (2017), Judy Baker and others list as urban problems lack of access to jobs, public transport and other infrastructure, and affordable housing (Baker and Gadgil 2017). These views are important to highlight not only because of the power of the international institutions from which they emerge, and which provides them with an easy legitimacy, the impact of which is clearly seen in domestic policies of low-income countries, but also because the discourse itself has consistently distanced itself from both empirical facts (for example, the decline in job growth) and theoretical perspectives that point to deeply structural factors which underlie the poverty of cities.

On the other hand, the decline of manufacturing, along with, relatedly, the growth of services as the predominant employer in urban areas, has generated much debate. A broad critical perspective on this of course has been that in the era of liberalisation/privatisation, industries, in order to be globally competitive, shifted to more capital- and knowledge-intensive sectors and production processes, thus leapfrogging the stage of labour-intensive industrialisation that had occurred in countries like China and South Korea. There is an emerging convergence on the idea that employment opportunities in the manufacturing sector need to be expanded. Thus, for example, Arvind Panagariya, otherwise known for his strong support for India's economic globalisation policies, has stated that an important reason for poverty and unemployment in India is that the manufacturing sector has remained stagnant, while it is a fact that in most poor, heavily populated countries that grow rapidly, manufacturing typically leads the way (for example, South Korea in the period 1965–75). Similarly, even as the World Bank remains a strong advocate for India's opening up to global markets and a private-sector-led industrialisation model, a World Bank publication has sounded a cautionary note: while acknowledging the importance of the tertiary sector in economic development, the authors state that 'it is unclear that India's human capital and infrastructure are adequately developed to allow India to leapfrog the labour intensive manufacturing stage and follow the growth path of an upper middle income or even an OECD-type economy' (Ahsan and Narain 2007). Others have described this as premature de-industrialisation.[9] As Ajit Ghose, author of the *India Employment Report* (2016), has commented, in history, remote and recent, countries at India's level of development experienced manufacturing-led and not services-led growth; for India too, the time is ripe for a transition to manufacturing-led growth (Ghose 2016).

Much of this critical discussion has based itself on the developmental histories of countries like China, Thailand and the East Asian giants. In each of these contexts, a period of labour-intensive industrialisation made it possible to expand the domain of manufacturing sector jobs for the first generation of industrial workers, mostly unskilled or semi-skilled. This period of growth was followed by the shift to globally competitive, capital-intensive and export-oriented industrial development, accompanied by the necessary changes in the labour market which saw the emergence of more skilled labour as well as the expansion of service sector work. For scholars who have consistently pointed to these developmental histories while at the same time have maintained a sustained criticism of India's low manufacturing employment, the position seems to be that India needs more thoughtful policies directed towards job creation, universal education and skill development during a particular phase of development, before a more full-fledged, globally competitive, capital-intensive and knowledge-based developmental model is adopted.[10]

Urban poverty and informality

The issues and debates outlined here provide a backdrop to an understanding of the ways in which urban poverty is linked to the domains of work and livelihood available to the unskilled urban workforce in India. Without going into the nitty-gritty of different and sometimes conflicting sources and interpretations of the employment structure in India, a simple and fairly accurate narration would be that around 41 per cent in urban areas were self-employed, 17 per cent were employed as casual labour and 41 per cent as regular salaried in 2009–10, as shown in Table 3.3. It is what these categories mean for an understanding of urban life which is important for the purposes here. Self-employed is a broad category. In their comprehensive report *State of Working in India*, Basole and Jayadev (2018) have shown that of the urban self-employed, close to 75 per cent were own account workers, that is, those who did not hire any wage labour, 21 per cent were unpaid contributing family members and 5 per cent were employers in 2015–16. This should convey that the largest majority of self-employed enterprises are small, petty units, run with the owner's own and family labour, at low levels of productivity and profit margins. The Periodic Labour Force Survey 2017–18 (GOI 2018) similarly

Table 3.3 Percentage distribution of urban workers by working status

	Self-employed		Regular salaried		Casual labour	
	Men	Women	Men	Women	Men	Women
1972–73	39.2	48.4	50.7	27.9	10.1	23.7
1977–78	40.4	49.5	46.4	24.9	13.2	25.6
1987–88	41.7	47.1	43.7	27.5	14.6	25.4
1993–94	41.7	45.4	42.1	28.6	16.2	26.2
1999–2000	41.5	45.3	41.7	33.3	16.8	21.4
2004–05	44.8	47.7	40.6	35.6	14.6	16.7
2009–10	41.1	41.1	41.9	39.3	17.0	19.6

Source: *Economic Survey of India*, several years.

indicated that 75 per cent of the self-employed do not hire, 26 per cent of workers employed in own account enterprises are unpaid helpers and only 4 per cent are employers.[11]

The institutional framework of employment is significantly related to the poverty of urban workers. Of urban wage earners, 35 per cent were formally employed and 67 per cent were informally employed in 2015–16 (Basole and Jayadev 2018). As shown in Table 3.4, more than 24 per cent of urban self-employed were poor, and close to half of casual wage earners were poor in 2009–10. Given that as many as 12.5 per cent of salaried workers were poor, this shows that many in the category of salaried workers might not have got even the minimum wage. Taking a closer look at construction work, which dominates employment of unskilled workers, 73.4 per cent were working as casual labour (Table 3.6) and 41.8 per cent were poor in 2009–10 (Table 3.5).

Table 3.4 Percentage of workers (15–64 years) in poverty in urban areas from 1983 to 2009–10

	1983	1987–88	1993–94	1999–2000	2009–10
Self-employed	43.8	40.7	33.5	32.1	24.1
Salaried	26.3	24.0	17.8	16.3	12.5
Casual labour	63.6	64.1	57.2	55.0	49.6
Total	40.1	37.8	31.5	29.7	25.2

Sources: *India: Urban Poverty Report 2009* (Hashim 2009: 81); NSS Employment and Unemployment Survey, 2011–12.

Table 3.5 Percentage of workers (15–64 years) in poverty by selected industries in urban areas from 1983 to 2009–10

	1983	1987–88	1993–94	1999–2000	2009–10
Agriculture	54.4	58.4	52.6	53.1	44.8
Mining	31.0	37.5	27.8	28.2	15.6
Manufacturing	42.1	38.5	30.4	29.6	24.5
Construction	51.4	50.6	44.4	43.9	41.8
Trade and hotels	40.9	37.5	31.5	29.2	21.4
Transport	39.6	38.4	32.2	32.8	25.9
Government and education	21.4	17.1	11.6	9.6	7.8

Sources: *India: Urban Poverty Report 2009* (Hashim 2009: 82); NSS Employment Unemployment Survey, 2011–12.

Table 3.6 Percentage of workers (15–64 years) by activity status and industry in urban areas, 2009–10

	Self-employed	Salaried	Casual labour
Agriculture	60.1	2.8	37.1
Mining	3.8	79.9	11.3
Manufacturing	39.6	46.7	13.7
Construction	16.4	10.3	73.4
Trade and hotels	69.8	23.7	6.5
Transport	40.6	43.5	15.9
Government and education	6.5	92.4	1.1

Source: NSS Employment Unemployment Survey, 2011–12.

The preponderance of poor urban workers in the two categories of self-employed and casual wage earners – the two domains of informal work – needs to be highlighted. There is thus a clear correlation between poverty, work and the institutional framework of work.

Competing theories on informality

The informality–poverty correlation – intuitive as well as obvious from the available information – has generated competing explanations and theoretical frameworks in what could be described as varying levels of abstraction and generality. To situate this theoretical discourse specifically in the Indian context, it should be mentioned that although the size of the informal economy has always been large, the scholarly concern with informality is fairly recent (dating to the 1980s). After independence, public political discourse and the Constitution itself firmly established the state's centrality in leading the developmental agenda. Public sector manufacturing, the large-scale, albeit regulated, private sector, central and state bureaucracies and large government-owned scientific and technological establishments provided the broad framework within which organised-sector employment developed and expanded. But this was indeed a miniscule proportion of the vast workforce, who largely worked in unregulated regimes, whether in self-employment or in casual wage labour, in a wide range of activities, both in rural and urban areas: farms, trading, construction, small and medium manufacturing, street selling, home-work, small eateries, private transportation, and so on.

A shared assumption, in liberal as well as in classical Marxist theoretical traditions, has drawn from the Kuznetzian paradigm that small and petty economic structures would eventually, in the course of development, be amalgamated into the broader framework of modern, large-scale, organised activities. Thus, within liberal or leftist thinking, informality was not theorised. However, the intransigence, as well as the steady expansion, of the informal economy in India, as in other developing countries, has generated many contemporary debates. This relates, first, to an expanded definition of what informality is. The most common definition of the informal sector for a long time seemed to be related to what are technically known as own account enterprises, where there is significant overlap of capital and labour, use of self and family labour, and which are typically characterised by limited investment in terms of capital and technologies and generate low returns. Own account enterprises broadly fall under the category of self-employment. In recent times, the scope of this definition has been extended from informal enterprises to informal employment, covering a whole range of wage work which fall outside of the formal, regulated sector. Increasingly, the gradual encroachment of informality into the formal sector has been noted, as public sector as well as large private sector companies have begun to maintain, along with a regular workforce, contract workers who may not have access to minimum wage, security of tenure and other employment-related benefits. In other words, the concept of informality has widened in scope to embrace the diverse forms of informal work in a variety of institutional contexts.

The literature on informal sector/informality, vast and – as economist Ravi Kanbur had termed it – in a mess (Kanbur 2009), sought to come to terms with both its intransigence and its bewildering diversity. Within the broad framework of accepting the permanence and universality of informality, there are two very different directions in which the literature seems to have moved.

First, there appears to be a broad scholarly convergence that as employment-related social insurance can no longer be practical or feasible (large numbers are self-employed, and wage earners may lack a clear, stable employer, as in construction work), this paradigm must be replaced with state-ensured social insurance. One of the earliest proponents of this paradigm was Manuel Castells. Castells emphasised that the informal economy is in fact universal, as similar arrangements are found in countries at very different levels of economic development. While many individuals who work in the informal economy are, as a matter of fact, poor, it is necessary to go beyond this characteristic and see informality as an emerging *process*, substantively linked to the emerging structure of production in the current scenario of global capitalism.

Castells' contribution was to show that informality is not merely a harking back to forms of production prevalent in the early stages of capitalism, but to see it as a function of capitalism as it is emerging in the present era.

> A key policy issue in this respect is finding the means to break the direct link between social benefits and employment in private firms. A new Social Contract in which governments would guarantee minimum living standards and security to people as people and not as workers, would do away with the most socially wrenching consequences of decentralization and informality. (Castells and Portes 1989)

The following discussion highlights what this perspective means for an understanding of informality in the current scenario.

Built into the Castellian more inclusive policy perspective on informal workers is an important concept, that the formal and informal are in a continuum, rather than opposed binaries. In this view, more or less regulation is what defines the formal and informal, and therefore the informal can, to an extent, be incorporated within the formal, by tweaking the structure of regulations as well as by bringing informal workers within the framework of state-sponsored social insurance. This view is seen, importantly, in the work of an international group of scholars, the Cornell-SEWA-WIEGO group,[12] whose ethnographic research on informal workers, mostly women, spans India, Mexico and South Africa. This group takes a broad, open-ended and loosely structured view of regulation and enforcement in the informal sector. For example, so-called orthodox, neoclassical economists would see wage regulation as leading to loss of employment. The Cornell-SEWA-WIEGO perspective is that a minimum wage, if it is not too high and not fully enforced, may not reduce employment, but it may help expand the bargaining space for wage earners and activists (Bali, Chen and Kanbur 2012). Thus, there is the possibility of at least the partial inclusion of the informal into the formal through greater regulation, and at the same time this perspective leaves enough room for adjusting the framework of regulation to the needs of efficiency and profitability.

Second, through government-sponsored social security intervention, it should be possible to address some of the critical aspects of the poverty and deprivation of informal workers. Access to education and skills would, over the long haul, enable those displaced from their traditional occupations to find alternative employment (Bali, Chen and Kanbur 2012). According to Ravi Kanbur, the study highlights the importance of non-party organisations like SEWA; while there is no shortage of government schemes, what is needed is intermediaries like SEWA to help access these schemes (Bali, Chen and Kanbur 2012).

A combination of a flexible regulatory regime, state-sponsored social security and NGO activism thus holds out the promise of the future incorporation of informal sector workers within the larger growth story of capitalism. An important point made by this group also is that the formal and the informal, although conceptually distinct, empirically are enmeshed.[13]

Overall, this framework speaks for the recognition of basic rights rather than workers' rights, and holds out the possibility of greater incorporation of informal sector workers through the recognition of basic rights. The idea that workers must now look to the state for insurance rather than to private employers, even within the framework of wage work, has found a great deal of purchase among scholars of Indian labour. A critique of this discourse is provided in Chapter 2. This perspective has obviously shaped policy thinking in a significant manner, as the political discourse on poverty and unemployment, indeed on development as a whole, has moved substantively away from addressing issues of work, wages and work-related social insurance to themes of state-sponsored social insurance, minimum income guarantee, universal basic income, and so on. Thus, the informal sector's permanence is recognised, as well as ensured, by getting the state to provide for their basic conditions of survival. What emerges from these perspectives, and what is important for the present discussion, is the effort to define informality into the mainstream capitalist structure in two ways: first, by understating the line of distinction between the formal and the informal, thus conceptually creating a more inclusive framework; and, second, by falling back upon state-guaranteed welfare to act as the basic mechanism of inclusion.

Contrarily, an alternative approach has seen informal workers in a domain of structured exclusion. Kalyan Sanyal's work allows us to see urban lower-class vulnerabilities within the broader framework of the relationship between capitalism and informality. In a widely acclaimed book (Sanyal 2007), he distinguishes between two domains of the informal sector. In the first, as a consequence of globalisation and increasing competition, firms are forced to resort to cost cutting by various practices such as downsizing, outsourcing, and so on. Importantly, the informalisation of the formal sector has meant that within public as well as the private corporate sectors, a significant percentage of the workforce is contractualised, that is, working under unregulated/informal regimes. These informalised practices, according to Sanyal, are taking place within the circuit of capital.

Second, and Sanyal's point of departure from other works on the informal sector, is that while informalisation of work within capitalist production provides an important clue to the nature of exploitation therein, informal production *outside* the framework of capitalism characterises what he calls *exclusion* within the capitalist system. Large numbers of both rural and urban underclasses continue to be displaced from their traditional means of livelihood, and separated from the means of production and survival; at the same time they cannot be incorporated within the capitalist structures of production, whether in agriculture or in industry. Thus it is that huge numbers become *self-employed*; given the nature of their operations, minimum capital investment, use of self and/or family labour, and meagre earnings at subsistence levels, their singular characteristic feature is that they are, for the most part, isolated from the dynamic growth structures of the economy, although they may not be disconnected (thus the home-based garment maker, who supplies to the garment factory owner, who in turn sells to local agents of global retailers, typically earns a subsistence living, although she is inserted into a global supply chain).

Sanyal's theorisation of the informal sector thus views informality as *both outside and necessary to capital*. He draws particular attention to the fact that, given the declining rate of growth of jobs in the manufacturing sector, even informal wage employment in industrial manufacturing has declined. Thus, there is a clear trend towards self-employment as the main source of livelihood for the informal labour force. While this labour force has no direct linkages to the formal economy, it nevertheless performs a vital function for capital in providing a peripheral basin which can absorb the ever-growing numbers who cannot be absorbed into the mainstream economy. In that sense, this outside of capital is necessary for capital to survive.

Other scholarly narratives of the informal sector approximate Sanyal's, but differ as to the structuration of informality. Thus, for example, Barbara Harriss-White has stressed that instead of the vertical movement of workers from subsistence to surplus production, workers are pushed horizontally from the rural, largely informal sector to petty production and casual wage work in the urban informal economy. Harriss-White (2010) sees the informal sector not only as manifesting economic inequality, but as closely structured by multiple sites of social discrimination, such as caste, tribe, religion and gender.

In these theorisations, the liberal as well as Marxist narrative of the transformative effect of capitalism is substantively challenged; what is highlighted is that an ever-larger space in the economy, in terms of numbers, is occupied by those pursuing livelihoods which are disconnected from the mainstream capitalist economy.

Thus, the literature on informality can be said to fall into two domains, broadly speaking, which can be categorised by the concepts of inclusion of informal workers within a welfarist paradigm and exclusion as a function of the structure of global capitalism. More recent theorisations have challenged the notion of exclusion, highlighting the intermeshing of capital and non-capital within petty commodity production (Gidwani and Wainwright 2014) and the graded linkages between the formal and the informal in non-factory labour, as in small workshops, individual home-based production or family labour (Mezzadiri and Lulu 2018). These debates turn on the question of class in the context of contemporary and emerging forms of informality, taken up again in the concluding chapter in this book.

Summing up, this chapter has presented information on rural–urban migration, urban employment structure and the relationship between informal work – in self-employment and wage work – and urban poverty. Even as international organisations interpret urban poverty as the spill-over of the poverty of poor migrants, scholars in India have suggested more structural aspects of urban poverty, seen in the decline of manufacturing employment and the stagnation of small towns and cities. As large numbers of unskilled and semi-skilled workers crowd into construction, low-end services and some segments of manufacturing in metropolitan cities, the unregulated and informal structure of such employment underpins their low incomes, multiple vulnerabilities and poverty. Subsequent chapters examine these questions in the context of the political economy of the state of Karnataka and its capital, Bangalore city.

Notes

1. See note 7 in Chapter 1.
2. The combined share of rural–urban (R–U) and rural–rural (R–R) streams for adult males has gone down from 66.7 per cent in 1999–2000 to 66 per cent in 2007–08 (Kundu 2012); the share of regular workers among R–U migrants at the place of destination is as high as 45 per cent, going up from 12 per cent at the point of origin, at two time points, 1999–2000 and 2007–08.
3. Thus, while the world average in terms of percentage of urban population is about 50 per cent, in India this figure is just over 30 per cent. The annual growth rate of urbanisation which was 3.21 per cent and 3.83 per cent during 1961–71 and 1971–81 respectively fell to 3.09 per cent and 2.73 per cent during 1981–91

and 1991–2001 respectively. During 2001–11, the annual rate of urbanisation increased to 2.76 per cent. Though the percentage of urban population to total population remains low, it has increased from 27.81 per cent in 2001 to 31.16 per cent in 2011 (Johnson 2011). This is low particularly in comparison to countries such as China, where the rate of urbanisation increased from 38 per cent in 2002 to 53 per cent in 2014.

4. The discussion on small towns and cities in India is wide ranging. For a sampling, see Dutta (2013) and Samanta (2014); most such studies highlight the neglect of small towns. A counterpoint is provided in a recent edited volume, Denis and Zerah (2017), where the editors argue that India's small towns have more dynamism and potential than is recognised and that the reality is more varied than the typical presentation of small towns as stagnant spaces.

5. The slow pace of job creation in rural areas makes the slow pace of urbanisation even more remarkable. Thus, between 1993–94 and 1999–2000, overall only about 9.4 million jobs were created in rural areas, while the rural labour force increased by 17.7 million workers (Sundaram and Tendulkar 2005, as quoted in Ahsan and Narain 2007). Aggregate employment in rural areas grew at a rate of 2.1 per cent between 1972–73 and 1983, but saw a decline to 1.7 and 1.4 per cent in the two subsequent decades. It has declined in absolute terms between 2004–05 and 2009–10 at a rate of 1.65 per cent per annum (Papola and Sahu 2012).

6. It should be noted that the decline in agricultural employment both in percentage and in absolute numbers in the decade from 1999–2000 to 2009–10, and particularly since 2004–05, has led some scholars to the opinion that the much-awaited structural transformation of the Indian economy is finally happening. Without going into this debate, I highlight that there seems to be an overall consensus that agricultural employment remains disproportionately high in India.

7. See, particularly, Das and Sen (2015), Papola and Sahu (2012) and Basole and Jayadev (2018).

8. See RoyChowdhury and Vani (2016); see also RoyChowdhury and Upadhya (2020).

9. Wherein manufacturing reaches its peak share in output and employment at much lower levels of national income, when compared to economies that underwent the transition earlier; see Rodrik (2016).

10. See also Kohli (2012) and Bardhan (2009).

11. In India, the National Sample Survey Organisation (NSSO) has been quinquennially collecting data on employment and unemployment, but from 2017 onwards the Periodic Labour Force Survey (PLFS) was launched by the NSSO to provide quarterly employment and unemployment data.

12. From 2004 to 2011, economists from Cornell University and activists from the Self Employed Women's Association (SEWA) and the Women in Informal Employment: Globalising and Organising Network (WIEGO) undertook participatory research in Ahmedabad, Durham and Mexico City.
13. An important work in this genre is Guha-Khasnobis, Kanbur and Ostrom (2006).

References

Afroz, N. 2020. 'Why the Government Cannot Afford to Repeat Its Mistakes in the Sunderbans'. *Caravan*, 30 May.

Ahsan, A. and A. Narain. 2007. 'Labor Markets in India: Developments and Challenges'. In *Job Creation and Poverty Reduction in India: Towards Rapid and Sustained Growth*, edited by Sadiq Ahmed, 293–338. New Delhi: Sage Publications.

Asian Development Bank (ADB). 2008. 'India: Promoting Inclusive Urban Development in Indian Cities'. Technical Assistance Report, Project No. 41609, Manilla.

Baker, Judy L. 2008. 'Urban Poverty: A Global View'. The World Bank Group, Urban Papers, UP-5. Washington DC.

Baker, Judy L., and Gauri U. Gadgil. 2017. *East Asia and Pacific Cities: Expanding Opportunities for the Urban Poor.* Washington, DC: The World Bank.

Bali, N., Martha A. Chen and R. Kanbur, eds. 2012. 'The Cornell-SEWA-WIEGO Exposure and Dialogue Programme: An Overview of the Process and Main Outcomes'. Working Papers 128865, Cornell University, Department of Applied Economics and Management.

Bardhan, P. 2009. 'Notes on the Political Economy of India's Tortuous Transition'. *Economic and Political Weekly* 44 (49): 31–36.

Basole, A., and A. Jayadev. 2018. *State of Working India*. Bengaluru: Centre for Sustainable Employment, Azim Premji University.

Bloom, D., and T. Khanna. 2007. 'The Urban Revolution'. Finance and Development Quarterly, International Monetary Fund 44 (3): 9–14.

Breman, J. 1978. 'Seasonal Migration and Cooperative Capitalism: Crushing of Cane and Labour by Sugar Factories in Bardoli'. *Economic and Political Weekly* 31 (33, Special Number): 1317–60.

Castells, M., and A. Portes. 1989. 'The World Underneath: The Origins, Dynamics and Effects of the Informal Economy'. In *The Informal Economy: Studies in Advanced and Less Developed Countries*, edited by Castells and Portes. Baltimore: Johns Hopkins University Press.

Das, D., and K. Sen. 2015. 'Where Have All the Workers Gone: Puzzle of Declining Labour Intensity in Organised Indian Manufacturing.' *Economic and Political Weekly* 50 (23): 108–5.

De Haan, A. 1994. *Unsettled Settlers: Migrant Workers and Industrial Capitalism in Calcutta*. Hilversum: Verolren.

————. 2002. 'Migration and Livelihoods in Historical Perspective: A Case Study of Bihar, India'. *Journal of Development Studies* 38 (5): 115–42.

Denis, E., and Marie Helene Zerah. 2017. *Subaltern Urbanization in India: An Introduction to the Dynamics of Ordinary Towns*. New Delhi: Springer.

Deshingkar, P. 2010. 'Migration, Remote Rural Areas and Chronic Poverty in India'. ODI Working Paper 323, Chronic Poverty Research Centre.

Dubey, A. R., Palmer Jones and K. Sen. 2006. 'Surplus Labor, Social Structure and Rural to Urban Migration: Evidence from Indian Data'. *European Journal of Development Research* 18 (1): 86–104.

Dutta, A. 2013. 'City Forgotten: The Fate of Small Towns in India's Urbanization.' *openDemocracy*, 18 September.

Gidwani, V., and J. Wainwright. 2014. 'On Capital, Not-capital and Development: After Kalyan Sanyal'. *Economic and Political Weekly* 49 (34): 40–47.

Ghose, A. 2016. *India Employment Report*. New Delhi: Oxford University Press and Institute for Human Development.

Gooptu, Nandini. 2009. 'Neoliberal Subjectivity, Enterprise Culture and New Workplaces: Organised Retail and Shopping Malls in India'. *Economic and Political Weekly* 44 (22): 45–54.

————. 2013. 'Servile Sentinels in the City: Private Security Guards, Organized Informality and Labour in Interactive Services in Globalized India'. *International Review and Social History* 58 (1): 9–38.

Government of India (GOI). 2017. *Report of the Working Group on Migration*. New Delhi: Ministry of Housing and Urban Poverty Alleviation.

————. 2018. *Annual Report: Periodic Labour Force Survey, 2017–18*. New Delhi: Ministry of Statistics and Programme Implementation.

Guha-Khasnobis, Basudeb, R. Kanbur and E. Ostrom, eds. 2006. *Linking the Formal and Informal Economy: Concepts and Policies*. Delhi: Oxford University Press.

Harriss-White, B. 2010. 'Work and Wellbeing in Informal Economies: The Regulatory Roles of Institutions of Identity and the State'. *World Development* 38 (2): 170–83.

Hashim, S. 2009. *India: Urban Poverty Report 2009*. New Delhi: UNDP and Ministry of Housing and Urban Poverty Alleviation, Government of India.

Johnson, C. 2011. *Managing Urban Growth*. Sydney: Metropolis Publications and Delhi: National Institute of Urban Affairs.

Kanbur, R. 2009. 'Conceptualizing Informality: Regulation and Enforcement'. Discussion Paper, No. 4186, Institute for the Study of Labor, Bonn.

Kasturi, Kannan. 2014. 'Workers Leave Agriculture, but Where Are They Headed'. *India Together*, 14 November.

Kohli, A. 2012. *Poverty amid Plenty in the New India*. Cambridge: Cambridge University Press.

Kundu, A. 2011. 'Politics and Economics of Urban Growth'. *Economic and Political Weekly* 46 (20): 10–12.

————. 2012. 'Migration and Exclusionary Urbanization in India'. *Economic and Political Weekly* 47 (26/27): 219–27.

Kundu, A. and N. Sarangi. 2005. 'Issues of Urban Exclusion'. *Economic and Political Weekly* 40 (33).

————. 2007. 'Migration, Employment Status and Poverty'. *Economic and Political Weekly* 42 (4): 299–306.

Mehrotra, S. 2019. 'Mega Challenges of Rural-Urban Migration.' *Business Line*, 3 October.

Mezzadiri, A., and Fan Lulu. 2018. 'Classes of Labour at the Margins of Global Commodity Chains in India and China'. *Development and Change* 49 (4): 1034–63

Mitra, A. 2010. 'Migration, Livelihood and Well-being: Evidence from Indian City Slums'. *Urban Studies* 47 (7): 1371–90.

Olsen, W., and R. V. Ramanamurthy. 2000. 'Contract Labour and Bondage in Andhra Pradesh'. *Journal of Social and Political Thought* 1 (2): 1481–5842.

Papola, T. S., and P. Sahu. 2012. *Growth and Structure of Employment in India: Long Term and Post Reform Performance and the Emerging Challenge.* New Delhi: Institute for Studies in Industrial Development.

Pattenden, Jonathan. 2012. 'Migration between Rural Raichur and Boomtown Bangalore: Class Relations and the Circulation of Labour in South India'. *Global Labour Journal* 3 (1): 163–90.

Ravallion, M., S. Chen and P. Sangraula. 2007. 'New Evidence on the Urbanization of Global Poverty'. *Population and Development Review* 33 (4): 667–701.

Reddy, D. N. 1990. 'Rural Migrant Labour in Andhra Pradesh'. Report submitted to the National Commission on Rural Labour, Government of India, New Delhi.

Rodrik, D. 2016. 'Premature Deindstrialization'. *Journal of Economic Growth* 21 (1): 1–33.

RoyChowdhury, S., and B. P. Vani. 2016. 'Work and Workers in the Services Sector: A Pilot Study in Bangalore'. Unpublished report, Institute for Social and Economic Change, Bangalore.

————. 2017. 'Self-employment: Broad Review of Dimensions and Diversity'. In *Employment Policy in Emerging Economies*, edited by Elizabeth Hill and Amitendu Palit. London: Routledge.

RoyChowdhury, S., and C. Upadhya. 2020. 'India's Changing City Scapes: Work, Migration and Livelihoods'. Unpublished report, ISEC and NIAS, Bangalore.

Samanta, G. 2014. 'Beyond Metropolitan Shadow: Growth and Governance of Small Towns in Eastern India'. *Jindal Journal of Public Policy* 3 (1): 52–70.

Samling, C. L., S. Das and S. Hazra. 2015. 'Migration in the Indian Bengal Delta and the Mahanadi Delta: A Review of Literature'. DECCMA Working Paper, IDRC Project No. 107642.

Sanyal, K. 2007. *Rethinking Capitalist Development: Primitive Accumulation, Governmentality and Post-colonial Capitalism.* London: Routledge.

Shah, Alpa. 2006. 'The Labour of Love: Seasonal Migration from Jharkhand to the Brick Klins of Other States in India.' *Contributions to Indian Sociology* 40 (1): 91–118.

Sharma, K. 2012. 'Rejuvenating India's Small Towns.' *Economic and Political Weekly* 47 (30): 63–68.

Srivastava, R., and A. K. Naik. 2017. 'Growth and Informality in the Indian Economy'. In *Labour and Development: Essays in Honour of T. S. Papola*, edited by K. P. Kannan, Rajendra Mamgain and Preet Rastogi, 189–214. New Delhi: Academic Foundation.

United Nations Human Settlements Program. 2007. *The State of the World's Cities Report 2006–7*. London: Earthscan.

4

A Political Economy Overview
Karnataka and Bangalore

Karnataka epitomises India's post-liberalisation developmental trajectory: high growth rates combining with continuing pockets of poverty and deprivation. These pockets are typically seen in terms of regional disparities, between the state's backward northern districts and the more advanced south, and between the urban and the rural. As discussed in this chapter, the state's glittering image as a leader in IT and ITES is at least partially darkened by slow progress on human development indicators and low levels of social sector expenditure. From the mid-1980s onwards, a growing, upwardly mobile, technical/professional middle class supported, as well as benefited from, the quick expansion of IT in Karnataka; on the other hand, large numbers of unskilled and semi-skilled workers remained outside of the technology-led growth. Even as successive agrarian crises caused dislocations from the farm sector, a declining rate of employment in manufacturing left them with little opportunities of absorption into the urban economy. These features of the state's political economy, presented below, foreground a discussion of the rise of Bangalore as India's Silicon Valley, where similar contradictions have played out.

Karnataka's growth rate (GSDP) increased from 5.3 per cent in 1980 to 7.3 per cent in the 1990s and stood at 8.3 per cent in the second half of the 1990s. During the latter part of the 1990s, Karnataka's agricultural, industrial and service sectors grew at average rates of 4.0 per cent, 9.2 per cent and 10.6 per cent respectively as compared to all-India averages of 3.6 per cent, 5.0 per cent and 8.7 per cent respectively. The growth rate of GSDP in Karnataka was 6.2 per cent in 2012 and 8.5 per cent in 2017–18. The growth rate of GDP for India was 5.5 per cent in 2012 and 6.5 per cent in 2017–18. Thus, the growth record in the state has been consistently higher than the all-India one.

As is well known, Karnataka's economic rise has been largely led by the service sector. The share of services in the state's GSDP was 65.15 per cent in 2018–19. The state has emerged as an IT hub, home to the fourth-largest technology cluster in the world, nineteen IT and ITES special economic zones (SEZs), five software-technology parks and dedicated IT investment regions. The central place of IT in the state's economy is important to highlight: export of electronics and computer software accounts for 39 per cent share in India's electronic and software exports, and 76 per cent of Karnataka's overall exports. In addition, there are vibrant automobile, agro-processing, aerospace, textile and garments, biotech and heavy engineering industries. As receiver of foreign direct investment (FDI), Karnataka stands third in the country, next to Maharashtra and New Delhi. A consistently high growth record and an impressive menu of modern, state-of-the-art industries, as well as rising exports, particularly from the 1990s onwards, have become Karnataka's most visible features.

There are disquieting features to this story as well: the poverty ratio (21 per cent) places Karnataka at the 20th position in the list of 35 states, close to the national average.[1] There has occurred a steady decline in poverty from 50 per cent in 1994 to 35 per cent in 2005 to 21 per cent in 2012. However, decline in poverty has slowed down since 2005, compared to other advanced states, such as in Maharashtra, where poverty declined from 38 per cent in 2005 to 17 per cent in 2012, and in Andhra Pradesh, where poverty declined from 30 per cent to 9 per cent during these years. Most remarkably, among the southern states, poverty in Karnataka continues to be the highest and well-being the lowest. In overall human development, Karnataka stands at the 11th position among 19 major states in India, and among the southern states, it is way behind Kerala (1st) and Tamil Nadu (5th) with respect to all indicators.[2] Table 4.1 provides information on Karnataka's poverty and Table 4.2 on its performance in human development index (HDI), comparative to other southern states.

There is thus an obvious duality in the state's developmental trajectory. High growth rates coupled with relatively high poverty demonstrate the

Table 4.1 Percentage of population below poverty line in Karnataka and other southern states, 2011–12

State	Rural	Urban	Total
Karnataka	24.53	15.25	20.91
Kerala	9.14	4.97	7.05
Tamil Nadu	15.83	6.54	11.28
Andhra Pradesh	10.96	5.81	9.2

Source: Economic Survey of Karnataka, 2013–14.

Table 4.2 Ranking in HDI and other indicators in Karnataka and southern states, 2011–12

State	Per capita income	Life expectancy at birth	Mean years of schooling	School life expectancy	Rank HDI
Andhra Pradesh	3,399	64	3.06	9.66	11
Karnataka	3,270	65	3.95	9.75	10
Kerala	5,263	74	6.19	11.33	1
Tamil Nadu	3,825	66	4.79	10.57	6
India	3,337	64	4.10	9.62	

Source: *Economic Survey of Karnataka, 2013–14.*

exclusivist nature of the growth pattern. Low human development indicators point towards inadequate state attention to social sectors. These are issues of concern in both academic research and policy debates. While a detailed discussion of the state's history and political economy would be out of place here, I highlight, briefly, three main features that have a specific bearing on the issue of urban poverty: first, regional imbalance in development between the northern and southern parts of the state; second, relatively low levels of public expenditure on social sectors; and, finally, the narrowness of urban growth, indicated by continuing dependence on agricultural employment, even as the structure of urban employment forces the crowding of large numbers of the urban workforce in low-paying, casual work.

Regional disparities

Bangalore Urban is central to Karnataka's economy, contributes nearly 36 per cent of the state's GSDP. Bangalore's prominence in Karnataka's development – currently associated with the IT wave which began in the 1980s – goes back to the state's earlier history. Southern Karnataka, under the enlightened leadership of the Maharajas of Mysore, took to modernisation early, and this led to the flourishing of industries, infrastructure, health, education and employment opportunities. In contrast, developmental initiatives were much delayed in north Karnataka (Prabhakar 2012).

Regional economic disparity between the northern and southern parts of the state had been first systematically recorded by the well-known D. M. Nanjundappa Committee, and since then endorsed by researchers and government documents. According to the committee, out of the 39 most-backward *taluk*s in the state, 26 are in north Karnataka and 13 in south Karnataka, and out of the total 61 relatively developed *taluk*s, 40 are in south Karnataka. The Hyderabad-Karnataka region in north Karnataka is comprised of the six most-backward districts, namely Bidar, Gulbarga, Bellary, Raichur, Yadgiri and Koppal. An eight-year Special Development Plan (SDP) had been recommended by the Nanjundappa Committee and special status was granted to northern Karnataka in 2012. However, successive governments have failed to implement the schemes for development of the region, which remains marked by weak industrial investment and infrastructure and severe droughts affecting agriculture. Thus, disparity has continued. According to the *Economic Survey of Karnataka* for the year 2018–19, only five districts, Bangalore Urban, Dakshina Kannada, Udupi, Chikmagalur and Shivamogga have per capita income above the state average of INR 1.42 lakh (1 lakh = 100,000) and all five districts are in south Karnataka (Table 4.3). Out of the 30 districts, 9 of the lowest 10 in the HDIs and per capita income belong in north Karnataka.

Regional disparity has further increased as the service sector in Bangalore has grown whereas agriculture, which is the backbone of most northern districts, has stagnated. The industrial strategy of Karnataka has been to prioritise industries such as IT, biotechnology, food processing, electronics and automobiles, which are mostly concentrated around the developed districts of Bangalore and Mysore (GOK 2014). Eight districts in southern Karnataka account for almost half of the total employment in the state: Bangalore (14.17 per cent), Dakshina Kannada (7.61 per cent), Belgaum (6.00 per cent), Mandya (5.95 per cent), Tumkur (5.72 per cent), Hassan (4.89 per cent), Mysore (4.87 per cent) and Shimoga (3.55 per cent).[3] Migration of technically qualified people in search of employment and the rise of a large number of private sector companies has also led to a further strengthening of the development of south Karnataka.

Table 4.3 District-level income disparity

Bangalore	Mysuru Region	Bangalore region (excluding Bangalore)	Belagavi region	Kalaburagi region
INR 370,003	INR 163,855	INR 126,328	INR 106,049	INR 95,887
128.5 per cent above state per capita income	1.2 per cent above state per capita income	22 per cent below state per capita income	34.5 per cent below state per capita income	40.78 per cent below state per capita income

Source: *Economic Survey of Karnataka, 2018–19.*

Table 4.4 HDI across the districts of Karnataka, 2012

Districts	Health index	Income index	Education index	HDI	Rank
Bangalore (Urban)	0.8151	0.7279	0.6538	0.729	1
Bangalore (Rural)	0.776	0.6204	0.5662	0.6484	4
Bidar	0.7647	0.5311	0.4443	0.5651	22
Chitradurga	0.7256	0.5356	0.4511	0.5597	23
Dakshina Kannada	0.8027	0.6796	0.5358	0.6636	3
Bagalkot	0.724	0.5431	0.4260	0.5513	24
Raichur	0.6444	0.5633	0.4336	0.5399	27

Source: *Economic Survey of Karnataka, 2018–19.*

Table 4.5 District-wise per capita education/health expenditure and education/ health development index

Bottom five EDI districts	EDI	Rank	Per capita exp.	Rank	Bottom five HeDI districts	HeDI	Rank	Per capita exp.	Rank
Bidar	0.49	27	1,252	12	Koppal	0.024	25	68	28
Koppal	0.50	26	495	21	Raichur	0.251	24	222	15
Bellary	0.50	25	229	29	Bellary	0.301	23	112	24
Raichur	0.526	24	467	23	Gulbarga	0.310	22	163	20
Gulbarga	0.529	23	468	22	Bagalkot	0.317	21	97	26
Top five EDI districts					*Top five HeDI districts*				
Chikmagalur	0.777	1	1,182	15	Dakshin Kannada	0.981	1	190	17
Kodagu	0.757	2	1,637	7	Udupi	0.958	2	81	27
Bangalore (U)	0.740	3	795	20	Bangalore (U)	0.952	3	1,524	2
Chitradurga	0.733	4	1,673	6	Mandya	0.858	4	1,783	1
Uttara Kannada	0.730	5	1,856	3	Bangalore (R)	0.833	5	171	19

Source: Gayithri and Raju (2016).
Note: EDI – education development index; HeDI – health development index.

Table 4.6 Urbanisation within Karnataka, 2011

Top five districts		Bottom five districts	
District	Urban population in %	District	Urban population in %
Bangalore	91	Kodagu	15
Dharwad	57	Koppal	17
Dakshin Kannada	48	Mandya	17
Mysuru	41	Chamarajanagar	17
Bellary	38	Yadagiri	19

Source: Economic Survey of Karnataka, 2018–19.

Table 4.7 Incidence of poverty by divisions in Karnataka

Division	Rural (in %)		Urban (in %)	
	NSSO 61st Round	NSSO 68th Round	NSSO 61st Round	NSSO 68th Round
Kalaburagi	56.9	37.1	58.6	41.5
Belagavi	42.7	29.5	47.1	28.2
Bangalore	36.6	18.8	9.1	5.5
Mysuru	18.5	12.6	23.4	8.9

Source: Niranjan and Shivakumar (2018).

The *Karnataka Human Development Report* of 2005 identified Raichur in north Karnataka as the most impoverished district of the state, followed by Gulbarga, Koppal and Bijapur, on all the HDIs (GOK 2005). These regional disadvantages and disparities have continued. As Table 4.4 shows, in 2012 Bangalore Urban stood first with HDI value 0.729, while Yadgir, Kalaburagi and Haveri were ranked as the last three with HDI values of 0.495, 0.534 and 0.539 respectively. Tables 4.5, 4.6 and 4.7 show the backwardness of the northern districts in terms of health, education, urbanisation and poverty. Kalaburagi division had the highest number of poor in 2011–12 (Table 4.7).

Public expenditure on human development

While I do not present a detailed analysis of the state's performance on the human development indicators, the following points could be briefly flagged.

Performance on human development is a function of both public expenditure on social sectors and of efficient utilisation of resources, that is, implementation of social policies. Regarding the first, there is of course an important link between budgetary resources and social sector spending. In the 1990s and early 2000s, the declining fiscal health of the state in Karnataka had posed constraints to investments in human development. A number of policy documents had drawn attention to the state's continuously rising fiscal deficit from the mid-1990s onwards[4] as well as growing public expenditure in the area of subsidies and services.[5] Even though curtailing subsidies became a recurrent theme in policy discourse, increasing subsidies and services continue to feature centrally in public expenditure, and the high growth of expenditure relative to revenue has had serious implications for spending on human development. Together, interest payments, salaries and pensions accounted for about 51 per cent of the rise in revenue expenditure between 1997–98 and 2001–02 (GOK 2005). In 2011–12, committed expenditure on salaries, pensions, interest, subsidies, administrative expenditure and devolution to Panchayati Raj institutions (PRIs) and urban local bodies (ULBs) constituted about 83 per cent of the total government expenditure. Containing the committed expenditure in light of the ever-expanding demands for welfare programmes is one of the key challenges (GOK 2013). However, as is well known, established subsidies, such as those in the power sector or in food subsidies, which have a clearly visible and large constituency, may be more difficult to cut than, say, public spending on primary education, where the benefits are long-term, unseen and therefore unidentified with any clearly visible political demand or constituency.

Successive governments have sought to address the problem of fiscal and revenue deficit through various tax reforms,[6] and over the years there have been some achievements in terms of the state's recovery in its fiscal position, as well as in its spending on social sectors. Social sector expenditure, as a percentage of GSDP, had declined from 6.32 in 1990–91 to 6.00 in 1998–99 and risen only marginally to 6.01 in 2002–03 (GOK 2005). However, during the years 2009–14, a significant increase in Karnataka's social sector expenditure was recorded, relative to GSDP, and was higher than other southern states (Table 4.8). Despite this rise, Karnataka's position, relative to other southern states, remains low on all indicators of human development (as shown in Table 4.2), thus calling attention to a history of low expenditure in the past two decades and to inefficient implementation of social sector policies.

Table 4.8 Social sector expenditure (SSE) as percentage of GSDP in southern states

State	2011–12	2012–13	2013–14
Karnataka	6.7	7.1	8.3
Kerala	5.5	6.0	6.2
Andhra Pradesh	6.9	7.5	7.7
Tamil Nadu	6.3	6.9	6.5

Source: *Economic Survey of Karnataka, 2013–14.*

This brief overview highlights that despite high growth rates, Karnataka's poverty and HDI profile compares unfavourably with other southern states. Uneven regional growth is reflected in deep poverty in northern Karnataka and grossly unequal achievements in human development indicators across districts of the north and south. Despite growth, successive governments in Karnataka have been unable to address these glaring features of inequity in income and access to human resources. These inequities cast a long shadow on the IT-led economic transformation of the state.

Urbanisation in Karnataka

The proportion of urban population in India as a whole increased from 18 per cent in 1961 to 31 per cent in 2011. In Karnataka, this growth was from 22 per cent to 38 per cent. While urbanisation in Karnataka has been above the national average, there are two important features about Karnataka's urbanisation process that are important to highlight. First, the number of towns in the state has not risen significantly. From 216 towns in 1901, the number increased to 286 in 1951, declined to 230 in 1971, and stood at 237 in 2009 (GOK 2009). The implications of these trends have not been studied systematically, but some preliminary points could be raised. Declassification of towns and stagnation in small towns and cities have been seen as symptoms of the lack of economic dynamism that sustains urban growth (Kundu 2012). In the case of Karnataka, the reduction in the number of towns shows that most of the urban growth has occurred on the basis of enlargement of existing towns, rather than the emergence of new towns. The growth of existing urban centres may happen partially on the basis of natural growth and partially of migration, but the developmental dynamism, which leads to the creation of new urban centres, is evidently lacking here.

The second point to note in this context is regional imbalance and concentration in urbanisation. More than 65 per cent of the urban population is concentrated in the three major transport corridors, namely

Bangalore–Belgaum, Mysore–Kolar and Mangalore–Karwar. Sixty-six per cent of the urban population is concentrated in 23 Class 1 cities. According to the *Urban Development Policy Report* (GOK 2009), one of the major factors contributing to the imbalance in Karnataka's urbanisation pattern as well as the state's development process is the concentration of economic activities in Bangalore and its emergence as a primate city. The urban population of Bangalore district accounted for 37 per cent of the state's urban population in 2011, and its share in the increase in urban population in Karnataka between 2001 and 2011 was 53 per cent (Pani and Chidambaram 2013). Table 4.9 shows that Bangalore's urbanisation is hugely advanced even when compared to the districts that feature next in urbanisation.

There is an overall consensus that the process of urbanisation in Karnataka has been overwhelmingly Bangalore-centric (GOK 2009; Pani and Chidambaram 2013). This is borne out by the prioritized attention of and spending by successive state governments on Bangalore's infrastructure, and the relative neglect even of other larger cities in the state. Mysore, the city second to Bangalore in population size, lacks an airport. A long-time aspirant to becoming the second industrial/commercial hub, Mysore suffers the disadvantage that the journey from Bangalore International Airport to the city (a distance of less than 150 kilometres), whether by train or car, amounts to half a day. The infrastructural support that Bangalore has received in the last decade, involving the construction of the Bangalore International Airport, the Metro Rail, an expanding public transport system, numerous flyovers and now an envisioned elevated road connecting the city centre to the highway leading to the airport, and the absence of comparable facilities in other cities stand testimony to successive governments' preferential commitment to Bangalore.

In recent years, policy makers and bureaucrats have made an effort to break this pattern. Thus, the announcement of the Smart Cities plan in 2014 was followed by the selection of six smaller cities (Belagavi, Davangere,

Table 4.9 Percentage of urban to total population in top four urbanised districts in Karnataka

District	Urban population in %
Bangalore	88.08
Dharwad	55
Dakshina Kannada	38
Mysore	36

Source: Economic Survey of Karnataka, 2013–14.

Hubli-Dharwad, Mangaluru, Shivamogga and Tumkur) for the grant of INR 500 crore from the central government and INR 500 crore from the state government, each, for infrastructural development. Bangalore as well as Mysore lost out in the race for this funding. The Karnataka Industrial Policy (2014–19) reserved jobs for locals in new industrial units and discouraged investments in and around Bangalore by offering special incentives for investing in backward regions, particularly in the Hyderabad-Karnataka region. Other state funding, however, continue to be Bangalore-centric. For example, the Atal Mission for Rejuvenation and Urban Transformation (AMRUT), a centrally sponsored scheme designed to ensure basic infrastructure in urban regions, covers 27 cities in Karnataka. As per the State Annual Action Plan for 2015–16, out of the total allocations made, Bangalore was allotted INR 800 crore and the next 14 big cities were allocated INR 160 crore each. While the higher allotment to Bangalore is justified by the much higher population size of the city compared to other cities, demographic and other associated imbalances continue to mark the pattern of Karnataka's urban development. The lack of growth, rather, decline, in the number of cities points to urban stagnation, on the one hand, and concentration of urban growth in Bangalore, on the other, indicates that the windows of urban opportunities are confined to the constricted urban space in the state.

The urban employment structure

The narrowness of urbanisation is further highlighted by the sectoral pattern of employment in Karnataka. As seen in Table 4.10, the share of agriculture in GSDP has steadily declined, along with a sharp decline in the share of industry over the years, while the share of services has risen steadily. In 2011–12, agriculture accounted for 55 per cent of the workforce, industry 18 per cent, while the service sector accounted for 26 per cent. As at the national level, in Karnataka too, agriculture's share in GSDP has reduced over the years, but the percentage of people dependent on agriculture has remained high, even as the share of services in GSDP has forged ahead. The rate of growth of rural non-farm employment (RNFE) too has remained low in Karnataka, compared to some other states, rising from 26.51 per cent in 2001 to 29.31 per cent in 2011. The all-India average in RNFE was 32.1 per cent in 2011. While in general RNFE is seen to be a positive development, enabling rural households to move away from dependence on agriculture and/or to augment incomes from agriculture, there is no conclusive evidence that RNFE in India has the dynamism that might address issues of rural unemployment and low incomes.[7]

Table 4.10 Karnataka: Sectoral share in GSDP (in percentage)

Karnataka	2009–10	2014–15	2016–17	2017–18	2018–19
Agriculture	16	13.40	11.53	11.67	11.18
Industry	29.10	24.79	22.94	22.45	23.67
Manufacturing	16.38	15.19	14.24	14.86	15.88
Services	57	61.82	65.53	65.88	65.15

Source: Economic Survey of Karnataka, several years.

It should be noted that in economically advanced states, as in Karnataka, Gujarat, Maharashtra and Tamil Nadu, there is an overall pattern of decline of the sectoral shares of industry and manufacturing in GSDP. Interestingly, Karnataka records the lowest shares for these sectors compared to these states. Highlighting particularly the case of Maharashtra, the share of industry and manufacturing in the state's GSDP was 33 per cent and 21 per cent respectively in 2017–18, while in Karnataka, the share was 22 per cent and 13 per cent respectively (Tables 4.11a and 4.11b).

Table 4.11a Share of industry in GSDP, selected states (in percentage)

State	2009–10	2010–11	2011–12	2012–13	2013–14	2017–18
Karnataka	29.10	28.66	28.36	26.34	24.68	22.27
Gujarat	41.85	37.55	37.97	38.29	35.82	–
Maharashtra	29.81	29.70	28.32	28.30	27.20	33.6
Tamil Nadu	30.16	30.56	30.15	29.58	27.97	–

Source: Economic Survey of India, several years.

Table 4.11b Share of manufacturing in GSDP, selected states (in percentage)

State	2009–10	2010–11	2011–12	2012–13	2013–14	2017–18
Karnataka	16.38	15.25	15.38	14.38	13.07	13.88
Gujarat	29.43	25.89	25.59	25.81	23.82	–
Maharashtra	21.03	21.05	19.51	19.54	18.09	21.3
Tamil Nadu	19.76	19.28	18.39	17.62	16.54	–

Source: Economic Survey of India, several years.

Overall, then, if a large number of people remain tied to agriculture, it is because of the lack of appropriate employment opportunities in urban areas. Industry's declining share in GSDP as well as in employment creation in Karnataka should be seen in the context of the emerging concern amongst scholars and policy makers (discussed in the previous chapter) regarding the overall trajectory of the growth process in India, which has not generated manufacturing sector jobs. In Karnataka, the decline of manufacturing has been a matter of concern for successive governments. The Manufacturing Task Force appointed by the Congress government in 2013 had provided, in its report, an ambitious target of raising the secondary sector's share in GSDP to 25 per cent by 2025.

The decline of industry and manufacturing in the state has occurred in the backdrop of the gradual erosion of two institutional domains that played a central role in the state's economic development: public sector manufacturing industries and the small-scale industries (SSI) sector. The decline of each of these sectors has occurred in the backdrop of economic policies of reduced state involvement in manufacturing: in the process of the shrinking of state-owned enterprise, the SSI sector, which had gained momentum in Karnataka as an ancillary to the large public sector industries, also declined. The dismantling of public sector manufacturing has been slow and politically contested but has remained a sustained process over successive governments. As early as 2002, the government of Karnataka, under S. M. Krishna of the Congress, a firm believer in private-sector-led growth, had initiated a programme of public enterprise reform by setting up the Public Sector Restructuring Commission to look into 78 public sector enterprises (PSEs) with a total of 162,000 employees. The commission had selected about 39 enterprises for privatisation and closure in two phases. Of these, 11 enterprises were closed down and 1 privatised. This led to about 10,000 workers to compulsorily opt for voluntary retirement scheme (VRS). However, eventually there was much foot-dragging on actual implementation and over the years the momentum for executing the commission's recommendations was lost. Powerful public sector trade unions have resisted possible loss of permanent blue-collar jobs and bureaucracies have resisted loss of positions of power and prestige associated with company directorships. Despite these counter tendencies, however, closure and privatisation have remained a sustained agenda of governments in the state. In 2011, the Karnataka government once again initiated a programme of reform, identifying 31 companies for possible closure. As of September 2012, 5 companies were dissolved or amalgamated. Of the remaining 26, 14 non-working and 3 working companies were identified for closure, and 8 working companies for privatisation. The number of PSEs decreased from 105 to 80 during the 2000s.[8] Second, Karnataka's industrial decline is reflected most glaringly in the SSI sector, which has registered a continuous decline in the number of registered units, total investment and the rate of growth of employment. The number of SSI units dipped from 47,883 in 2001–02 to 37,054 in 2003–04 and rose only to 43,647 in 2006–07. During this period, employment in the SSI sector in Karnataka fell from 73,195 to 57,515 (Kalasanavar 2013).[9]

The decline of industry in general and of the public sector and SSI sector in particular indicates certain features of Karnataka's political economy that are important to highlight. As Table 4.12 shows, in urban areas of Karnataka, the percentage of working population in regular salaried employment has increased, although it is lower than the all-India figures in this category. While the increase in regular salaried employment in general can be seen as a sign of progress, it is also true that this increase has occurred mostly in contractual employment, that is, in short-term or fixed-term work. Second, the percentage of casual workers has remained higher in Karnataka than the all-India percentage from 1993–94 to 2009–10. As unskilled workers earning a daily wage, casual workers are typically at the bottom of the heap in the urban labour market. A large percentage of urban workers in Karnataka working as casual wage labour earn less than the minimum wage, work under conditions of great insecurity and have no access to social insurance. These themes are taken up in the next three chapters on lives and livelihoods of informal workers in Bangalore. Average wages of regular and casual workers in Karnataka are below those in other states.[10]

Table 4.12 Percentage distribution of workers by category of employment in urban areas

Type	Karnataka				India			
	1993–94	1999–2000	2004–05	2009–10	1993–94	1999–2000	2004–05	2009–10
Self-employ-ed	41.3	38.8	42.1	38.3	42.4	42.2	45.4	41.1
Regular salaried	36.0	39.6	38.6	39.4	39.5	40.0	39.5	41.4
Casual labour	21.8	21.6	19.3	22.2	18.3	17.8	15.0	17.5

Source: *Economic Survey of Karnataka*, several years.

As the *Economic Survey of Karnataka* points out, the share of casual employment in the state is noticeably high for all population categories. The survey underlines that casualisation in the state is a conspicuous phenomenon and increasing casualisation has profound implications on the labour market from a policy perspective.

> When work is casual and irregular, the people depending on such kind of employment will have little or no opportunity to enhance their skill base, which is critical from the standpoint of bettering employment and livelihoods. Therefore, immediate policy interventions are required to shift the workers from the casual status to other two statuses in the state. (*Economic Survey of Karnataka 2012–13*)

Chapter 3 provided a broad discussion of the debates, both academic and policy oriented, around the concept of urbanisation of poverty. Interestingly, the *Economic Survey of Karnataka* (2012–13), published by the Government of Karnataka, has stated that the urbanisation of poverty in Karnataka has been witnessed in recent decades, with the decline in urban poverty being much slower than the decline in rural poverty. Thus, the pace of poverty reduction in rural Karnataka has been 32 per cent between 1993–94 and 2011–12, while the pace of poverty reduction in urban Karnataka has been 18.9 per cent over this period (Table 4.13). What is more telling is a comparison with two other economically advanced states, Maharashtra and Tamil Nadu, where the urban poverty ratio in 2012 stood at 9 per cent and 7 per cent respectively, in contrast to Karnataka's 15 per cent, and the rate of decline or urban poverty was much sharper in both states (Table 4.14). The debate on poverty reduction in India, particularly the comparative performance of different states, is wide ranging, including contestations over what constitutes the poverty line. Without engaging with that debate, this brief overview is meant to highlight that Karnataka's performance in urban poverty, as in overall poverty reduction and in human development indicators, as discussed earlier, has been low in comparison with other economically advanced states, even though the growth performance has been consistently above the national average.

This section drew attention to the contrasts between high growth rates on the one hand and regional disparities and faltering performance on human development indicators on the other. The narrowness of urban growth in seen in two ways. First, urbanisation has been confined to three major urban corridors. The decline of small towns and cities as well as the hyper-development of Bangalore city highlights this narrowness.

Table 4.13 Decline in poverty in Karnataka

Year	Rural (in %)	Urban (in %)
1993–94	56.5	34.2
2004–05	37.5	25.9
2009–10	26.1	19.6
2011–12	24.5	15.3

Source: Economic Survey of Karnataka, 2013–14.

Table 4.14 Urban poverty, selected states (in percentage)

States	1994	2005	2012
Karnataka	34	26	15
Maharashtra	30	26	9
Tamil Nadu	34	20	7

Source: Economic Survey of India, several years.

Second, and relatedly, while Karnataka's economic growth has been urban-led, that is, largely driven by the growth of cutting-edge global industries and services, large numbers of the rural workforce has remained tied to agriculture despite its diminishing role in the state's economy, registering the absence of work opportunities in urban areas. Increasing casualisation of urban employment and lower wages of casual workers compared to the national wage rates indicate that a large percentage of the urban workforce is unable to benefit from the technology- and services-led economic growth model. I turn now to a more specific discussion of Bangalore which extends the points raised here.

Bangalore, city of technology-led growth

Known since pre-independence times as the garden city or retirees' haven, Bangalore has undergone many transformations. The fourth largest city in the country, Bangalore's population stands at about 12 million currently in the city and 20 million in the Bangalore Urban area. Shifting boundaries have attended Bangalore's expansion. In 2007, the Government of Karnataka issued a notification to merge 100 wards of the erstwhile BMP, or the Bangalore Mahanagara Palike (the municipal corporation), with 7 city municipal councils (CMCs), 1 town municipal council (TMC) and 111 villages around the city to form a single administrative unit. The city council was renamed as Bruhat Bangalore Mahanagara Palike (BBMP).

Bangalore's development in the first four decades of independence was closely aligned to the development of science, technology and the state sector. Green and sprawling campuses of large public sector companies and institutions, providing housing, schools and hospitals for employees, produced a cushioned lifestyle for a growing middle class. Coupled with a year-long unusually pleasant climate, the city gained a profile of quiet prosperity that was somewhat unique in the Indian context.

As the era of economic reforms began, from the late 1980s, successive governments in Karnataka, across political parties, pushed an economic reform agenda that underlined the need to curtail public expenditure, wind down loss-making public sector units and provide multiple incentives for the private sector to lead the state's economic growth. Bangalore has occupied the cutting edge of this shifting developmental paradigm as the icon of India's IT revolution, a major hub for MNCs, international banking, finance and hospitality. Sprawling campuses of state-owned companies were transformed into shadows of the past as much of their land was put up for sale, units were shut down, some companies were folded up and the permanent workforce in the public sector was gradually downsized and contractualised.

Bangalore has transformed itself from a city anchored in the public sector and a thriving SSI sector to a city whose growth is driven by large private capital both in manufacturing and in services. The city changed its profile from the quiet affluence of the retired bureaucrat's bungalow to a strident materiality: world-class residence, leisure and entertainment, global commerce and business. With the increasing visibility of a cosmopolitan and knowledge class in the city's landscape, Bangalore now stands as the signal of India's arrival.

Much has been written about Bangalore's technology-led rise, the dramatic growth of IT and ITES, as well as biotechnology, as the epicentre of this trajectory in the last few decades, and the wide-ranging impact of the IT revolution in shaping the city in the last four decades, and I will not cover that ground again here.[11] What stands out from that history is the gradual evolution of a technology- and knowledge-based paradigm of urban development, which was largely the product of state thinking and policy, and which the state was able to successfully push through by proactive and efficient facilitation of private capital, both domestic and foreign. As far as IT and biotechnology were concerned, the central government and successive state governments in Karnataka moved in synchrony. From slow beginnings in the 1970s with state-led initiatives in IT, the central government moved quickly to the increasingly favoured model of harnessing and facilitating private capital as the principal driver of this sector. Thus, from the mid-1980s, there were a series of policy initiatives towards greater opening up to FDI in this sector, technology transfers, reduction of license requirements and import duties for software, as well as tax exemptions on profits made on software exports. As is well known, exports dominate the Indian IT industry, being 79 per cent of the industry's total revenue. The industry's share in total Indian exports increased from 4 per cent in 1998 to about 25 per cent in 2012. The IT industry's share in GDP went up from 5.8 per cent in 2009 to 9.5 per cent in 2015 and was 7.7 per cent in 2017.[12]

In Karnataka, 55 per cent of GSDP is generated by IT and ITES. Exports of IT and electronic products from Karnataka account for 38 per cent share in India's electronics and computer software exports and 76 per cent share in Karnataka's total exports. Currently, 40 per cent of India's IT industry is located in Bangalore and accounts for 34 per cent of India's total IT exports. The city headquarters about 80 per cent of global IT companies, and out of 870 MNCs who have research and development (R&D) centres in India, 700 are located in Bangalore.

The existence of an unusually large number of scientific and technical education institutions in the city provided the initial advantageous starting point for Bangalore in terms of a ready supply of technically trained and skilled manpower. Several central public sector companies were set up in Bangalore soon after independence, such as Indian Telephone Industries, Hindustan Machine Tools, Bharat Electronics Limited and Bharat Earth Movers Limited. They have acted as drivers of Bangalore's fast growth. Overstaffing in the traditional government-owned industries resulted in skill supply for other enterprises and plenty of specialists, many of whom became entrepreneurs on their own account. The private sector took advantage of the large number of engineers and skilled workers trained in the public sector companies (Van Dijk 2003).

While these institutional factors certainly created a framework of knowledge preparedness, what perhaps most significantly and consistently pushed the city towards becoming India's knowledge capital was a series of state policies and initiatives. Karnataka was the first state to announce a comprehensive IT policy as well as to create a separate government department of IT at an early date. The setting up of software technology parks, of Electronic City and Whitefield as state-of-the-art spaces to house IT clusters, bespeaks a close state–private sector collaboration which underlies the prominence of IT in Bangalore. Successive state governments have made available land and infrastructure to the IT industry, and the policy framework has continued to provide a plethora of supports: 100 per cent foreign equity, corporate income tax exemption up to 90 per cent, duty free imports, access to dedicated data communication links, custom bonding and export certification at a single point. Bangalore is the seat of giant domestic players in IT such as Infosys, WIPRO and TCS as well as large MNCs like Accenture, Apple India, Dell International and IBM. Information technology has a huge and stridently visible presence in the city, dwarfing older industries and defining the city's physical and cultural landscape.

If large companies, both foreign and domestic, form the core of the industry, the gradual spread of a network of start-ups, the beginnings of what is being called a start-up culture, and the state's clear signals of support have ensured that the technology revolution has developed a broader base among younger, new entrants who are willing to take risks, engage in innovations and participate in the city's ever-expanding techno-industrial space. An extraordinary range of interests engage start-ups in Bangalore – from transport and finance (self-driven car rentals and credit) and marketing (intimate wear and used goods) to advertisement (coffee/tea cup branding) and real estate (top-end co-living arrangements for young professionals). These demonstrate the rapidly changing face of the urban consumer market and the ways in which IT has transformed the way of doing business. In 2016, the Karnataka government had announced the Innovate Karnataka policy for financial support equivalent to INR 300 crore in the form of grant/equity through its various funds to start-ups and micro, small and medium enterprises (MSMEs) in IT. However, the financial structure of most start-ups is much higher, between USD 15 and 60 million, raised from the capital market, demonstrating the firm anchoring of start-ups in private/global capital. As the start-up initiative took hold, the IT-driven business model spread beyond the Whitefield and Electronic City tech parks to older residential/commercial localities like Marathahalli in the south-east, Indira Nagar in east central and Koramangala in the south, signalling the deeper penetration into the city of an emerging entrepreneurial-consumer culture, now led by a new generation of young industry leaders, many of whom have come from other states or have recently returned from the United States and Europe.

India's biotechnology industry is comprised of about 800 companies valued at USD 11 billion, growing annually at 20 per cent. In Bangalore, there are 294 biotech companies, including large and medium and around 65 start-ups. Karnataka was the first state in the country to introduce a Biotechnology Policy in 2001, followed by the Millenium Biotechnology Policies of 2014 and 2017. This policy framework encourages investments in new technology platforms of life sciences for effective, multi-disciplinary collaborations, with streamlined incentives and concessions for large investments. The aim of the policy clearly was to encourage R&D in emerging technology areas. It is important to highlight the central role envisioned by the state for itself in supporting entrepreneurs in this sector. The Karnataka Biotechnology and Information Technology Services (KBITS) played a central role in providing financial support to start-ups in this sector. Unlike start-ups in IT, which are largely service-driven, based on market research of demand, and generate quick profits, start-ups in biotechnology have a long incubation period and high risk of failure. As such, funding from government, rather than from the capital market, plays a larger role in the setting up of biotech start-ups. In a recently conducted survey, 84 per cent of existing start-ups in the sector attributed government funding from the KBITS, which has a dedicated start-up fund. The government of Karnataka mobilised INR 2,000 crore funding for investment in start-ups through government intervention alone.

Beyond financial support, a network of institutions was created which provides guidance, mentorship, training and facilities for research. The specific educational and research institutions in this sector are the Institute of Agro Bio Technology, Institute of Bioinformatics and Applied Biotechnology, the Centre for Human Genetics and a number of Biotechnology Finishing Schools. The growth of the biotechnology industry in Bangalore is also anchored in a close relationship between the state and scientific research/ academic institutions. Institutions like the Indian Institute of Science, the Jawaharlal Nehru Centre for Advanced Scientific Research, the Raman Research Institute and the National Centre for Biological Sciences have set up intellectual property cells and established dedicated biotechnology start-up/entrepreneurship cells.

A key player in the biotechnology domain is the Bangalore Bioinnovation Centre (BCC). Situated in the Bangalore Helix Biotechnology Park, which is a developing bio-cluster in Electronic City, the BCC is a state-of-the-art incubation centre for biotechnology start-ups. Created by the KBITS, renamed as the Karnataka Innovation and Technology Society (KITS) under the Government of Karnataka's Department of Information Technology, Biotechnology and Science and Technology, the BCC also receives funding from the Government of India's Department of Biotechnology. An example of the close state–business relationship in this sector was the creation of the Idea2POC (proof of concept) in 2016 organised by the Karnataka government's Start-Up Cell, which had a dedicated INR 10 crore fund for 26 start-ups in biotechnology, of INR 50 lakh each. This award was implemented by the BCC.

Thus, a dense network of academic and research institutions and state agencies and programmes specifically designed for this sector and supported by state funds provide the broader support structure within which biotech start-ups are emerging and are expected to flourish. In this sector the state is not only providing financial support and incentives for an envisioned explosion of talent and entrepreneurship, but is also providing the institutional backbone (land, infrastructure, mentorship) for the rise of a new generation of science/technology-trained, highly skilled, research-oriented entrepreneurs who are expected to take the sector to the next level. Biotechnology start-ups indeed represent the emerging leadership roles of a new crop of entrepreneurs, who may be recent returnees from US or European universities after the completion of doctoral or post-doctoral work, or may be faculty in the city's premier research institutes, or entrepreneurs with a background in science and a nose for business.

Innovate Karnataka, an umbrella brand, was another key intervention in this chain of state-led initiatives to support technology and innovation. The mandate of Innovate Karnataka, launched in 2017, was to encourage innovations in emerging domains: blockchains, artificial intelligence, nanotechnology, digitisation of health, agriculture and other areas. Several Centres of Excellence were set up under this programme, including one each in Mysore and Hubli, in an effort to regionally broaden the base of the innovation initiative. Bangalore led the race for funding, achieving 366 projects out of the 7,000 that were selected for funding. Other programmes, such as Elevate 100, were similarly designed to bring financial and mentorship support to entrepreneurs whose projects were selected from a competitive platform.

While IT, ITES and biotechnology define the cutting edge of Bangalore's economic dynamism in the last four decades, other industries such as automobiles, pharmaceuticals, aerospace, food processing, cement, textiles and garments have also expanded in terms of capital investment, technology and the role of FDI. Some of these changes are associated with broader policy shifts relating to the opening up of the economy. These varied sectors represent a combination of the old and the new. The export-oriented ready-made garment industry is a new and expanding sector, exporting primarily to branded retailers in the United States and Europe. Tucked away in the city's older, and sometimes declining, industrial areas, the garment industry is labour intensive and predominantly an employer of female, unskilled labour. Framed by employment practices that have been widely criticised as marked by low wages and unregulated working conditions, the garment industry is inserted into the global supply chain of apparel exports, but represents a contrasting profile to the glittering world of innovation and technology parks.[13]

An older industry such as automobiles has changed its profile. From a slow and sluggish sector dominated by a handful of domestic manufacturers up until the 1970s, the automobile sector became one of the drivers of India's economic growth, with high participation in global value chains. In the liberalisation and post-liberalisation period, the industry rode on rising domestic demand. Increasingly restrictions on FDI were removed and import duties on components were lowered, and a large number of MNCs entered the automobile sector to take advantage of the expanding domestic demand as also trained manpower and lower wages. While initial entry was through joint ventures, several MNCs now hold all or the greater share of the equity in a sector where 100 per cent FDI is now allowed. Bangalore is one of the main automobile hubs in south India, along with Chennai and Hosur. A large number of foreign players have entered the space of auto manufacturing in Bangalore. Out of the top 20 automobile companies in the city, as many as 9 are MNCs, headquartered in Japan, Germany, the Netherlands and Switzerland. As the sector, particularly the passenger car segment, now moves towards digitisation and automation, a fast-changing digital technology will increasingly shape investment, production processes and employee profiles (Miglani 2019).

The complex, changing and many-layered system that characterises Bangalore's industrial economy is not the principal focus of analysis in this book, and I do not further elaborate on this. The brief outlines presented here of the IT, ITES, biotechnology, automobile and garment sectors are designed to provide a limited window to the changing paradigm of industrial growth that has guided government policies, and their impact on the city's industrial landscape. As technology, digitisation and automation define the drivers of growth, whether in services or in manufacturing, an expanding technically skilled class of professionals and entrepreneurs, powered by government and private funding, both domestic and international, and plugged into globally competitive processes and prices, comes into its own and deepens its hold over the city's economy.

On the other hand, an unskilled or semi-skilled workforce remains outside these domains of economic dynamism. The decline of the public sector as well as the small-scale sector, discussed in the previous section, is seen pronouncedly in the context of Bangalore, as large numbers of workers were displaced from these domains. While globalisation has brought some opportunities to sections of the urban lower classes in Bangalore, there is as yet no substantive analysis of the precise nature of these opportunities. The next section presents information on the city's employment structure, drawing attention to declining opportunities of employment in industry and manufacturing; the decimation of the public sector and SSI sector; and a growing percentage of workers in salaried wage labour, but predominantly in informal sectors of employment, which signals the growing precarity of the urban workforce.

Structure of employment in Bangalore city

The pattern of sectoral growth and employment in Bangalore city replicates the patterns at the state and national levels, particularly in the decline of industry. As Table 4.15 shows, from the mid-1990s onwards, there has occurred a steady decline in the share of the secondary sector (industry) and of registered manufacturing in Bangalore's gross domestic district product (GDDP). Commensurately, the share of the tertiary sector in GDDP has steadily increased. Urban employment is dominated by the tertiary (service) sector rather than by the secondary (manufacturing) sector. Within the tertiary sector, urban employment is concentrated in trade, hotels and restaurants, finance, insurance, real estate and business services, and community, social and personal services. In 2004–05, these service sectors accounted for 66 per cent of the total employment in Bangalore. This was higher than in million-plus cities (62 per cent) and in urban India (57 per cent) (Narayana 2011). By 2012–13, the share of services in employment had risen to 73.25 per cent (Table 4.16).

Table 4.15 Sectoral share in GDDP, Bangalore (in percentage)

Year	Secondary sector	Registered manufacturing sector	Tertiary sector
1993–94	48.92	38	47.96
1999–2000	39.23	29	56.72
2004–05	35.41	27	62.91
2010–11	37.37	NA	NA
2012–13	30.22	21	68.79

Source: Narayana (2011) and GOK (2014).

Table 4.16 Sector-wise percentage of employment in Bangalore, 2011–12

Sector	Percentage of employment
Primary	0.20
Secondary	26.55
Tertiary	73.25

Source: Employment and unemployment situation in cities and towns in India, NSS 68th Round (July 2011–June 2012), NSSO.
Note: Employment data is based on usual status employment in principal and subsidiary activities of the persons in the age group of 15 and above.

In Bangalore, self-employment increased marginally from 32 per cent to 34.5 per cent from 2004–05 to 2013–14 and casual work declined by more than half – from 16 per cent to 8 per cent (Table 4.17). The structure of employment becomes clearer when we see that in Bangalore the share of labour force in wage or salaried employment is higher compared to other cities and other forms of employment. The share of wage salaried employment increased from 48 per cent in 2004–05 to 55 per cent in 2011–12 (Table 4.17). In urban India as a whole, the share of wage salaried employment was 42.8 per cent in 2011–12 (Table 4.18). It is noteworthy that the share of manufacturing sector employment is much lower in Bangalore (21.3 per cent) as compared to urban India (24.3 per cent) (Table 4.18). The comparison is even more telling with regard to million-plus cities, where in 2011–12 manufacturing sector employment stood at 36 per cent. As the service sector constitutes 73 per cent of employment in Bangalore, one would assume that much of what is described as regular or salaried employment is to be found in the service sector.

Table 4.17 Distribution of workforce according to usual principal activity status in Bangalore Urban area (in percentage)

S. No.	Workforce	2004–05	2011–12
1.	Wage/salaried employment	48	55
2.	Self-employment	32	33.5
3.	Casual labour	16	8.4
4.	Unemployed	4	3.1
5.	Total	100	100

Source: Computed using 63rd (2004–05) and 68th (2011–12) Round Unit level NSSO data on employment and unemployment.

Table 4.18 Distribution of workforce (different categories) in Bangalore Urban area and Urban India (in percentage)

S. No.	Category	Bangalore Urban	Urban India
1.	Wage/salaried employment	55	42.8
2.	Manufacturing sector	21.7	23.6

Source: Computed using 68th Round Unit level NSSO data on employment and unemployment, 2011–12.

Both in manufacturing and in services, much of the unskilled employment is informal in nature. Salaried employees in the informal sector may be denied minimum wages, security of tenure and other employment-related benefits. This is by and large true of sectors such as construction and ready-made garments, and in the lower rungs of the service sectors, such as domestic work, security, maintenance, hospitality, retail, and so on. The point to underline here is that while the figures indicating relatively large percentage of persons employed as regular and wage salaried look good, micro studies of salaried and regular employment reveal a somewhat different story of precarious employment defined by the classic features of the informal sector, that is, unregulated wages, uncertain tenure and absence of insurance. These features of Bangalore's informal economy have been discussed in detail in Chapters 5, 6 and 8.

A broad policy perspective on restructuring and reducing the number of public enterprises has been in place in Karnataka since the mid-1990s. In the case of Bangalore, this is of particular relevance since its growth has been synonymous with the existence of a large number of PSEs, at both central and state levels. Since the mid-1990s, the city has seen the gradual erosion of this structure, through closures, privatisation, contractualisation of employment, closure of PSE units, downsizing, and sale of PSE land (RoyChowdhury 2003, 2010). Among state-owned enterprises that have been closed down, some of the more prominent names are NGEF, shut down in 2002, in which about 6,500 employees opted for VRS, and Mysore Lamps, which closed in 2003 and 1,046 employees took VRS. Other units that have closed down or have been privatised are the Karnataka Soaps and Detergents, KAVIKA, Mysore Electrical Industries, Binny Mills, Minerva Mills, and so on, affecting the lives and livelihoods of large numbers of their employees. The impact of public sector restructuring on Bangalore's economy in general, and on employment in particular, is under-researched. A survey conducted in 2003 found that about 68 per cent of VRS takers in state-government-owned units remained unemployed (Rajeev and Dasgupta 2003).[14] Several central-government-owned PSEs located in Bangalore have restructured, by closure of particular units, leading to loss of employment of the permanent workforce. Public sector employment has been reshaped not only through closures, but also through downsizing via VRS, unwillingness of managements to fill up superannuated positions, replacing permanent jobs with contractual work, and so on.

In most PSEs, the last two decades have seen a gradual reduction of permanent positions in the areas of maintenance, security and hospitality. As a permanent workforce diminishes in number through retirement and golden handshake schemes, contracting agencies are invited to cater to these services. Workers appointed through contracting agencies are given a minimum salary but do not have access to security of tenure, pension, medical leave, housing and schools on campus.

If employment in organised manufacturing industries and the state sector has stagnated, the situation in the SSI sector further reflects the grimness of the situation with regard to industrial employment. The SSI sector has been affected in the state as a whole (as discussed earlier). In Bangalore, particularly, a large number of SSI units had developed as a satellite structure to the large public sector; the extinction of many SSI units was a result of the drying up of orders from declining public sector units. A study of the SSI sector in Bangalore division highlights that the decline of SSIs in the city had begun from the latter half of the 1990s. Following the announcement of a 25 per cent capital investment subsidy (CIS) in 1993, 3,339 units received subsidy during the period 1993–94 to 1998–99. Bangalore Urban district (Bangalore city and outlying areas) had 36 per cent share in the total CIS. Of these, 82.46 per cent of the units had closed down when the survey was conducted in 2001 (Gayithri 2003). In the subsequent period, there has been some improvement in the situation. The number of registered units in Bangalore increased from 902 in 2007–08 to 1,370 in 2011–12, but employment declined from 38,870 to 34,470 during this period.[15] The decline of the SSI sector is clearly seen in Bangalore city in areas like the Peenya Industrial Estate, which had been set up in the 1970s by the Karnataka State Small Industries Development Corporation (KSSIDC) to provide space to about 800 SSI units spread across 250 acres of land. The largest such estate in Asia, most units in Peenya acted as ancillary to Bangalore's public sector units. While many PSEs came under threat in the post-reform era, SSI units also faced declining orders as well as increasing competition from both multinational and domestic manufacturers, as a large number of items formerly reserved for the SSI sector became de-reserved. At the same time, as government attention to the SSI sector declined, the Peenya Industrial Estate faced huge shortages in power, water and road infrastructure.[16]

In terms of industrial employment, two main sectors have expanded significantly during the last two decades, both in the context of globalisation of the city. First, there has been a sustained boom in the construction industry as a result of the growth of IT, ITES, financial services, hospitality and entertainment and up-scale housing requirements of the city's upwardly mobile sections. Second, the relatively new ready-made garment export industry developed as part of the emerging global supply chain in garment production and retail. Both sectors have played an important role in fuelling the city's economic growth as well as employment opportunities for unskilled labour. However, the workforce is largely migrant, non-unionised and lacking collective bargaining rights to improve their incomes and living standards over time as well as access to education and skills that could lead to occupational and social mobility inter-generationally.[17]

What has Bangalore's overall economic dynamism – particularly, vastly increased volume of services like hospitality, entertainment, transportation, retail selling, luxury accommodation, corporate colonies, medical services, and so on – meant for the city's poor? The study of lower-class livelihoods in slums (presented in Chapters 5 and 6) highlights that there is no easy bridge between slums and the city's modern economy. Slum households lack access to skills and opportunities necessary to obtain a foothold even in the lower rungs of the service sector. A large number of the urban poor are engaged in wage work in traditional occupations like head-load bearing, unskilled construction work and domestic work. These domains are marked by unprotected wages and absence of social security. Many slum dwellers are engaged in self-employed activities – in petty trade and services – with low investment and income. A new class of service sector workers has indeed emerged, those with education up to class 10 or 12 and working in Bangalore's vast and multiplying service domains such as hospitality, maintenance, security, retail, and so on. Recent studies of the workforce and the nature of work in these sectors indicate a high degree of variation in compensation and employment conditions, marked by insecurity of tenure and the extractive role of contracting agencies.[18]

This broad overview indicates certain patterns of exclusion inherent to the structure of the city's economy as it has evolved in the past three decades. Bangalore provides an appropriate location for examining the paradoxes of growth: as a city that has provided space for remarkable economic and technological dynamism and the rise of technologically anchored classes of professionals and entrepreneurs and, at the same time, retains a large workforce that is unable to access the opportunities introduced by the city's rapid growth. The next chapters (5, 6 and 8) narrate that story of exclusion, looking at urban livelihoods through the lens of slums and employment in construction and ready-made garment industries.

Notes

1. Kerala has a poverty ratio of 12 per cent and Punjab 15.9 per cent.
2. In terms of specific human development indicators, Karnataka's infant mortality rate (IMR) in 2011 was 35 per 1,000 live births, whereas Kerala's was 12 and Tamil Nadu's was 22. In terms of nutritional deficiency of children below the age of five, Karnataka's rank was 18th.
3. Ibid.
4. Fiscal deficit increased from 2.40 in 1990–91 to 3.54 in 1998–99; after that it decreased to 2.28 in 2006–07 and 2.24 per cent in 2007–08, and rose again to 2.94 per cent in 2012.
5. The total quantum of direct subsidies increased from INR 2,992.65 crore in 2001–02 to INR 5,661.11 crore in 2007–08 to INR 4,541.59 crore in 2010–11, recording a rate of growth of 4.26 per cent per annum (1 crore = 10 million). In terms of components, the largest direct subsidy goes to the power sector; power subsidy constituted 77 per cent of the total in 2001–02, 81.5 per cent in 2002–03 and reduced to 40.58 per cent in 2007–08, but after that there is a continuous increase to 68.90 per cent in 2011–12. In food, similarly, a low of 12.48 per cent in 2007–08, which increased to 28.28 per cent in 2009–10 and then declined to 13.62 per cent in 2011–12. In addition to direct subsidies, there are huge expenditures involved in the provision of various goods and services provided by the government, for which there is no equivalent recovery made. The unrecovered cost in 1990–91 amounted to INR 1,653 crore and increased by 455 per cent to INR 9,164 crore in 2007–08. For a discussion on these themes, see Gayithri and Deshpande (2012).
6. In 2001, a Tax Reform Commission was set up and various reforms in improving the structure of sales tax, introducing value-added tax (VAT), reforms of excise, transport and stamps, and registration taxes have since been introduced. These reform measures showed some results. The tax–GSDP ratio improved from 8.1 per cent in 1999–2000 to 8.6 per cent in 2000–01, to 8.9 per cent in 2001–02, and 9.5 per cent in 2004–05. Although there was a dip during 2008–09 and 2009–19 to 9.0 and 9.1, the tax–GSDP ratio has risen continuously since then (10.1 in 2010–11, 10.7 in 2011–12, 10.3 in 2012–13 and 10.38 in 2013–14) (*Economic Survey of Karnataka: 2013–14*: 36). As part of state efforts to better manage its finances, the Karnataka Fiscal Responsibility Act was enacted in

2002. Revenue receipts (as a percentage of GSDP) declined from 16.55 per cent in 2006–07 to around 15 and 14 per cent during 2007–08 and 2010–11 respectively, but there has been a gradual increase to 16 per cent and above from 2011–12 to the present.

7.   The recent NSSO 73rd Round (2015–16) data shows that over 90 per cent of rural non-farm enterprises are own account enterprises, that is, they do not hire labour. Thirty-five per cent of the rural non-farm enterprises are in manufacturing, while the rest are in services, of which 50 per cent are in trading, and the largest number in this category, again, are own account enterprises, which are most likely to be small, petty shops. See Rajeev (2020) and Biradar and Kusugal (2010).

8.   For a discussion of the impact of restructuring in state-government-owned enterprises, see Rajeev and Dasgupta (2003). For a discussion of restructuring of central government public sector manufacturing enterprises in Bangalore and the impact of these processes on labour, see RoyChowdhury (2003, 2010).

9.   Several studies have drawn attention to the deceleration of the SSI sector, particularly from the period after the programme of economic reforms began in Karnataka. Looking at the period 1995–2003, a study of the impact of the World Trade Organization (WTO) agreements on Karnataka's SSI sector stated that the WTO agreements had implications on all SSIs, whether in export or in the domestic sector, as most sectors became exposed to global and enhanced domestic competition. According to this study, the highest number of closures and sickness was evident in the post-WTO period in the smaller SSIs (Narayana 2005; see also Narayana 2011). The annual growth in employment fell from 6.59 per cent in 1995–96 to 3.6 per cent in 2002–03 (Kalasanavar 2013).

10.   Average wage for regular workers in Karnataka was INR 487 per day in 2011–12, in Haryana INR 777, New Delhi INR 589. Casual wages were also significantly lower. Female regular workers' average wage in 2011–12 was INR 392 per day, 62 per cent and 57 per cent of equivalent average wages in Haryana and New Delhi respectively. Average wage for female casual workers in Karnataka was below the national average at INR 102 per day in 2011–12.

11.   See, particularly, Heitzman (2004) and Upadhya (2006).

12.   See Dhar and Joseph (2019), Rastogi (2019) and Van Djik (2003).

13.   See discussion in Chapter 7 of this book.

14.   See Rajeev and Dasgupta (2003).

15.   *Economic Survey of Karnataka*, several years.

16.   For a discussion of the adverse impact of WTO on competitiveness in the SSI sector in Karnataka/Bangalore, see Narayana (2011).

17.   These themes are presented in subsequent chapters.

18.   For service sector workers, see RoyChowdhury and Upadhya (2020).

References

Biradar, R. R. and N. S. Kusugal. 2010. 'Rural Non-aEmployment in Karnataka: Emerging Issues and Evidences'. *Journal of Rural Development* 29 (2): 181–97.

Dhar, B. and R. K. Joseph. 2019. 'India's Information Technology Industry: A Tale of Two Halves'. In *Innovation, Economic Development, and Intellectual Property in India and China*, ARCIALA Series on Intellectual Assets and Law in Asia, edited by Liu K. C. and U. Racherla, 93–117. Singapore: Springer.

Gayithri, K. 2003. 'Industrial Incentives in Karnataka'. In *Volume and Composition of Budgetary Subsidies in Karnataka*, Monograph, edited by Govinda Rao. Institute for Social and Economic Change, Bangalore.

Gayithri, K. and R. S. Deshpande. 2012. 'Government Subsidies in Karnataka'. Institute for Social and Economic Change, Bangalore, mimeo.

Gayithri, K. and K. V. Raju. 2016. *Financing India's Development*. New Delhi: Cambridge University Press.

Government of Karnataka (GOK). 2005. *Karnataka Human Development Report*. Bangalore: Planning, Programme Monitoring and Statistics Department, Government of Karnataka and United Nations Development Program (UNDP).

———. 2009. 'Urban Development Policy'. Department of Urban Development, Government of Karnataka. Available at http://www.indiaenvironmentportal.org.in/files/Urban%20Development%20Policy.pdf (accessed 20 April 2021).

———. 2014. *Sixth Economic Census*. Bangalore: Directorate of Economics and Statistics. Available at https://des.kar.nic.in/docs/Sixth%20final%20Economic%20Census%20Report.pdf (accessed 20 April 2021).

———. Several years. *Economic Survey of Karnataka*. Bangalore; Directorate of Economics and Statistics, Government of Karnataka. Available at http://karenvis.nic.in/Content/EconomicSurveyKarnataka_8184.aspx (accessed 20 April 2021).

Heitzman, J. 2004. *Network City: Planning the Information Society in Bangalore*. New Delhi, Oxford University Press.

Kalasanavar, H. S. 2013. *An Economic Analysis of Small Scale Industries in Karnataka*. Bangalore: KASSIA.

Kundu, A. 2012. 'Migration and Exclusionary Urbanization in India'. *Economic and Political Weekly* 47 (26/27): 219–27.

Miglani, S. 2019. 'The Growth of the Indian Automobile Industry: Analysis of the Roles of Government Policy and Other Enabling Factors'. In *Innovation, Economic Development and Intellectual Property in India and China*, ARCIALA Series on Intellectual Assets and Law in Asia book, edited by Liu K. C. and U. Racherla, 439–63. Singapore: Springer

Narayana, M. R. 2005. *WTO Agreements and Small Scale Industries in Karnataka State: An Exploratory Study of Current Policy Issues, Interventions and Future Policy Options.* Bangalore: Department of Industries and Commerce, Government of Karnataka.

————. 2011. 'ICT Sector: Globalization and Urban Economic Growth – Evidence from Bangalore (India)'. *International Journal of Urban and Regional Research* 35 (6): 1284–301.

Niranjan, R. and Shivakumar, 2018. 'Poverty among Socio Religious Groups in Karnataka by Using NSSO Data'. *International Journal of Creative Research Thoughts* 6 (1): 479–98.

Pani, N., and G. Chidambaram. 2013. 'Evaluation of the Processes in the Implementation of JnNURM in Karnataka'. Karnataka Evaluation Authority, Planning, Programme Monitoring and Statistics Department; National Institute of Advanced Studies, Bangalore.

Prabhakar, J. 2012. 'Socio-cultural Dimensions of Development in North Karnataka'. Working Paper, Centre for Multi-disciplinary Development Research, Dharwad.

Rastogi, V. 2019, 'India's Export and Import Trends, 2018–19'. India Briefing. Available at https://www.india-briefing.com/news/indias-export-import-trends-2018-19-18958.html/ (accessed 20 April 2021).

Rajeev, M. and A. Hariharan. 2020. 'Time to Focus on Rural Farm Economy'. *Deccan Herald*, 8 June.

Rajeev, M. and P. Dasgupta. 2003. 'Karnataka Public Enterprises'. World Bank, New Delhi.

RoyChowdhury, S. 2003. 'Public Sector Restructuring and Democracy: The State, Labour and Trade Unions in India'. *Journal of Development Studies* 39 (3): 29–50.

————. 2010. 'Class in Industrial Conflict: Case Studies from Bangalore'. In *Globalization and Labour in China, India and the West*, edited by John Harriss and Paul Bowles, 170–88. New York: Palgrave and Macmillan, 2010.

RoyChowdhury, S. and C. Upadhya. 2020. 'India's Changing Cityscapes: Work, Migration and Livelihoods'. Institute for Social and Economic Change, Bangalore, and National Institute of Advanced Studies, Bangalore.

Upadhya, C. 2016, *Reengineering India: Work, Capital and Class in an Offshore Economy*. Delhi: Oxford University Press.

Van Dijk, M. P, 2003, 'Government Policies with Respect to an Information Technology Cluster in Bangalore, India'. *European Journal of Development Research* 15 (2): 89–104.

5

New Slums
Migration, Livelihoods and Living

This chapter presents a discussion of four slums, which are settlements of migrants who came to Bangalore not earlier than 2002. At the time of the study, the households had been in residence on an average of 8 to 10 years. Several households were found to be circular migrants, that is, they left the city to go back to their home villages regularly for several months of the year, typically during the harvest season.

The relationship between migration and urban poverty has engaged development scholars for a long time. As discussed in Chapter 3, and to briefly rehearse here, the spillover thesis (that urban poverty is mainly the reflection of rural poverty, carried over by poor migrants) continues to inform policy discourses mainly emerging from international organisations. In criticism, migration scholars in India have pointed out that the poorest do not migrate; the relatively better-off/better-informed among the rural population are those who are able to actually move to cities and towns (Kundu 2007, 2014). Mitra (2006, 2010) has suggested that while there is obviously a distinct association between rural and urban poverty, the total inflow of rural–urban migrants – and the percentage of migrants to total urban population – is not high enough to justify the spillover thesis; Mitra also points out that many of the urban poor have been residing in cities for several decades; thus the poverty of migrants may be related to urban poverty at the margin. Chapter 6 in this book shows that contrary to the claim that the urban poor are predominantly new rural–urban migrants who fail to take advantage of urban opportunities, old inner-city slums in Bengaluru combine limited opportunities for economic mobility with deep pockets of poverty and marginalisation of households that have been in urban residence for two or three generations. I have called this category the 'old poor'. The discourse on urban poverty has in fact gone beyond the spillover thesis to recognising structural dimensions of the political economy of cities – decline in manufacturing jobs and an increasingly technological paradigm of development that marginalises the unskilled and semi-skilled urban workforce, whether migrant or non-migrant. In this sense, the poverty of migrants can be seen to be a symptom rather than a cause of urban poverty.

The specific dynamics of the poverty of migrants must of course remain a huge concern for both scholars and policy makers. The chapter provides information and analysis of households who might be called the new poor: recent migrants who live in fragile settlements in the city's peripheries, work mainly on construction sites and leave frequently to return to the village. As discussed in Chapter 3, there is an ongoing debate over whether or not migrants benefit from migration: are they able to climb out of poverty, gain better access to well-being? Several studies have highlighted the continuing social and economic marginalisation of migrants, and the coercive role of labour contractors and urban employers. On the other hand, the World Bank and other international agencies have continued to maintain that the city provides a ladder that even the poorest can step on to. On similar lines, a recent volume on circular migration has stated that migration is important for sustaining, and in some cases improving, rural households. Studying migrants from the poorest regions as well as socially marginalised groups from more prosperous areas, the volume concludes that circular migration makes important contributions to rural households and to the construction sector, and draws attention to the need for policy interventions at the points of destination (Deshingkar and Farrington 2009). Other studies (Mitra 2006) have suggested that while urban opportunities are limited, migrants may still grasp at the possibility of getting a subsistence living, which may not be possible in rural areas. Mitra (2010) on the basis of a study of four cities in north India suggested that, over time, migrants may achieve some improvement in their levels of income and well-being. Pattenden (2012) in a study of seasonal migrant workers from Raichur district in northern Karnataka concluded that they move from one site of exploitation, small agrarian capital, to another site, the building industry in Bangalore. Highlighting low earnings of unskilled construction workers, he nevertheless found that they are able to use their urban base as some kind of negotiating platform vis-à-vis their seasonal rural employers.

These somewhat contrasting, sometimes overlapping perspectives on migration suggest that the migration–poverty relationship is both complex and varied, and possibly elude any precise judgements. The present chapter provides information on multiple vulnerabilities in the lives of migrant labour in Bangalore's slums: income, work availability, housing, children's education, and so on. Compared to the older slums (Chapter 6), where a range of different occupations are found, particularly in the lower rungs of the service sector, and some degree of social and economic mobility has been gained in particular pockets, households in newer slums were crowded into the construction sector and faced a narrower scope of choice and economic opportunities. At the same time, built into the lives of migrant households is a set of vulnerabilities related to insecure housing, with the possibility of evictions, and inadequate basic services such as water and toilets, and hardly any provision for education of children.

Beyond these descriptive narratives, what frames the analysis are the institutional framework of work and the representational mechanisms available to migrant workers. The chapter underlines that across occupations, informality and absence of regulation create a context where migrant labour is prevented from claiming a decent livelihood. Second, there is no systematic attention to this workforce from state or non-state actors. NGO intervention has been low in this cluster of slums, while political representatives across parties and across the different levels of democratic representations (city corporation, state legislative assembly, national parliament) have shown little interest in these communities. Given their itinerant lives as circular migrants, most households lacked the necessary papers relating to voter identity, and therefore were not attractive to local politicians. In the absence of grassroots organisations, the slum households lacked the necessary bridges for access to broader representational channels. This political economy framework suggests that while subsistence living may be available to the migrants, it may be difficult to translate this into substantive well-being or even inter-generational mobility.

Bangalore has attracted an increasing number of technically skilled migrants, primarily from other states in India. Skilled labour (those possessing technical qualifications, diplomas or graduate degrees) constituted 11.68 per cent of migrants in 1981 and 16.47 per cent in 1991, and by 2011 this proportion had gone up to 23.86 per cent (Mukhopadhyay and Sivaramakrishnan 2013). On the other hand, a study conducted in Bangalore in 2012 found that the majority of the migrants continue to be either agricultural labourers or farmers before migration (Sridhar, Reddy and Srinath 2012). This study further shows that factors such as large size of household, small size of agricultural holding and poor public services in rural areas contribute to rural–urban migration to Bangalore. Rural-to-urban migration is most prevalent amongst low-skilled workers who engage in circular migration, that is, who have some employment in their villages and come to the city for seasonal work. Short-duration mobility is higher amongst the poor as compared to middle-class households. In Karnataka, rural-to-rural migration is highest amongst SCs (73 per cent),

STs (78 per cent) and OBCs (58 per cent). In contrast, the share of SCs (14 per cent) and STs (16 per cent) in rural-to-urban migration is lower than the average (21 per cent), OBC (20 per cent) and others (25 per cent).

Migrant slums: socio-economic profiles

The chapter examines four slums in Bengaluru city:[1] Veerupakshanagar in Hebbal (north), Narayanpura in KR Puram (east), Chamundinagar in Banashankari (south) and Ashrayanagar in Peenya (west). The choice of these slums was determined both in terms of geographical representation and newness of the settlement. Residents in these slums are recent migrants who have been in the city for about 0–15 years, on an average 5–8 years. The settlements do not date further back than 2002. The sizes of the slums range from 250 to 400 households, except in the case of Ashryayanagar, which is one of the largest slums in the city with 2,000 households. In each of the slums, 50 households were selected for responding to a questionnaire designed to elicit basic information relating to the socio-economic profile of the slum dwellers. Thereafter, in each slum, several focus group discussions were held, in which other households (that is, those who were not respondents to the questionnaire) as well as slum leaders (members of slum-based caste associations), wherever relevant, also participated; particular care was taken to include women in the discussions.

In terms of the origin of migrants (Table 5.1), households in Veerupakshanagar and Narayanpura slums were predominantly from north Karnataka, hailing from the districts of Gulbarga, Dharwad, Raichud and particularly from two *taluk*s, Shapur and Yadagiri. In Ashrayanagar and Chamundinagar slums, the households were mainly from southern Karnataka, particularly from Mangalore, Udipi, Chikmangalor, and a few from Andhra Pradesh, Tamil Nadu and Kerala. In the case of Chamundinagar, around half the households had in-migrated from different parts of Bangalore, particularly from Hosakarehalli. The regional origin of migrants is related, as the discussion below reveals, to the education and skill levels of the migrants, and their subsequent life and livelihood trajectories in the city.

Broadly speaking, each of the four migrant settlements emerged when the present residents set up temporary shacks on public land or land on which ownership was disputed but which did not prevent locally influential persons from extracting rent from migrants. Most households studied in the four slums did not possess any land in their village of origin, and their members had been working as agricultural workers or daily-wage earners in public works and had earned an income below INR 2,000 per month.[2] At such low

Table 5.1 Place of origin of migrants

Slum	North Karnataka	South Karnataka	Tamil Nadu	West Bengal	Bihar	AP	Other	Total
Veerupakshanagar	46	1	0	0	0	1	2	50
Narayanpura	18	16	10	4	0	1	0	49
Ashrayanagar	4	44	2	0	0	0	0	50
Chamundinagar	2	37	10	0	1	0	0	50

Source: Author's field research.

income and asset levels, migration had obviously been led by distress. Each of the slums had a young profile, in terms of age of the first migrant or the head of the household, as most had migrated when they were in the working age. The education pattern confirms the conventional understanding that the typical migrant enters the urban labour market with low levels of education and frequently as illiterate and unskilled labour. In the four slums studied, a large majority were illiterate, and a small number were literate but without formal schooling (Table 5.2).

Across the slums, we found that the largest numbers work as unskilled labour in the construction industry (Table 5.3). The wages received by construction workers varies not only by skill, but also by gender and size of the project. Between 2010 and 2017, the minimum wage of an unskilled construction worker in Karnataka was raised from INR 135 to INR 385 per day (GOK 2017). With the revision, an unskilled worker in Bangalore (zone 1 city) can earn a monthly income of about INR 10,000. As unskilled workers are frequently seen to work as couples on the same project, the income of a worker couple could go up to INR 20,000. However, this is an entirely hypothetical

Table 5.2 Education patterns of migrants (first migrant or head of the household)

Slum	Illiterate	Literate but without schooling	Up to class V	Up to class VIII	SSLC	PUC	Graduate	Total
Veerupakshanagar	32	2	7	7	2	0	0	50
Narayanpura	28	1	4	5	9	2	0	49
Ashrayanagar	26	1	3	9	8	2	1	50
Chamundinagar	16	0	8	11	11	3	1	50

Source: Author's field research.

Table 5.3 Current occupational structure

Slum	Unskilled construction	Skilled construction	Self-employed	Driver	Maid servant	BBMP	Other (salaried /regular)	Total
Veerupakshanagar	42	1	3	0	0	3	1	50
Narayanpura	40	6	1	1	0	0	1	49
Ashrayanagar	26	10	4	1	2	0	1	44
Chamundinagar	21	10	1	7	8	0	3	50

Source: Author's field research.

projection. In reality, within the slums studied, workers rarely, if ever, get to work all six days of the week, and frequently the daily wage falls well below the minimum, to about INR 220–50 per day. Women may receive wages as low as INR 180–220 per day. Many workers reported their monthly income to be about INR 12,000–14,000, even when both husband and wife were working on the same construction site. Individual monthly earnings could be as low as INR 7,000–8,000.

The number of skilled workers was much less. According to the revised rates in 2017, a skilled worker in Bangalore (zone 1 city) would get INR 405 per day; the monthly minimum wage of such a worker could thus be INR 10,530 for 26 days of work. While this is the minimum wage, there are significant variations based on location, experience, network, size of project, and so on. We found that skilled workers who have lived in the city for many years and have developed channels of contact with more than one contractor or agency may find work in large private or public projects in the city, and could earn up to INR 600–800 per day and may even have a small space for bargaining. Thus, their monthly earnings, ranging from INR 16,000 to INR 21,000, could be well above the minimum wage, even when they may not get work all six days of the week. In contrast, a very different picture appeared in the migrant slums. Skilled workers who are recent migrants have an unsure footing in the city and are entirely dependent on a single agent (contractors or subcontractors) for work. Their earnings as masons and plumbers, on an average, are between INR 300 and INR 450 per day; monthly incomes could range from about INR 7,800 to INR 11,700, and unavailability of regular work made their monthly income lower. Depending upon the size of the project and availability of work, a skilled male worker could earn up to INR 13,000 per month. Women construction workers are rarely skilled. In any case, skilled construction workers who earn in the higher brackets are already partially gentrified and, therefore, it is very rare that the wife of a skilled construction worker would work at a construction site, as it is considered one of the lowest in the occupational hierarchy by working-class families.

Moving on to other occupations, while there was only one BBMP (the city council) sanitation worker in the group studied, it should be highlighted that wages in this sector vary according to whether a worker is a regular BBMP employee or a contractual employee. The BBMP employs 2,500 workers on its rolls as regular workers, who earn up to INR 14,000 per month. Around 18,000 men and women are contractual workers who earn INR 6,000–7,000 per month, and the non-payment of salaries of contract workers is a huge issue in the city. In another work, drivers of three wheelers, of which the largest number, seven, were found in Chamundinagar slum, reported earnings of about INR 15,000 per month. In other salaried, regular work, which could include salespersons in small shops, the wages varied from INR 6,000 to INR 8,000 per month (Table 5.4).

Returning to construction workers, who constitute the majority in the group, the reported monthly earnings may appear to be unexpectedly low, particularly in context of the cost of living in Bengaluru. Even allowing for a certain amount of under-reporting of incomes, the discrepancy between what could be the monthly income based on the calculation of the stipulated minimum daily wages in various categories and the actual monthly earnings needs to be highlighted. First, across the settlements studied, it was uniformly reported that construction workers, on an average, do not get work for more than 3–4 days per week, amounting to 12 to 14 days of work per month. The daily wages therefore do not translate directly into monthly income (in terms of 26 working days per month). Therefore, while there is a stipulated daily wage, there is no guaranteed monthly wage in this sector.

Table 5.4 Work and wages

Work	Number of workers	Average wages per month
Construction (skilled)	26	INR 13,000
Construction (unskilled)	135	INR 8,500
Self-employed	9	INR 5,000
BBMP sanitation worker	3	INR 8,000
Three-wheeler driver	9	INR 15,000
Regular salaried	6	INR 8,000

Source: The income of construction workers is based on discussions with skilled and unskilled workers in the slums studied.

Second, the average wage of unskilled workers in other sectors, even when there is a regular monthly wage, is approximately comparable. For example, waiters in low-cost eateries earn as low as INR 4,500; semi-skilled young persons, who have undergone short periods of training, and who serve behind coffee counters in high-end cafes may earn INR 7,000–8,000; while security guards employed in apartment buildings in middle-income neighbourhoods earn between INR 6,000 and INR 8,000 per month (RoyChowdhury and Vani 2016). In this context, the monthly average earnings of migrant, unskilled construction workers, who may find work only for 12–15 days per month, do not appear to be unreal. Finally, of course, the household income would be more than the monthly wage of an individual worker because in most households there were one or two part-time earners besides the head of the family. It should also be highlighted that driving and sales jobs fetch higher earnings; however, the representation of recent migrants in these relatively higher-income occupations is low, and the largest number flock to unskilled construction work.

Within the broad features of occupation and income presented above, there are certain variations between the settlements, which provide some insight into the nature of opportunities available to migrants in Bangalore. Ashrayanagar and Chamundinagar slums shared some similarities, which distinguished them from the other two slums. As Table 5.2 shows, in each of these two settlements, compared to the other two slums, illiteracy rates were lower; the number of those who had studied up to class 8 as well as up to high school was higher; and, remarkably, both slums had one graduate each. As shown in Table 5.3, in both slums the share of unskilled workers amongst construction workers was lower, and skilled workers higher, compared to the other two slums. The occupational profile appeared more diversified. There is a possible correlation between the place of origin and educational/occupational levels. In contrast to the other two slums where migrants were predominantly from north Karnataka, these housed more migrants from south Karnataka. South Karnataka, as is well known, has a better record of human development, particularly in education, as compared with other parts of the state.[3]

A closer look at the occupational and family structure in these two slums revealed certain paradoxical features. It was found that in Ashrayanagar and Chamundinagar the number of working adults is much lower than in the other two slums (Table 5.5). A possible clue to understanding this situation emerged during discussions in the slums. In both slums, many women pointed out that they were unable to find work, but would not choose to work in construction. On deeper probing, it appeared that as part of households with

Table 5.5 Number of working adults and dependents in slums

Slum	Total number (including all adult members of the households)	Number of working adults
Veerupakshanagar	198	112
Narayanpura	215	102
Ashrayanagar	219	78
Chamundinagar	177	89

Source: Author's interviews at slums.

some degree of education, and where the men were employed in semi-skilled or skilled occupations, the women, as well as their families, saw themselves as part of a gentrified community. As such, the idea that the woman of the family should work in construction sites was not acceptable to these families. In this scenario, lacking skills, the women's only choice was to work as domestic help. However, as newer migrants, they encountered many obstructions in this sector. In upper-middle-class neighbourhoods and in newly emerging up-scale residential areas (luxury apartments or villas that house middle to high-end IT employees, gated communities of recently returned non-resident Indians (NRIs) and expatriates, all part of Bengaluru's booming new economy), women domestic workers earn anywhere between INR 8,000 and INR 10,000 for full-time work (eight hours) and can earn INR 15,000–18,000 as live-in housekeeper. As new migrants, women in these two slums do not have access to networks or connections that can get them well-paid domestic-service jobs in up-scale neighbourhoods. Thus, migrant women in Ashrayanagar and Chamundinagar found only part-time work in middle-class or lower-middle-class households in surrounding neighbourhoods where salaries were expectedly low. The work that these women do is basic (cleaning) rather than work that requires some skill (typically, cooking and childcare). Thus, the average wage earned by women (confined predominantly to part-time domestic work) in these settlements is as low as INR 3,500–4,000 per month. In the absence of opportunities in manufacturing or in better-paying service work, unskilled women from these slums can find only low-paid, part-time domestic work or prefer not to work, leading many households to be in poverty because of the larger number of dependents. What is to be highlighted is that although the migrants in these two settlements have better resources as compared to the other two slums studied, in terms of literacy, education, as well as higher representation in occupations that fetch higher incomes, their access to work is extremely limited.

In contrast, in Veerupakshanagar and Narayanpura, although education levels are much lower, the number of working adults is significantly higher. In most households in these two settlements, both husband and wife (and possibly children, although not stated openly) are working members, the largest numbers being unskilled construction workers. As migrants from northern Karnataka, with low levels of literacy and education and emerging from conditions of acute want, these men and women are prepared to do any kind of work.

To conclude this section, the relatively higher literacy and education levels of particular migrant communities does not provide them with access to better opportunities: there are no available avenues of skilling, nor can migrants enter factory work in which typically unskilled workers are trained on-the-job. Migrant communities thus face an opportunity structure which pulls them to the lowest-paid work, in construction and domestic service. Even within these two sectors, given a combination of disadvantages relating to being recent migrants, lacking a foothold in the city and primarily lacking skills, they are pushed to the lowest rungs of unskilled, irregular and part-time work. The distribution of occupations and structure of incomes across the slums clearly indicate that migrant households are confined to low levels of earnings.[4] I turn now to other indicators of vulnerability, namely children's education, housing and basic services.

Channels of mobility – children's education

Low incomes/earnings of slum households is reinforced by the fact that access to wider opportunities remain severely limited for migrants as well as their children. For adult members of the household, there is little scope for skill formation or for moving up the occupational ladder and into better-paying jobs.[5] Children of migrants, by and large, are unable to access school education. Thus, households remain trapped in low-skill, low-income occupations with little scope for mobility even inter-generationally. Most households are typically unwilling to provide accurate information on whether children are going to school or staying at home, and across the slums an impression was given that most children between the age of 6 and 14 are going to school. However, over several visits, we were able to gain the information that of a total of 247 children in the age group of 6–14, as many as 45 were out of school. Children in this category dropped out of school at some stage or another. In this age group, 33 children were illiterate and 7 were literate but had not gone through formal schooling (Table 5.6).

Table 5.6 Information on children aged 6–14

Slum	Total number of children (6–14)	Number of children reported as going to school (6–4)	Children reported as not going to school (6–14)
Veerupakshanagar	59	36	12(23)
Narayanpura	52	48	2(4)
Ashrayanagar	72	63	1(9)
Chamundinagar	64	55	2(9)

Source: Author's field research (figures in parentheses in the last column show actual number of out-of-school children, which was higher than what was reported).

For younger children, those in the age group of 0–6 years, the Integrated Child Development Services (ICDS) scheme enacted in 1976 had introduced the concept of *anganwadi*s as a one-stop crèche to provide pre-school education and nutritional care to small children and expectant mothers. Under the Sarva Shiksha Avignyan (SSA) scheme, it is mandatory to have at least one *anganwadi* in every slum. The discussion below shows that access to schools and *anganwadi*s was limited.

In Veerupakshanagar slum, there was no *anganwadi* or a school nearby. Most of the children old enough to go to school had been left behind in the village of origin in the care of relatives, and it was reported that they were either helping relatives in agricultural activities or attending the village school. In this slum, many children were working as helpers at construction sites, although no exact estimates were available. In Narayanpura slum, a government-run primary school as well as an *anganwadi* are located close to the settlement but hardly any children from the slum were enrolled there. In Ashrayanagar slum, 35 children were enrolled up to class 4 in a government-run primary school located not far from the slum. The rest, 28, were reported to be enrolled in private schools in the neighbourhood. One *anganwadi* had been opened in the slum with assistance from an NGO and is attended by 5–10 children. Here, afternoon meal is provided by the International Society for Krishna Consciousness (ISKCON) temple. In Chamundinagar slum, an *anganwadi* is run by the Association for Promoting Social Action (APSA). Some children in this settlement were enrolled in a nearby private school.

In Ashrayanagar and Chamundinagar, parents sent their children to both public and private schools, and an *anganwadi* had been provided by an NGO. In contrast, in Veerupakshanagar, there was no school or *anganwadi* available, and Narayanpura had low enrolments in both the *anganwadi* and the primary school. With more children in school and in *anganwadis*, both Ashrayanagar and Chamundinagar slums appeared to confirm the analysis earlier that the communities in these two slums have higher leanings towards literacy and education as compared to households in the other two slums.

Much has been written on why poor children do not attend school or drop out. In the case of recent migrants to the city studied here, a specific set of circumstances led to a large number of children being out of school. A commonly cited reason was that there was no one to take the children to school and bring them back, as, for the parents working at construction sites, the day starts at 8 a.m. and ends at 6 p.m. Many parents left their children at home in the care of older siblings or neighbours, or took them along to the construction site, where they either worked or, if they were too young, played around at the site.[6] Additionally, there is an inherent instability in their lives as they move from site to site and may change their dwellings due to evictions. Given this instability as well as low incomes, the propensity to send children to schools is very low.

If the work and life structure of migrant construction workers prevent them from actively seeking to put their children to school, state intervention has been conspicuously absent in this domain. Broadly speaking, through the SSA, the government has given itself the mandate of providing tent schools that are designed as a bridge to provide basic education to children of migrant workers and enable them to move on to mainstream government schools. I have discussed elsewhere the plight of tent schools (RoyChowdhury 2017). Briefly, tent schools failed to act as effective mechanisms of intervention in the lives of migrant children, as they were fund starved and poorly run, with abysmal infrastructure and poorly paid teachers. The scheme was eventually withdrawn. Ironically, the slums studied in the present chapter did not even come under the purview of tent schools. Although three of the four slums had access to *anganwadis*, these had been provided by NGOs, rather than by the government, and were beset with the typical problems relating to inadequate funds. In each of the slums, it was seen that the *anganwadis* were used by parents for childcare for a few hours and for the midday meal, rather than as a space for active learning. The findings thus indicate that state intervention has been minimal in providing educational facilities for the children of migrants. Thus, if lack of education and skills caused migrants to be tied to low-paying, unskilled work, it seems unlikely that the city would provide their children with the stepping stone out of the cycle of low skills and low incomes.

Housing and basic services

In each slum, the most immediate and visible vulnerability appeared to stem from the lack of decent housing. Families were crammed into shacks made of the ubiquitous blue tarpaulin propped up with bamboo poles. Broadly speaking, there was no electricity, water, sanitation or toilets. Several communities have been residing in these settlements for the last 5 to 10 years or longer. As the discussion in the Introduction and Chapter 7 indicates, new housing projects are typically designed as redevelopment schemes for slums which have been notified or recognised by the government. Non-notified slums, which house migrants who have moved to the city recently, are rarely taken up for redevelopment by state-sponsored housing projects. The lack of housing is, of course, closely connected to the issue of the urban poor's right to urban land (discussed in Chapter 7).

Living in temporary and unauthorised shelters, migrant communities are at constant risk of eviction. Out of the four slums studied here, two had experienced eviction, with different outcomes. The dynamics and outcomes of evictions were determined by differential access of slum households to the support of political parties and civil society associations. Demolition had taken place in Narayanpura slum in June 2009. Out of 300 households, about 100 shacks were demolished by the BBMP. Subsequently, with the help of some local leaders, the evicted families were allowed to return and reconstruct their shacks. Ashrayanagar slum faced demolition by the BBMP in May 2006. Due to active intervention by a local leader belonging to the Bahujan Samajvadi Party (BSP), temporary shelters were rebuilt, and the community was rehabilitated on the same piece of land.

As a result of the sustained engagement of a local NGO, in Chamundinagar slum, under the Basic Services for Urban Poor (BSUP) scheme of the Jawaharlal Nehru National Urban Renewal Mission (JNNRUM) for the construction of permanent houses for slum dwellers, the Karnataka Slum Development Board (KSDP) started a two-phase housing programme in December 2010.[7] Every household paid INR 25,000 to receive land entitlement documents.

Apart from the fundamental insecurity associated with an ever-present threat of eviction, the physical environment within slums is marked by multiple insecurities. None of the settlements studied had access to any kind of drainage system or waste collection. Each settlement presented a similar sight: waste piled high in a corner of the settlement, stray dogs roaming around and the stink of rotting garbage. In Narayanpura slum, the entire space is surrounded by mounds of garbage dumped by BBMP vans in an open space. Adjacent to the slum is a large space, which used to be a pond and which, over the years, has become choked with garbage. Three of the four slums pay a daily or a monthly charge to private water tanks or water carriers.

The state's attention had been for the most part absent in the domain of any kind of service delivery or, at best, such attention appears to be opportunistic and sporadic. Thus, only in the case of one slum, Chamundinagar, direct intervention by a BJP Member of the Legislative Assembly (MLA), who was seeking votes, led to the sinking of bore wells, installation of hand pumps and construction of toilets under the Valmiki Ambedkar Awas Yojana (VAMBAY) scheme by the KSDP. The toilets, however, had fallen into disuse due to lack of maintenance, thus demonstrating that there is no sustained interest on the part of the elected representatives to ensure service delivery. The VAMBAY scheme, applicable to all slums, had not even reached the other slums studied.

Perhaps the most commonplace but at the same time the starkest measure of deprivation was the absence of toilets, private or community. In each of the communities studied, the lack of toilets and the forced use of public spaces on a daily basis, year after year, remains a source of severe physical and emotional stress, particularly for women. Many reported that they suffer from ailments on account of not being able to relieve themselves when needed (they can only go in groups and prefer to do so in the evening and very early morning), suffer infections from unhygienic conditions in which they relieve themselves and the younger women are particularly traumatised by the threat of men lurking nearby and the complete lack of privacy. It must be remembered that many of these families are very recent migrants and the women lack the aggressiveness required to survive in urban slums. Accustomed to wide open spaces, trees and forest lands in their rural setting, it is a daily struggle for these women to negotiate densely populated streets and roads to reach a field that stinks of human and other waste, unprotected by trees and exposed to the gaze of anyone walking past. The story of migration cannot be told without this subscript of the despair of women.

Ration card, which acts as an address proof, entitles the holder to low-priced food grains and fuel through the public distribution system (PDS). The ration card is also an identity card for claiming social security benefits such as old age, disability and widows' pensions, for getting Bangalore Water Supply and Sewerage Board (BWSSB) water connection, access to government hospitals, admitting children to government schools and accessing poverty alleviation and slum development programmes. In the present study, it was seen that less than half of the slum dwellers possessed ration cards. Most households are unable to claim a ration card because they cannot provide a permanent address or proper documentation for their place of residence. Lacking any kind of ownership or certified tenancy rights to the rooms in which they live, migrant communities are prevented by home owners from using their addresses. Almost all the migrants were in possession of the Aadhaar card, under the national digitised identification system which was introduced by the Congress-led UPA government in 2005. For most migrant workers, Aadhaar cards had been issued to them on the basis of their permanent addresses in their home villages. This did not entitle them to ration cards in Bangalore, where they lacked address proofs. In 2014, the central government decided to allow migrants to change the addresses on their Aadhaar cards by self-declaration.[8] However, migrant workers inevitably came up against the refusal of their landlords to certify their city addresses. Essentially, therefore, they lacked the papers that would entitle them to welfare benefits relating to food grains at controlled prices, children's education and free medical services in public hospitals.

Brief outline of the construction industry in Karnataka

As construction workers constitute the largest occupational group across the three slums that were studied, it may be worthwhile to note some of the important features of the industry in Karnataka, as well as the laws and institutions surrounding it. In 2009–10, construction workers constituted 10 per cent of the total unorganised workforce, and the industry accounted for 12 per cent of GSDP. The construction industry is the second-largest employer after agriculture. Infrastructure development has been a central agenda of successive governments in Karnataka.[9] In Bangalore, the construction industry has expanded greatly, following the city's recent IT-driven growth. There are some 1.5 million workers involved in construction work in the state. In Bangalore city, the strength of the construction workforce is over 0.35 million, although the enumeration of this workforce can only be approximate, given the cyclical character of a large proportion of the migrant workforce (GOK 2010).

A number of legislative measures have been taken, both at central and state levels, to address wages, working conditions and other welfare-related measures relating to workers in this sector. Most significant among these are the Building and Construction Workers (Regulation of Employment and Conditions of Service) Act, 1996, and the Building and Other Construction Workers Welfare Cess Act, 1996.[10] By these Acts, state governments are empowered to create welfare boards in which construction workers will be registered, and through which they can claim a number of benefits relating to pension, accidents, medical- and children's education–related expenses, and so on. The Karnataka Building and Other Construction Workers Welfare Board was set up in 2006. The board's mandate is in the domain of welfare provisions – accident insurance, medical support, educational assistance for children, loan facilities for housing, and a pension scheme. The claims recognised by the state and sought to be implemented through the board do not speak of income and housing, the two most important points of deprivation in the lives of construction workers. The number of workers registered with the board is low, and awareness and implementation of the welfare measures remain partial and inadequate. Across different domains, construction workers are systematically denied access to the benefits (water and toilets at the workplace, sick leave, accident or other insurance) even though these have been mandated by the Building and Other Construction Workers Welfare Cess Act of 2006 in Karnataka.

A survey of 169 workers, working for private builders, conducted in 2011 (Prasad, Rao and Nagesha 2011), reported that 25 per cent of workers were receiving wages less than the minimum wages stipulated by the Government of Karnataka. Findings of another study of 365 construction workers in Bangalore confirmed that many were receiving low pay and had little access to state-sponsored benefits (Premchander et al. 2014). In my earlier study of three construction worker communities, I found that close to 48 per cent were not receiving the minimum wage (RoyChowdhury 2017). Thus, the minimum wage has limited significance in the lives of construction workers, not only because they do not find a full month's work, but also because the minimum wage stipulation is frequently flouted. On the other hand, workers in large government infrastructure projects earn a higher wage than what is available to those working for private builders of commercial and residential complexes. The wage structure of workers employed in the construction of the Bangalore Metro Railway was considerably higher (Madhu Sudan 2013). The wide range of incomes available to construction workers across similar functions clearly point to the unregulated nature of the industry. As far as other benefits under the welfare board is concerned, few had access to information and implementation mechanisms. Prasad, Rao and Nagesha (2011), in the study mentioned earlier, found that about 76 per cent workers were not even aware of the welfare board.

Some of the legislatively guaranteed benefits were inappropriate for the targeted beneficiaries. To take an example, the welfare boards are in principle required to provide scholarships for children of construction workers, but this applies only to those pursuing studies at the 5th grade and above, and only if the student is staying in a hostel. In principle, the Right to Education Act (2009) provides basic and free education to all, and there are additional supports for children of SCs and STs. The reality of course is that few have the opportunity to attend school, there are a large number of drop-outs amongst those who do and, as the discussion in the previous section has pointed out, many children of construction workers start working in the construction industry from a young age. Thus, in the absence of educational interventions in the early school years of these children, the provisions for scholarship for high school and college students appear to be unrealistic.

Civil society, political parties and politics in slums

A complex set of networks exist between slums and the political and administrative authorities. In the context of their fragile identity – lacking a permanent and legal address, or even ration cards – migrants in slums tend to rely on an informal set of linkages to local politicians and bureaucrats, frequently mediated by NGOs or other local-level associations. NGOs typically come into slums with given mandates, which could be helping youth to acquire skills and jobs, creating women's credit groups, helping slum folks to get their ration cards or fill out their pension forms, and so on. Most NGOs are professional organisations working to make a set of resources or welfare provisions accessible to slum dwellers, that is, facilitating access to benefits. Other mediators include local politicians (corporators, MLAs), slum leaders, and community- or caste-based organisations. An undefined mutuality – set of benefits, resources, claims and rewards – typically marks the exchanges between such mediators and slum households. For example, slum-based local leaders help households claim their old age/widow pension from the relevant government office, or ration card, or funeral expenses and, in a quid pro quo, expect that their preferred political party be supported by the slum dwellers or expect support in admitting outsiders to the slum, to consider just a few examples. From the relatively structured (social-work-oriented NGOs) to the unstructured (slum leaders, local strongmen, corporators, MLAs), slum dwellers engage with a wide range of social organisations and political actors. How effective are these connections?

In Chamundinagar slum, one can clearly see the impact of sustained NGO presence, as APSA has been actively involved here for several years. The discussion above has shown that compared to other slums in the cluster, Chamundinagar has better access to amenities like public taps, borewells, *anganwadi*s and Sulabh toilets. In remarkable contrast to the other three slums, all residents of this slum have received both PDS and voter ID cards. APSA has been working in Chamundinagar slum for close to 15 years. APSA volunteers assist households in filling forms, forming self-help groups (SHGs) and resolving day-to-day problems associated with access to basic amenities. APSA has also helped the households to form various associations: the Chamundinagar Slum Nivasigala Sangha formed in 2010 is a small savings group; the Association for Promoting Social Action Swosahaya Sangha was formed in 2003. In addition, there are three Stree Shakthi Sanghas (small micro-credit groups mobilising women), the B. R. Ambedkar Sangha and the Dalitha Sangharsha Samiti.

As a result of APSA's sustained activities here, a large number of adults have voter ID cards. The slum, therefore, has attracted the attention of local politicians. Chamundinagar slum is in ward no. 16 under the Giri Nagar constituency, which has been a BJP stronghold for several decades. Giri Nagar is part of the Bengaluru South constituency. The late Ananth Kumar, a senior leader of the BJP, had been elected from this constituency for five consecutive parliamentary terms. Similarly, Ravi Subramaniam of the BJP has had a long innings as MLA and has, over a period of time, shown interest in the slum (discussed earlier) by facilitating the installation of public taps and borewells with motors as well as obtaining PDS cards for the households. The local corporator has been elected from the BJP in 2010 and again in the 2015 BBMP elections. Thus, Chamundinagar provides an example of a slum where a city-based NGO has not only provided some basic facilities, but has also encouraged the formation of associations and committees. These grassroots-level organisational efforts and the fact that most residents in the slum have obtained voter ID cards have served to establish direct links with politicians. The sustained presence of a single party, the BJP, and across different levels of representation, local corporator, state assembly and Lok Sabha, has brought a certain coherence in terms of governance of basic needs.

In contrast, Ashrayanagar, although a much larger slum, has not drawn the attention of NGOs. Ashrayanagar slum is located in ward no. 38 (also known as HMT Ward), under the Rajarajeswari Nagar constituency (Bangalore South). The parliamentary (Lok Sabha) seat here has gone to a Congress candidate from 2009 onwards. In the state legislative assembly, the present MLA, Muniratna Naidu, elected to this constituency in 2013 and re-elected in 2018, is a member of the Congress Party. Although historically this constituency has been a stronghold of the Congress Party, the results of recent assembly and corporation elections have revealed a pattern of positive movement towards the BJP. The elected MLA in the 2008 assembly elections was from the BJP and more than half of the nine wards in this constituency elected councillors from the BJP in the 2010 and the 2015 BBMP elections. The tenure of the Congress MLA, since 2013, has been fraught with tensions with BJP corporators as well as by at least two corruption scandals relating to public works projects for which bills were submitted to the government but which did not actually happen. In 2016, BJP corporators had demanded the resignation of the Congress MLA. In 2017, three women corporators from the Janata Dal (Secular) (JD[S]), BJP and the Congress staged a demonstration in the Council Hall protesting the abusive behaviour of Muniratna and his associates. Asha Suresh, the woman corporator from the Congress, has been locked in a conflict with Muniratna although they belong to the same party. In 2015, residents of the ward, in support of Asha Suresh, signed a petition calling for the resignation of the MLA. As a further fallout of this conflict, Suresh in the 2018 assembly openly campaigned for a JD(S) candidate in this constituency and was attacked by some residents of the slum. Politically, therefore, the constituency is fragmented, and hardly any developmental work has taken place here as a whole.

The BSP has been involved in Ashrayanagar slum for over a decade.[11] Lacking a political base in Bengaluru, the BSP has been relatively less interested in working for votes and more in grassroots development work. As a predominantly caste-based party, the BSP's interest in the slum was to develop the political profile of Dalits through grassroots organisations. Manasandra Muniyappa, state president of the BSP, started some organisational work with Dalits in Ashrayanagar in the early 2000s. During the evictions of 2005, Muniyappa prevailed upon then Chief Minister H. D. Kumaraswamy to allow the community to reoccupy the land. Since then, the BSP has been active in the slum, stepping in during crises to address day-to-day issues as well as in grassroots organisational work. Grassroots association activities in this slum are closely aligned to the BSP. The BSP Sangha and the Ambedkarvada have around 200 members, undertaking maintenance of the area and day-to-day needs of the community. Two SHGs have also been formed. BSP leaders encourage direct meetings with the residents to solve routine problems.

In Ashrayanagar slum, of the 2,000 odd households, not more than 300 have voter ID cards (most adults in the slum return to their native villages during elections because they are often paid by political parties to do so). Therefore, they form an insignificant proportion of the voting population at the ward-level elections (to elect the councillor) as well as at the constituency-level elections (to elect the MLA). Given the absence of any active NGO, the only active presence is that of the BSP, which is not interested in contending elections and therefore has not facilitated the political registration and activation of the community. This possibly explains the lack of interest in this slum on the part of the two main political parties, the BJP and the Congress. Neither party has ever been involved in issues relating to the slum. This scenario underscores the political marginalisation of this migrant community and, in a microcosm, highlights why issues of deprivation in migrant slums do not feature in the public policy agenda of successive governments.

Veerupakshanagar slum is part of Kodigehalli ward (no. 8) in the Byatarayanapura constituency (Bangalore North). This constituency has traditionally been a Congress stronghold, although since 2004, the MP (Lok Sabha) from this constituency has been from the BJP (Sadanand Gowda). The current MLA, Krishna Byregowda (elected in the 2013 and in the 2018 assembly elections), was the Minister for Agriculture in the Congress government of 2013–18. Of the seven wards under this constituency, four councillors are from the BJP. Thus, here too, the local voting pattern has led to some kind of fragmented leadership as far as the politics of the constituency as a whole and that of the ward in particular is concerned. The slum community pays a monthly rent to a private landowner, who has an obvious interest in keeping the rental arrangements informal without granting the tenants any claim to permanence. The slum dwellers have, therefore, not been able to provide the proof of address required to obtain a below-poverty level (BPL) card or a voter ID card. Lacking the basic document of identity as citizens, the dwellers do not exercise their voting rights in the city and as such do not show up on the radar of any political party or leader. In Veerupakshanagar, neither were there any slum-based associations nor had any outside NGO shown any interest in the slum. Most householders here have retained a pronounced migratory character, frequently returning to their native place for the harvest season and for elections and, most importantly, many in the slum have left their children behind in their native villages. The city, then, for these migrants is predominantly a space for earning a meagre livelihood.

Narayanpura slum is part of the KR Puram assembly constituency (North Bangalore). It was one of the 10 villages that were included within the BBMP limits when the Greater Bangalore area was formed in 2007. Once a part of the Mahadevpura City Municipal Council and surrounded by villages, KR Puram quickly became one of the most preferred neighbourhoods among MNCs as industries and particularly the IT sector identified it as a new and upcoming area. KR Puram typifies the contradictions of urbanisation in terms of both uneven, inequitable development and the inadequacies of governance. The emerging presence of IT and other industries brought an influx of middle- and upper-class young people to the area; their demand for residences close to their work pushed up the price of real estate and led to the construction of a large number of high-rise apartment buildings, in addition to office spaces. The plethora of construction led to the inevitable influx of migrant labour in search of work. The stark contrasts between these two streams within the same neighbourhood represent the emerging contradictions of development in Bangalore. Narayanpura slum, as seen earlier, typifies the multiple vulnerabilities of migrants facing an unregulated employment market and the absence of state attention to basic services and human resources.

The pattern of political representation shows similar elements of fragmentation as described in the two cases earlier. While the Lok Sabha seat has gone to a BJP member in 2009 and 2014 (and again in 2019), the state assembly seat has been held by a member of the Congress Party since 2009. Of the nine BBMP wards in KR Puram, six are represented by corporators of the Congress Party and the remaining by BJP members. These divisions across the vertical of local, assembly and parliamentary representation creates a situation of fragmentation and lack of focus of political energies. Narayanpura slum as a part of ward no. 56 in the KR Puram assembly segment was unfortunate to have been associated with two successive corporators, one each from the BJP and the Congress, who were disqualified on corruption and harassment charges. More than 200 individuals in Narayanpura slum have strong affiliations with a political outfit called the Samatha Sainik Dala (SSD). Several households have strong connections with the BJP. The settlement is thus politically diverse.

On the margins of the economy and the polity

Within a democratic framework, there are two channels through which issues related to the urban poor are articulated to state agencies for policy and action. The first is that of NGOs, and the second of slum committees, caste or community associations, and political parties. In the four cases described in this chapter, the involvement of NGOs was limited. Only in one slum, Chamundinagar, where the NGO APSA had been working for over a decade, were there some visible signs of greater access to basic amenities, as compared to other slums. NGOs, as a rule, come into slums with limited funds that are bound to specific projects, such as building toilets, repairing roads, laying sanitation pipes, or organising a primary school. APSA's involvement with the migrant slum in Chamundinagar is similarly confined to creating specific facilities. The project-specific approach obviously precludes addressing broader issues of urban deprivation related to employment and income or governance of social welfare.

Across the slums, the activities of political parties and of elected representatives, particularly at the level of local (city council) government, revealed patterns familiar to most observers of local politics in India: corruption, intimidation and indifference to the plight of migrants, broadly, and to specific slum-level issues, locally. The discussion earlier has shown that interest on the part of politicians was kindled only when the slum community in question was seen as a potential vote bank (in the case of Chamundinagar) and here political parties became actively involved in campaigning as well as providing some infrastructure and resources. In slums where most migrants were not voters, there was little or no interest on the part of political parties or of local political leaders. Local politicians had made little effort to establish contact with these slum dwellers for mobilisation or representation. The intervention of parties in these communities has happened only at the time of eviction, demolition and/or during elections. Thus, in Ashrayanagar slum, during the demolition drive of the BBMP in May 2006, the BSP intervened to rebuild temporary shelters for many households. We found that several leaders in the community have active affiliation with the BSP. However, given the BSP's marginal political presence in Karnataka, this affiliation did not bring any other gains to the slum dwellers.

Interventions by political parties or NGOs remained sporadic and confined to activities such as providing taps, toilets, and so on. There was no sustained activity even in these spheres. For example, even if a set of toilets is built, there is no effort to ensure proper maintenance and functioning of the service. Even a steady connection with a political party, therefore, did not translate into sustained or broad-based gains that would address the central issues of deprivation relating to civic facilities.

To return to the points raised at the outset of the chapter, mainstream development literature has held that although not all rural migrants may be able to avail of urban opportunities, yet, by and large, cities remain dynamic spaces of growth and mobility. The study of migrant slums shows that the city provided work to migrants at low subsistence levels. The institutional framework of informality created a context where work was insecure and irregular, wages were low, and there was little scope for mobility for an unskilled workforce. The broader context of course is created by the fact that there has been little growth of jobs in the manufacturing sector for the unskilled workforce. This economic structure underpinned the vulnerabilities and stagnation of migrant households.

Development literature has increasingly held that in a profit- and incentive-based and private-sector–led growth model, the poor, instead of looking to private employers for higher wages or work-related insurance, must look to the state for social benefits. Migrants lack the necessary proof of identity, which is the first step in claiming social benefits. The analysis in this chapter has shown that two central resources, housing and schools, constituted crucial points of deprivation for these communities. Governments have not been proactive in reaching needy households. Migrants are highly unorganised and sometimes transitory communities. Their daily struggle for existence typically precludes organised effort to pursue government benefits. They are then caught in a cycle where, lacking a clear identity as citizen or worker in the city where they earn a livelihood, these households can claim neither state benefits nor the attention of political parties.

Notes

1. Each of the slums is under BBMP (Bruhat Bengaluru Mahanagar Palike) jurisdiction, that is, Greater Bengaluru area. Some are on land owned by the Bengaluru Development Authority (BDA), others on private or disputed land.

2. In the point of origin from north Karnataka, more than 50 per cent of the migrants were earning less than INR 1,000 and about 34 per cent were earning between INR 1,000 and INR 2,000. While there is some under-reporting of incomes, we do know that daily wages in rural north Karnataka can be as low as INR 30–40 per day, without availability of work on all days of the week. The share of workers from south Karnataka in these lowest wage categories was comparatively lower.

3. The occupational background of migrants from south Karnataka in the point of origin showed that about 60 per cent had been working as daily-wage earners in agriculture and public works and 35 per cent had been engaged in skilled work and self-employment in non-farm activities, whereas amongst those from north Karnataka, only 4 per cent had found such employment and 96 per cent were working as daily-wage earners in agriculture or public works. Broadly speaking, this structure of employment reflects the differential development of the two regions, insofar as in rural south Karnataka there appeared to have been at least some opportunities for skilling and self-employment in non-agricultural activities, whereas in the rural north, unskilled daily-wage work appeared to be the only means of livelihood.

4. An attempt was made to identify the number of households in poverty in each slum by using the total income and the number of members of the household. This exercise yielded very high poverty levels, although there was certainly a range. However, I have not included this information in the analysis for the following reasons: first, there was clearly some under-reporting of income and,

second, the poverty of slum households could be calculated only on the basis of income which was reported, and I did not have an opportunity to cross-check, for example, by looking at consumption levels. Ownership of assets, again, was a problematic category as the households were clearly in two spaces, their urban slum tenements, where they lived to work, and their rural habitats, where they returned again and again. Given the inaccuracy and incompleteness of the data on earnings as well as assets, the poverty-level information has not been included in the analysis.

5. Observations on occupational mobility are limited by the fact that the households studied have been in Bengaluru for not more than 10 years on an average. However, it was found, over many qualitative discussions, that the approximate patterns that emerge from our study of limited opportunities for occupational mobility match the understanding of the slum dwellers and slum leaders on this issue.

6. The issue of child labour in the construction industry has been explored in RoyChowdhury (2017). This paper looked at construction workers in different segments of the industry (public and private, as well as in labour colonies).

7. Under the first phase, 168 houses are under construction and the second Phase will complete the construction of all 384 houses.

8. Amendment to the Prevention of Money Laundering (Maintenance of Records) Rules, 14 November 2019, Gazette Notification, Government of India.

9. Several projects such as the Karnataka State Highways Improvement Project, the National Bank for Agriculture and Rural Development (NABARD)– assisted Rural Infrastructure Development Fund scheme, the Pradhan Mantri Gram Sadak Yojana, and so on, have been in place since the early 2000s. Central to these programmes has been the task of building state highways and rural connectivity roads. During 2012–13, 3,710 kilometres of state highways had been taken up at an estimated cost of INR 1,423 crores, and a total budget allocation of INR 500 crores had been made. The Rural Infrastructure Development Fund has been implemented in five phases. Such projects are supported through funding by the government and other agencies (such as the World Bank and the Asian Development Bank). In Bangalore, infrastructure projects such as the international airport, the Nandi Infrastructure Corridor Enterprises (NICE) road connecting the city to Mysore, and a large number of highways and overbridges to ease traffic congestion have created a large infrastructural base. The rapid expansion of the IT industry has meant large private construction projects involving business, commerce, residences and entertainment.

10. The salient features of the Building and Other Construction Workers Welfare Cess Act are the setting up of an advisory committee at central and state levels to advise the governments on issues related to construction workers; make provision for registration of each establishment within a period of 60 days

from the commencement of work, in order to ensure that builders maintain compliance with the laws; make provision for registration of building workers as beneficiaries under this Act; and, importantly, make provision for the constitution of a Building and Other Construction Workers Welfare Board by every state government. By the Cess Act, builders are required to pay a given percentage of the project cost (as cess) to the board, through which workers' welfare expenditures would be met. Other important laws covering migrant construction workers are the Inter State Migrant Workers (Regulation of Employment and Conditions of Service) Act, 1979, and the Contract Labour Regulation and Abolition Act, 1970.

11. In the 2009 Lok Sabha elections, the BSP fielded candidates in all 28 constituencies in the state, and all lost. Similarly, in the 2014 Lok Sabha elections, the BSP lost in all the 18 constituencies in which it had fielded candidates. In the 2013 Assembly elections, the BSP lost in each of the 20 constituencies in which it had fielded candidates. There has been a gradual decline in the vote share of the party since 2009.

References

Deshingkar, P and J. Farrington, eds. 2009. *Circular Migration and Multi Locational Livelihood Strategies in Rural India.* Delhi: Oxford University Press.

Government of Karnataka (GOK). 2010. *Annual Report.* Bangalore: Ministry of Labour.

———. 'Minimum Wage Notification for Construction Workers'. Labour Commissioner's Office, Bangalore.

Kundu, A. and L. R. Saraswati. 2012. 'Migration and Exclusionary Urbanization in India'. *Economic and Political Weekly* 47 (26/27): 219–27.

Kundu, A. and N. Sarangi. 2007. 'Migration, Employment Status and Poverty: An Analysis of Urban Centres'. *Economic and Political Weekly* 42 (4): 299–306.

Madhu Sudan. 2013. 'Consrtuction Workers in the Bangalore Metro Railway Corporation Ltd'. CIVIC, Bangalore.

Mitra, A. 2006. 'Labour Market Mobility of Low Income Households'. *Economic and Political Weekly* 41 (21): 2123–30.

———. 2010. 'Migration, Livelihood and Well-Being: Evidence from Indian City Slums'. *Urban Studies* 47 (7): 1375–90.

Mukhopadhyay, Partha and K. Sivaramakrishnan. 2013. *How to Govern India's Cities: Towards Needed Transformation.* Delhi: Centre for Policy Research.

Pattenden, J. 2012. 'Migration between Rural Raichur and Boomtown Bangalore: Class Relations and the Circulation of Labour in South India'. *Global Labour Journal* 3 (1): 163–90.

Prasad, R. S. N., K. V. Rao and H. N. Nagesha. 2011. 'Study on Building and Other Construction Workers Welfare Schemes and Amenities in Karnataka'. *sasTECH Journal* 10 (1): 59–66.

Premchander, S., V. Premilla, S. Banu, K. G. Meenakshi, H. Manjunath and T. Prema. 2014. 'The Socio-economic Status of Migrant Construction Workers in Bangalore and Intervention Plan to Improve Their Livelihoods'. *Urban India* 34 (January–June): 88–112.

RoyChowdhury, S. 2017. 'New Paradigms of Labour Relations: How Much Do They Explain?' In *Political Economy of Contemporary India*, edited by R. Nagraj and S. Motiram, 179–202. New Delhi: Cambridge University Press.

RoyChowdhury, S., and B. P. Vani. 2016. 'Work and Workers in the Services Sectors: A Pilot Study in Bangalore'. Institute for Social and Economic Change, Bangalore.

Sridhar, K. S., V. Reddy and P. Srinath. 2012. 'Is It Push or Pull: Recent Evidence from Migration into Bangalore, India.' *Journal of International Migration and Integration* 14: 287–306.

6

Old Slums

Cities of the Global South have witnessed the emergence of a newly affluent, highly mobile upper class, dramatic changes in consumption patterns, rapidly changing information and communication channels, and the exclusion of some from these processes. Disparities are hardly new to cities in developing countries, anchored as they are in highly unequal structures shaped by the privileged access of elite castes and communities, in traditional societies, to learning and increasingly to professional skills and other resources. Social and economic exclusions were structured into this urban framework where manual, unskilled work was performed by lower castes and underprivileged communities. In the current era, however, urban inequalities have a different face. As cities become sites of spectacular wealth and consumption, the widening chasm between those who can access the benefits of global marketisation and those who remain on the margins, or are in structurally disadvantageous positions within it, becomes starker. Many cities of the developing world are caught within these sharply emerging contradictions of wealth and deprivation.

These contradictions are blatantly visible in Bangalore. Bangalore's rapid economic rise, riding on the IT revolution and a facilitating policy environment for private capital, both domestic and foreign, has been discussed in Chapter 3. While this growth trajectory has brought some opportunities to a few sections of the urban lower classes in Bangalore, there is as yet no substantive analysis of the precise nature of these opportunities, and, more importantly, whether these translate to increased access to economic and social resources for the urban poor and their progeny. The questions examined in this chapter are: What happens to the urban poor in a context of rapid economic growth of the city? What are the channels through which the urban underclass get drawn into the city's growing economy? What are the modalities of inclusion and exclusion?

The decline of large state-owned manufacturing industries and of the SSI sector frames Bangalore's political economy of the last few decades. With the folding up of factory jobs, unskilled workers are employed predominantly in he construction industry and in the lower rungs of the service sector. In what ways do these macro features reflect in the lives and livelihoods of slum dwellers?

This chapter is about inner-city slums, where most people were found to work in casual wage employment, self-employment in petty trade, or as salaried workers in services. Bangalore's inner-city slums narrate a story of exclusion wherein many households remain tied to traditional occupations (head-load bearers in the city market areas, construction workers, contract street cleaners employed by the city corporation, domestic workers, freelance waste pickers, pushcart sellers, small-time vegetable/fruit/flower sellers, and so on). While domestic workers and city corporation employees may receive a monthly salary for part- or full time work, the income of others depend on availability of work, contacts with contractors, links to larger retail markets or the day's waste picking. The few who have made it to jobs in the service sectors of the so-called modern economy (waiters in clubs or restaurants, sales persons in small shops or showrooms, delivery boys, security personnel, and so on) have gained a modicum of social prestige, but their work is informal, with unregulated wages and working conditions.

In the present study, inner-city slums represented pictures of some degree of economic dynamism, but also of astonishing stagnation and marginalisation. The study draws attention to the distance between slums and the supposed market of urban opportunities. With the decline of jobs in the manufacturing sector, where unskilled or semi-skilled urban labour typically and historically have found employment, slum dwellers are pushed and confined to low-paying occupations. The absence of state regulation of these occupations underpins their economic hardships, while the lack of state attention to providing education leads to the replication of their disadvantages over generations.

Slums in Bangalore

The poor in Bangalore live in a large variety of habitations and spaces: notified slums (the government is responsible for providing basic services to notified slums), non-notified slums, temporary squatter colonies, pavements and railway stations, and labour camps, which are temporary shelters provided by builders to migrant construction workers. This chapter is based on research on notified slums.

The city's poor can physically as well as conceptually be divided into the old poor and the new poor. The new poor are those who may have migrated to the city anywhere between 1 and 15 years and are typically found living in temporary settlements in the city's peripheral areas. As non-notified slums, these settlements do not fall within the purview of slum-development projects. Occupationally, the new poor in peripheral slums are predominantly in the construction industry, the largest number as unskilled labour. Chapter 5 presents a discussion of such settlements, anchored in debates on the relationship between migration and urban poverty, and whether the city makes a difference to the poverty of migrants.

The present chapter provides a discussion of inner-city slums that have existed for 40–70 years and are inhabited by second, and sometimes third, generation of original residents. I have called them the 'old poor'. As notified or recognised slums, these old settlements of the poor are entitled to certain basic services to be provided by the government. Additionally, slum dwellers may demand property rights to the land they occupy and, as older residents of the city, they may have a closer set of links with political parties and civil society associations than recent migrants do in peripheral slums. In contrast to new slums that mainly house construction workers, older inner-city slums represent a diversity of occupations, incomes and standards of living, although they are predominantly characterised by low incomes, multiple vulnerabilities and low levels of basic amenities.

Older slums in particular highlight the embeddedness of poverty and inequality in a city that has grown rapidly in the post-independence era, and particularly since the 1980s, as a consequence of the IT revolution. Slums that are 60–70 years old, and households that have lived in these slums over two or three generations, represent a pattern of systemic, structural exclusion of urban poor communities.[1] This reflects both the narrow and exclusivist growth trajectory of global cities such as Bangalore, where the unskilled and otherwise resource-poor communities are left out, and state indifference to the task of providing necessary support to slum residents to enable them to access opportunities for education, skills and decent employment.

Compared to cities like Mumbai, Kolkata, Meerut and Faridabad, the percentage of slum dwellers in Bangalore is low at about 20 per cent. However, the growth of slums, as well as of the slum population, in Bangalore needs to be underlined (Tables 6.1 and 6.2). While the number of slums increased steadily, the increase in the number of people living in slums was more dramatic. The population of slums increased by ten times during 1971–2000.

Table 6.1 Growth of slums in Bangalore

	No. of slums	Growth rate (per cent)
1971	195	NA
1981	273	40
1991	401	46.88
2001	480	19.7
2011	542	12.91

Source: Madheswaran and Vani (2017).

Table 6.2 Growth of slum population in Bangalore

	Population (millions)	Growth rate (%)
1971	3.15	NA
1981	3.48	10.47
1991	3.65	2.85
2001	9.78	167.94
2011	13.86	41.71

Source: Madheswaran and Vani (2017).

Growth of slums and slum population is frequently attributed to population growth, caused in part by in-migration. The rate of growth of population in the Bangalore metropolitan area increased from 21 per cent during 1951–61 to 36.9 per cent during 1961–71, to 76.8 per cent during 1971–81, declined to 40.6 per cent during 1981–91 (Schenk 2001) and further declined to 37.69 per cent during 1991–2001). During 2001–11, the rate of growth increased to 46 per cent (Directorate of Census Operation, Karnataka 2011). The increase in the rate of growth of population has been attributed partly to the redrawing of the boundaries of the Bangalore Urban district, and there is as yet no systematic analysis of the relationship between population growth and growth of slums. While the growth of in-migration to Bangalore Urban is obviously closely related to the city's population growth, there is no easily established systematic link between the flow of migrants to the city and the growth of slums. As mentioned earlier, large numbers of migrants live in the city's peripheral, unrecognised settlements, and also constitute an iterant, cyclical population. Interestingly, earlier studies found that migrant heads of slum households had declined from 60 per cent in 1973 to 36 per cent in 1992 (Ramachandran and Subramanian 2001). It should also be noted that

3 out of every 10 slums in Bangalore have existed for over 40 years (Schenk 2001). According to Ramachandran and Subramanian, the role of migration in explaining slum growth has declined significantly, particularly where the old inner-city slums are concerned. As such, we need to carefully consider the nature of continuing or deepening urban poverty as manifested in the growth of inner-city slums.

The extent of poverty in slums remains a matter of debate, as also the fact that slums are not the only locales of urban poverty. Nevertheless, slums represent, in some sense, the darkest side of urban deprivation in terms of exclusion of a large number of people from social status, economic security and social mobility as well as from basic amenities of life like water and sanitation. In one of the few early works which study slums over time, Ramachandran and Subramanian (2001) re-surveyed in 1992 8 slums that had been part of an 11-slum survey conducted in 1973. This re-survey enabled the authors to make a comparison across time, to chart changes that had occurred at the household level in terms of access to basic amenities, education, employment, and so on.

Spread across the core, intermediary and peripheral areas of the city, the re-survey offered interesting points for consideration: while education had improved, the study recorded increased levels of child labour at the same time, and while income had risen, lower status and semi-skilled occupations had increased. What would these imply for an overall understanding of the situation of the urban underclass? In another landmark study on this theme, Anirudh Krishna (2013) examined socio-economic mobility in 14 slums in Bangalore by looking at the occupations of grandfathers, fathers and sons in the same household. The study found that the majority of slum residents were engaged in low-paying and precarious work in services and trade, and different generations did not practice vastly different occupations.

The present chapter highlights the complexity and multilayered nature of the problem of understanding that confronts us, and one of the first things to note is that within the urban underclass, as seen in slums, there is a high degree of variation in terms of work availability, returns to labour, earnings, assets, skills, opportunities, and future life chances. This diversity is perhaps the most important characteristic feature of informal work, which provides an important clue to understanding slum economies. Slums provide an appropriate domain to study this diversity. This chapter highlights diversities at different levels: within the same slum, between slums within the same ward, and slums within the same municipal jurisdiction. While there were slums in which a large number of households, if not all, belonged to the BPL category, there were others where we found large variations in incomes, consumption, education levels and other such factors. Second, within the same ward, we found slums that were significantly different in terms of income levels, career paths, availability of physical infrastructure, and so on (within ward no. 46 in K. S. Garden slum, there was some degree of occupational diversity, and household income per month went as high as INR 15,000–22,000. In the neighbouring Cement Huts slum, almost all 400 households were waste pickers, and the income of many households did not exceed INR 5,500 per month).

Livelihood and income in slums

This section discusses the livelihoods and income of slum dwellers based on a study of 300 households across six slums located in J. C. Road, close to Lalbagh, the central commercial hub of the city. This area was selected in order to study older slums (in existence for 50–80 years) and to gain an understanding of slum living in the heart of the city. The slums are: K. S. Garden, Ramanna Garden, Papanna Gardens, Vinobha Nagar, Cement Huts and Rajagopal Gardens. The number of households in each slum ranged from 300 to 500. As mentioned, the slums are old settlements that were set up between the 1940s and 1960s primarily because large numbers of unskilled migrants in search of work had moved from Tamil Nadu, Andhra Pradesh and the northern parts of Karnataka to Bangalore in search of work. As the households represent second or third generation of settlers, most slum dwellers speak a combination of Kannada and what they consider to be their mother tongue, Tamil or Telugu. The majority of the households were SCs and two slums had a few Muslim families. Information regarding occupations and income has been provided in Tables 6.3, 6.4 and 6.5. The tables are based on information collected from 250 slum households and excludes Cement Huts slum, where we found the majority of the households (over 90 per cent) deriving their incomes from a single occupation, that is, work relating to waste picking and selling. As such, Cement Huts is presented as a case study. Information on K. S. Garden slum, though included in the tables, is also presented as a case study as it has a relatively large number of higher-income-earning families.

Chapter 7 provides detailed discussion on the land and housing situation in slums. These details are not repeated here. But briefly, the physical infrastructure in the slums were found to be in a state of extreme squalor; large households occupied one-room minimal spaces, using common, frequently dysfunctional toilets. Public areas in the slums were found to be scenes of great decay: used for heaping waste, selling a few stale vegetables and children freely defecating in the open.[2]

This chapter focuses mainly on income and occupation, which are seen as the primary domains of exclusion and marginalisation. Slum dwellers in Bangalore are employed in a wide range of economic activities: auto/bicycle repairing, small eateries, autorickshaw driving, pushcart vendors, rag pickers, and so on. In each of these activities, they may be working either as self-employed or as wage earners. An autorickshaw driver or a small tea-shop owner may own the vehicle or the unit or, alternatively, may be working for a wage. Some occupations, for example, head-load bearing, construction work and domestic work, feature a monthly salary or a daily wage. It needs to be noted that the information on occupations and income (Table 6.3) is an approximation and not exact. For each category of occupation, a range of incomes was reported from which an average was drawn. However, it is important to note the variability of income in several of these categories. For example, for workers who work as coolie labour or head-load bearers, the number of days of work varies a great deal, depending not only on work availability, but also on the individual's propensity to find work on a regular basis, which, again, is determined by age, health, addiction to alcohol, and so on.

Of the 250 households surveyed, 26 per cent were coolie labour or head-load bearers in the city market area (Table 6.4). The largest number, then, were occupied in one of the lowest income categories, earning INR 5,000–6,500 per month (Table 6.3). Among other low-return work were those in the category of self-employed (15.6 per cent), where the average earnings were around INR 4,500–5,500. This category covered a wide range of activities involving minimum capital investment and own or family labour: owning a small corner tea shop, selling a few vegetables on the pavement, pushing a cartload of fruit, hawking plastic goods or glass bangles on a pushcart, mobile tea selling, selling toys and magazines at traffic lights, and so on. Flower sellers (in the category of self-employed) constituted a significant percentage (10.9 per cent) and they have been categorised separately in the survey (Table 6.3 and Table 6.4).

It is important to underline the diverse structures in these domains of work. Flower sellers who source their material in large quantities from the wholesale flower market and have large volumes of sale in the city's main markets (for example, in the Malleswaram 12th Cross Market, K. R. Market or Yeshwantpur), particularly during festivals or wedding seasons, can make

Table 6.3 Major occupations and average incomes found in six slums in J. C. Road

Major occupations found in six slums	*Average income per month*
Coolie labour (head-load bearer in city market area)	INR 5,000–6,500
Construction worker (unskilled)	INR 7,000–8,000
Rag picker (BBMP contract worker)	INR 5,000–7,000
Auto driver	INR 9,000–12,000
Maid servant (part-time)	INR 5,000–5,500
Flower seller	INR 6,000–8,000
Skilled labour (electrician, plumber, auto/two-wheeler repairing, steel/metal work, welding, cable, carpentry, tile fitting)	INR 10,000–22,000
Self-employed (vegetable vendor, tea shop owner)	INR 4,500–5,000
Chowltry work (part-time) (cleaner in wedding halls)	INR 3,500
Government service (Bangalore Municipality: sweeper, maintenance work)	INR 14,000–20,000
Social worker	INR 9,000–10,000
Office assistant in private office	INR 9,000–12,000
Watchman in apartment building and retail shop	INR 5,500–6,500

Source: Author's field research in slums.

Table 6.4 Percentages of households dependent on different occupations

	Coolie labour	*Auto driver*	*Maid servant*	*Flower seller*	*Skilled labour*	*Self-employed*	*Others*
Vinobhanagar	50.0	1.7	3.4	0.0	36.2	5.2	3.4
K. S. Garden	36.7	7.0	15.6	0.0	18.8	7.0	14.8
Ramanna Garden	38.0	10.1	30.4	0.0	7.6	3.8	10.1
Papanna Gardens	3.9	3.9	0.0	15.6	19.5	54.5	2.6
Rajagopal Gardens	6.1	12.1	7.1	36.4	23.2	12.1	3.0
All slums	26.1	7.5	12.0	10.9	20.2	15.6	7.3

Source: Author's field research in slums.

a profit of INR 15,000–16,000 per month. In contrast, the typical flower seller whom we met in the slums are women who buy flowers at higher prices (compared to prices in the wholesale market) in the local market, string them into small garlands and they and/or their children sell these in nearby apartment complexes, at traffic lights or as lone sellers on the pavement near the slum. Long hours of labour, low productivity, limited markets and low profit margins (INR 6,000–8,000 per month)[3] characterise their work. Domestic servants constitute 12 per cent of the households surveyed. As in flower selling, domestic work too is highly diverse in terms of the labour market and wage packages. The salary for an eight–nine-hour workday would be a little over INR 12,000 per month. However, by and large, domestic work in the city is structured around part-time work. Women from slums frequently only have the option of part-time work and may end up earning no more than INR 5,000–5,500 for half a day's work, sometimes even less. Flower selling and domestic work, predominantly jobs done by women, were among the lowest-paid work. Sweepers employed on a casual/contract basis earned between INR 5,000 and INR 7,000 as employees of the contractor or contracting agency rather than of the BBMP directly. Those who were in permanent service with the BBMP, as maintenance personnel, were entitled to a wage of INR 14,000, but could earn as much as INR 20,000 per month, depending on years of service. The section titled 'Diversity in Slums' presents a detailed discussion on waste collectors who are not employed by the BBMP.

Together, the lowest-paying occupations, coolie labour, self-employed, flower sellers and domestic servants constituted 62 per cent of those studied (Table 6.4). The study highlighted that 62 per cent of the households were dependent, wholly or partially, on incomes that ranged from INR 6,000–8,000 (flower seller, self-employed) to INR 5,000–6,500 (coolie/head-load bearer/part-time domestic help). In terms of income, then, more than half of the households surveyed had at least one earner whose income would be placed at below the urban poverty line.[4]

Moving on to other kinds of work, the average return to skilled work of any kind was obviously higher than returns to unskilled labour. Here, the institutional framework as well as the availability of work determines differential earnings. Those with skills such as electrical and plumbing work, tile-fitting and even carpentry have found a growing market in the expanding construction industry. Monthly incomes in these kinds of work could be between INR 10,000 and INR 22,000 depending on experience, networks, connections with contractors, and so on. A highly experienced, skilled plumber or tiles fitter connected to multiple contractors can earn up to INR 25,000 per month, given regular work availability. Higher incomes, however, do not come with social insurance or even regular availability of work.

Other occupations in the slum in which only a very few were engaged, and in which higher incomes were possible, were those of watchmen in offices, shops and apartment buildings, and helpers in high-end hotels. Here again, the variations are important to note. The few slum residents who worked as watchmen in apartment buildings in middle-class localities earned between Rs 6,000 and Rs 8,000 per month. On the other hand, security guards, employed through agencies, who guard multi-storey apartment buildings, gated villas, plush offices in the IT sector and top-end hotels can earn between INR 15,000 and INR 25,000.[5] A very small number belonged to the category of office assistant or receptionist in travel/transport agencies, where the income could be around INR 9,000–12,000. The entry of slum dwellers into these growing areas of the private sector had been very limited.

Poverty in slums

It was difficult to arrive at precise figures relating to poverty levels in the slums. There is frequently an element of under-reporting of income. Household-level information on income can be supplemented through consumption data, which is difficult to collect, or can be fully confirmed on the basis of detailed surveys of wages and earnings from specific employments in which a large number of slum dwellers are engaged. While such data is generally unavailable on a macro basis, our survey attempted in a very small way to fill this gap (Table 6.3). Nevertheless, as mentioned, there is a great deal of variation in incomes in most informal occupations. Given the difficulties of arriving at precise figures, in this study I have not attempted to arrive at poverty figures.[6] Drawing on the information presented in the previous section, this section presents some qualitative insights into the dynamics of work and poverty in the slums studied.

The information reported in the tables shows that the largest number of households depend on the lowest-paid work. Read together, Tables 6.3 and 6.4 provide a closer look at the occupational and income structure within these slums, and a window into the dynamics of poverty. In Ramanna Garden, households dependent upon the lowest-income category (coolie labour and maidservant) constituted 68 per cent of this slum. Similarly, in Papanna Gardens, 70 per cent of the households surveyed were dependent on self-employment and flower selling, occupations in the lowest-income category. While the households might be dependent on more than one income, typically, it was found through focus group discussions that the lowest-pay categories appeared in the same households; for example, there were a large number of households where the husband and wife were coolie labour and domestic worker/flower seller respectively.

Average monthly incomes in the different occupations appear to be astonishingly low, even though there is a range. Research into several other occupations and earnings of the urban underclass, particularly of unskilled workers, have confirmed similar levels of income. Chapters 5 and 8 of this book are on unskilled migrant construction workers and young women garment workers starting their first job. In both sectors, earnings may be around INR 7,000–8,000 per month. Recent research on the lower rungs of the service sector has shown that in cafés and beauty parlours, both expanding domains in the city's service sector, semi-skilled young workers (who have undergone quick trainings of four–six months) can be paid INR 6,000 – 7,000 per month, and sometimes even less. In these domains, employees can be denied even a weekly holiday, can be dismissed without notice or can have their wages cut in case of absence due to illness or family emergencies. The fact that large numbers of informal workers in the city are willing to accept this level of precarity highlights the extreme vulnerability of the workforce facing an economy where a large supply of unskilled labour is available, and where the world of work is marked by a complete absence of regulation. The very low incomes of slum dwellers in this study, therefore, need to be seen in the larger context of work and wages in the informal sector in Bangalore (RoyChowdhury and Vani 2016; RoyChowdhury and Upadhya 2020).

At the outset, it was mentioned that slums demonstrate a high degree of variation in terms of income. This variation is seen within the same slum as well as between slums that are within the same ward and in close physical proximity. From discussions held with slum leaders and slum communities, we attempted to arrive at a rough approximation of categories of households within the slums – categories that the slum dwellers themselves suggested to us is a good way of describing the changes that have occurred in the community. In the first category were households who had 'done well', their income ranging from INR 15,000 to INR 20,000 per month. These were households with at least two earning members and typical occupations were permanent government service, a regular fruit or vegetable shop in the city market areas (both in the traditional domain), skilled labour, office assistant in private offices, organised waste collector, helper in five-star hotel, receptionist or saleswoman, and social worker with NGOs (all of these in the domain of the so-called modern economy).

The next category was termed as 'just managing', typically represented by the coolie labourer/vendor (male) and domestic servant/flower seller (female) duo (couple). Coolie labourers and domestic servants may not find regular work. Despite the constraints, such families were managing to keep themselves afloat and send their children to school. In the opinion of slum residents, continuing to send children to school was a sign of sorts that the family was not in crisis. If an older child completed (or dropped out after) Secondary School Leaving Certificate (SSLC) and started to work, it signalled an increase in the family's income. Such families remained afloat unless affected by a major illness, accident, death or some other crisis. In such situations, they could quickly descend into the 'very poor' category (Krishna 2010).

In general, the third, the 'very poor', category was typically represented by large households where coolie labourers/daily wagers were sole earners or women garment workers were sole supporters of their families. In addition, there were single-member households consisting only of an older widow or the very old, disabled or sick, who lived alone or as a couple, dependent on relatives or neighbours; those who had some kind of addiction, again dependent on the charity of neighbours or relatives; and those who begged, living on the fringes of the slum and may not have a roof over their head.

Diversity in the slums

In order to highlight this variation across the three categories, as also to identify what the reasons are that some households make it out of poverty, others remain on the brink and yet others remain in abject want, I present case studies of two of the slums in our cluster, K. S. Garden and Cement Huts, both within a few yards of each other within ward no. 46.

K. S. Garden presents a picture of relative prosperity in pockets of the slum, where several households appear to have crossed over to relatively higher incomes, but others remain in conditions of great precarity, while in Cement Huts, a large number of households are confined to low-paying, unregulated garbage picking, and have been so for several generations.

K. S. Garden slum: While the distribution of occupation in this slum is not significantly different from that of the other slums, we found that the clue to the relative prosperity (confirmed through repeated visits, opinions of slum leaders and NGOs, focus group discussions in the slum) could possibly be found in the category of the 'other' (Table 6.4). In this slum, the category 'other' constituted 14 per cent of the surveyed households, the highest in the slums surveyed. In this category, several persons in K. S. Garden slum were earning between INR 12,000 and INR 20,000. These occupational categories were the following:

1. Permanent employee in the city corporation or in state-owned companies (in cleaning, maintenance, gardening)
2. Attendant/messenger in government office
3. Owner of fruit and vegetable shop in a city market, or owner of scrap business
4. Office assistant in a travel agency
5. Watchman working through a security agency
6. Helper in a top-end club in a wealthy neighbourhood
7. Social worker employed by an NGO
8. Plumber or mason working with a construction company
9. Receptionist in an office or salesgirl/cash counter operator in a shop or small supermarket

While categories 1 and 2 represented the older, organised sector government employment with a scaled salary and pension, which have become scarce over the decades, in category 3 was the rare trader who had managed to build a decent-size business in a city market; each of these was in the traditional domain, and was represented by an older generation (45–60 years of age). In categories 4–10 were younger persons, in the age group of 25–40, who had somehow managed to get a foothold in the private sector via the seemingly modern economy of the city. About 50 youths in the slum had managed to receive some kind of computer training. Of these, about 25–30 women were working as receptionists in small offices or showrooms or at cash counters in small supermarkets. In other words, they had stepped out of the traditional low-paying occupations. As seen in Table 6.4, in addition to the category 'other' (14 per cent), we found skilled labour (18 per cent) and three-wheeler driver (7 per cent). Thus, 39 per cent of the households have at least one member earning within the higher brackets. The families of persons in these occupations with relatively higher incomes appeared to have a standard of life that was higher (compared to other households) in terms of being able to send their children to private English-medium schools or for computer training, afford metered water supply, build individual toilets in their houses, and so on.

What has enabled groups of households/individuals within slums to move into higher-order earnings? Social connections had worked. The son or the brother of a person who had a permanent job with the BBMP would get a similar position, particularly in case of death or retirement of the incumbent. Those in government service had been able to give a push to a son or a brother to attend an English-medium school and/or obtain computer training, and eventually to find some kind of employment in a private office. Such persons had started with a slight edge over others, which they had utilised. For those who had actually been able to find a regular salaried position in the private sector, mostly in services, the channel was typically through connections of a family member or information from a friend or neighbour. However, even those with basic computer training frequently remained unemployed or only partially employed.

The opportunities which had been available to some residents had therefore been entirely contingent in nature, wherein learning basic computer skills or a smattering of English and being able to find a job as a waiter or an office messenger was a matter of chance and a constellation of fortunate circumstances. Occupational trajectories of the apparently successful in the slum appeared as accidental spin-offs. There had not been any systemic, policy-based effort on the part of state agencies or of civil society to channelise the urban underclass into the city's growing economy (discussed again in the next section). Therefore, connections to the growing sectors of the city's economy remained limited to a few households in the slum. Their prosperity, clearly visible in a specific set of markers mentioned earlier, was not reflected in the condition of the slum as a whole.

Most remarkably, coolie labour and maidservants accounted for 52.3 per cent of the households surveyed, thus indicating that a large number of households remained in the low-income categories of work. Households in these categories frequently had two members (husband and wife) working as coolie labour and domestic servant/flower seller. They managed to pull along and educate their children up to a certain point, unless struck by a crisis related to death, accident or illness. Their children frequently drop out before the 10th grade and find work in similar occupations.

The 'very poor' in this slum, as described in focus group discussions, were the pushcart vendors, head-load bearers and petty vendors who collected a few waste vegetables from the city market and sold in the slum, and who were typically single earners in large families. Households which were combinations of the aged, the physically dependent and individuals with serious addictions were also part of the category of the 'very poor', dependent on donations from relatives and neighbours.

During repeated visits to the slum, alongside the relative prosperity of some households, the slum presented pictures of extreme want: in the inner roads that snake through the slum there would be older men and women, visibly in poor or failing health, sans medical or other care, their level of destitution obvious as they languish on the roadside or near a temple within the slum; women sitting on the inner slum streets with a few vegetables laid out in front for selling; loitering children, obviously out of school; and men who had been unable to find any work on a particular day in construction sites or in the city market.

The city's growing economy, predominantly the service sector, has had an impact in terms of expanding job opportunities, reflected in the relative prosperity of a number of households. As outlined earlier, such mobility appeared to be the result of individual, isolated and often accidental factors that linked the slums to the city's modern economy. There were no educational or employment-related policies that could provide a systemic bridge between the slum and the new economy; this accounted for the large number of people who remained outside its margins.

Cement Huts slum: Cement Huts, a few metres down the road from K. S. Garden, is known to be predominantly a slum of waste collectors. There are 400 households here of about 2,400 inhabitants. Of approximately 1,200 working adults, around 900 are waste pickers. The slum is 70–80 years old and about 70 per cent of the people living here are, and have always been, waste collectors or street sweepers. Bangalore's vast army of labour engaged in the collection and disposal of waste can be grouped into three categories: first, permanent employees of the BBMP; second, a much larger number who are indirectly employed by the BBMP through contractors or contracting agencies;[7] and a third category who are engaged in waste disposal independently of the BBMP. The community of waste pickers in Cement Huts are in the third category, which features a complex and varied structure of activities, described below. Although a rag-picking community, only a few individuals from Cement Huts work for the BBMP. The business of rag picking goes on here at various levels and is connected to different types of waste-disposal networks in the city, bringing highly differential earnings, depending upon the type of network that the individual waste picker is connected to.

In the mid-1990s, an NGO named Mythri had started work in the slum; their main activity was centred around an Australian grant through which they built roads, toilets and provided water taps. Additionally, Mythri, along with the NGO Waste-Wise, had put through a programme of connecting some of the rag pickers of this slum to Electronic City, the IT tech park, and a few five-star hotels in central Bangalore. This was the beginning of organised scrap collection in the slum. About 150 individuals became connected to the Mythri–Waste Wise initiative. Groups of four to five persons began to work for companies in Electronic City, collecting waste from these companies for a weekly payment. In a second model, the collectors became contractors who themselves paid the hotels in order to collect their waste. The contractor then paid groups of persons from the slum to do the actual work of collection and sorting/segregation. After the segregation, the principal contractor then sold the material. Mythri, additionally, organised some members of the slum, primarily women, to begin selling the collected waste to a set of scrap dealers at fixed rates.

As Mythri's activities remained confined to not more than 150 persons from Cement Huts slum, many who were not included were disappointed and frustrated. Over the years, the role of Mythri as well as of Waste Wise receded, although the structures and networks they had created continued to be operational. Some enterprising individuals followed the Mythri model and organised their own scrap business. They bought the waste collected by the people in the slum and sold it to wholesellers in the neighbouring market area. In this system, those in the slum who pick the waste are paid the day's market price for each kilogram. At the bottom of the heap are mostly women, the old and the infirm, and children, who are unconnected to any kind of organised activity. They may or may not, and most often do not, have any fixed time or places for collection. They sell their daily collection at any price they can get to local scrap dealers.

The organisation of work and gradation of incomes in the slum (Table 6.5) highlight a number of issues. First, Mythri provided a limited number of slum households the vital links to organised scrap collection. Over the years, new groups of young men in the slum were able to take advantage of the information and networks already available and climb on the bandwagon of organised scrap business.[8] These beneficiary groups were the more resourceful persons in the slum: men who were relatively young and who had some organisational skills. On the other hand, a large number of men and women linked to these organised activities as pickers and sorters receive very low daily earnings. Further below are others outside the loop of organised collection; their meagre incomes depend entirely on the hours they are able to work, their collection on a particular day, and the variable rates at which they can sell the collected scrap. Thus, even as a part of the community got drawn into a network of organised collection, for those who did the actual picking and sorting of waste, whether connected to organised collection or not, earnings remained low and precarious. A pattern of exclusion inherited from the past reproduced itself. There has been no effort on the part of the state or of NGOs to visualise a programme that could include larger numbers of this rag-picking community into a framework of organised collection.

Table 6.5 Work and earnings through rag picking in Cement Huts slum

Category of work	Earnings per month
(1) Principal contractor with hotels or companies	INR 15,000–22,000
(2) Waste pickers and sorters who work for (1)	INR 3,500–5,500
(3) Independent scrap business (selling collected scrap to whole sellers)	INR 10,000–12,000
(4) Individuals collecting from streets and selling to (2) or to neighbourhood scrap dealers.	INR 2,500–3,500

Source: Author's field research in Cement Huts slum.

Cement Huts slum presented not only a picture of low incomes and precarity, but also of time standing still for most members of the community. In a focus group discussion with 20 women in the slum, it was revealed that 17 of them collected waste from roadside waste bins and heaps and sell either to plastic and paper scrap dealers in the Chickpet area or directly to scrap dealers operating from within the slum. Aged between 40 and 70, the average earnings of these women ranged from INR 50 to INR 80 per day, that is, between INR 1,500 and INR 2,400 per month. They were not the sole earners in their households. Their husbands and sons, working either as scrap collectors or coolie labour in the city, earned between INR 5,000 and INR 6,000 per month. Of the 20 women, 2 came to the slum after marriage; the rest had been born and brought up in Cement Huts slum as children of rag pickers, married residents of the slum and continued in this occupation. In these 20 households, there were 28 of the next generation, between the ages of 6 and 18. Eight children between the ages of 6 and 12 were going to school. Twenty children ranging from ages 10 to 18 had dropped out of school as early as in fourth grade and 16 of them were engaged in rag picking.

In a typical household, women rag pickers were married to men who were coolie labourers or ragpickers; both men and women represented the second generation of Cement Huts residents; a large number of the third generation had either taken to rag picking or were idle after dropping out of school. In a few cases, they were found to be working as coolie labour. A very small number had been able to get jobs in some kind of services such as a messenger boy in a small office, domestic helper or as packer of produce in a supermarket. This community, residing in the heart of the city, represents a stunning spectacle of stagnation, material degradation and neglect in the lives and livelihoods of three generations of slum dwellers.

A comparison of K. S. Garden and Cement Huts shows that there is an ongoing process of integration into the modern sectors of the city's economy. A large number of households in K. S. Garden still remained tied to traditional, low-paying occupations. However, compared to the other slums in the cluster, there was a relatively larger presence of those who had been able to move into higher income jobs. These individuals had found a foothold in salaried employment through access to education and social networks. In Cement Huts, an initiative led by an NGO, although small in scope, had triggered off a process whereby several waste-collecting households transitioned to becoming scrap dealers or scrap contractors. However, as described earlier, the study highlights the continuing ghettoisation of the second and even the third generations in low incomes generated from isolated, roadside waste picking, or even working as pickers and sorters for waste contractors, highlighting the failure of the state and civil society to reach into their marginalised lives and livelihoods.

Future of slums

We have no problems, only we are poor.
If any government or NGO representative asks, jobs will be our only demand.

This section is on youth aspirations and educational/vocational and employment opportunities available to youths in the age group of 18–24, typically who have dropped out after a few years of schooling. A study of 58 young adults was conducted across two slums, Cement Huts (selected because of the preponderance of scrap picking as an occupation amongst the adult population) and Ramanna Garden (selected for its low occupational and economic profile, as discussed earlier). The objective was to examine whether new avenues and opportunities had opened up for young men and women in these slums.

Across the two slums, 58 young adults (26 women and 32 men) were met over six days of focus group discussions. Of the 26 women, 18 had dropped out of school before completing the class 10 examination. The reasons cited were financial problems, failing in class, not understanding maths and English or not being interested in studies. Two young women had passed class 10 and had dropped out after that due to financial reasons. Only 6 had completed the Pre-University Course (PUC, or terminal two years of high school) level. Of the 26 women, 20 stayed at home, 2 were part-time domestic helpers,

1 worked as a vegetable packer with an eight-hour day and a weekly payment, 2 worked in garment factories, earning INR 7,000–8,000 per month, and o1 worked in a courier service, earning INR 9,000 per month. The focus group discussions revealed the serious limitations of state and civil society interventions in the lives of young women in slums. About 10 of the young women had taken beautician and tailoring courses offered for free by a local NGO, Bosco. However, none of them had been able to find jobs as these were unavailable or they would have to travel too far to work. Post training, there had been no hand-holding interventions to find them suitable placements within manageable distances. During discussions, the young women told us that their only problem was that they were poor. About half the women in the group were already married. However, married or single, the shared concern was that none of them had jobs, and the clear articulation was 'jobs would be our demand, when asked by any government or NGO representatives'. Several women felt that the family's economic situation was responsible for them not being able to continue studying. Out of the 26 women, 11 stated financial reasons for discontinuing studies after class 10. There was a general feeling that only families with regular sources of income were in a position to support their daughters if they wanted to study.

A generational change had indeed occurred, and young women in the slums were no longer inclined to go into scrap collection or domestic service, which their mothers and grandmothers were still engaged in. Women working in garment factories or in the new services economy, like courier and vegetable packing, demonstrated for others the possibility of a regular income from an eight-hour job. This possibility remained a distant dream for most of the women in the group, and the absence of jobs or work had become a point of anguish and continuing frustration.

Of the 32 young men, 6 had studied to the PUC level, and in this group, 4 had been to college, 1 of them having a B. Com degree. Twenty-two had dropped out before completion of the class 10 examinations. A large number, therefore, did not have a school-leaving diploma. Eighteen stated 'not interested' and 'failed in exam' as reasons for dropping out. Six stated financial difficulties as the reason. Of the 32 young men, 18 were working in various capacities, the incomes of 8 ranged between INR 10,000 and INR 20,000, 2 earned less than INR 10,000 and 1 reported income as more than INR 30,000. They worked in a variety of occupations: driving three wheelers, working as office helper, sales counter person, delivery boy, and so on. As many as 14 were unemployed, having been unable to find suitable work.

Scrap collection or coolie work was taken up by youths in the slum who had not had any schooling and were barely literate. These occupations were obviously not a preferred option for youths who had even a few years of school education. However, there were no bridges that the youth in the slum could traverse in order to reach the market of opportunities available in the city. No skill development programmes or schemes, either government or NGO sponsored, had reached the youth. Their professional ambitions were to work in MNCs, set up a dance school, become a gym trainer, and so on. These dreams faltered primarily due to lack of opportunities. The dancer and the gym trainer said that they would never be able to set up their own schools or gyms as they wanted to do. 'We can try hard but nothing would change.'

An important element in the lives of dropouts was that they remained unemployed or partially employed. Their days were spent hanging around the slum, watching movies on their phones, chatting, and some were clearly involved in drugs. What explained their lackadaisical lives, and the fact that they apparently did not need to work for regular incomes? The youths themselves provided the answer. The school curriculum was difficult. The future provided no incentives to work hard in school. Their peers who had completed 10th or 12th grade had remained jobless. The fathers of the jobless youths work as auto drivers, tempo drivers, coolies and scrap collectors. The mothers work as domestic maids or scrap collectors. The parents continue to support their unemployed children who have dropped out of school.

This situation highlighted the failure of institutional intervention at multiple levels. First, no systems were in place to help first-generation learners cope with school curricula. Second, the Skill India policy had been framed particularly with the mandate of rehabilitating school dropouts.[9] Despite the hype around the Skill India policy, government and non-government skilling programmes had failed to reach out to the slum youth. While there was some interest among the youth in the idea of skilling, they were not aware of the different options available under various skilling programmes, or the placement services offered by skills training institutions. Therefore, despite the generational change in terms of a shift from the community's traditional occupations, the roadblocks to social and economic mobility for school dropouts stem from the absence of skilling and employment opportunities. What framed this situation of course was the larger political economy where factory jobs have dried up and the service sector, despite its spectacular growth, does not offer regular employment and a clear career trajectory to dropout slum youth.[10]

Political parties and slums

The six slums studied here fall under two wards (ward nos 145 and 146) under Chickpet constituency in the Bangalore South zone.[11] The constituency has a varied history in terms of support to political parties. At the council (city corporation) level, the Congress has been the majority party since 2006. At the level of assembly elections, a member of the BJP was voted as MLA during 2003–08; thereafter, R. V. Devraj of the Congress Party was elected as MLA for two consecutive elections and was MLA for the period 2008–18. In the 2018 assembly elections, there was a change to the BJP with the election of one Uday Gurudachar. In the Lok Sabha elections (to the parliament), the constituency has consistently voted for the BJP, as the political persona of the well-known BJP leader Ananth Kumar dominated the Bangalore South zone for more than a decade, from 2004 until his death in 2018. Eventually, in the 2019 elections, the Lok Sabha seat was won by a young, first-time BJP candidate, Tejaswi Surya.

During these years, slum dwellers have benefited very little from state policies. In the cluster of six slums, Vinobha Nagar was the only slum that received cash loan assistance for building houses. Why housing policies and projects, particularly those associated with the JNNURM, did not reach the other slums is a complex story (discussed in Chapter 8 in detail). Here, I highlight two main points. First, slum residents' most consistent and long-drawn-out demand has been for property rights (*hakku patra*) on the land which they occupy. Successive governments have provided selected slum households with Possession Certificate, which offers security of tenure, but not an inheritable or saleable right. Second, slum residents have been largely indifferent to new housing projects insofar as these do not meet their demands for property rights and have also opposed the coming of multi-storey housing projects as their interest is to retain the ground floor which allows both living and livelihoods (small shops, cycle repairing units, livestock, and so on). The battle, then, has been for the *hakku patra*, and several slum-level leaders have won and lost their position as interlocutors, depending on their promises and their capacity to negotiate with state agencies on this issue.

On the side of the state, an important actor in this drama has been R. V. Devraj, a real estate developer-cum-politician with close links to the constituency. Devraj won successive elections to the Karnataka assembly, and an important plank of his election promises had been the *hakku patra* promised to slum dwellers. The *hakku patra* remained elusive even as Devraj finally lost to a BJP candidate in the 2018 assembly elections. R. V. Devraj's political career, seen in the context of the slums that he has represented for many years, reflects the ways in which the urban poor and their interests are bypassed even as local leaders rise to positions of power riding on the support of slum households. The son of a city market vegetable merchant, Devraj's rise in the Congress, and to different positions of power in government, represents the space that democratic politics allows to non-elite members of the society. Devraj's career spans several election victories from the Chamrajpet and Chickpet constituencies, and his political rise is often traced to his close association with former Congress strongman and chief minister, S. M. Krishna. On the other hand, Devraj's career has a chequered history, with police and legal cases against him for repeated violations of law, relating particularly to land.[12] Devraj's immunity to legal issues that have been raised against him time and again reflects the easy protection that Indian politicians enjoy vis-à-vis the legal system. Given this background, it is easy to see why Devraj has been, at best, indifferent to slum dwellers' demands for *hakku patra*, as he himself is a stakeholder in the complex structure of the land market in the inner-city areas in which he has a significant political presence as a member of the Congress Party.

The other side of the question of course is the political preferences of voters. Devraj lost in the assembly elections, once in 2004 to Zameer Ahmed, member of the Janata Dal party, and in 2018 to a BJP candidate. Zameer Ahmed of the Janata Dal, similar to Devraj, did little for the slum dwellers' demand for land. Uday Garudachar, a member of the BJP, won this assembly seat in the 2018 elections. Presently, it is too early to assess his performance as MLA. However, the election of Garudachar from this constituency brings to light certain unique features of the democratic process as it works in the Indian context. A successful real estate developer, Garudachar is also the owner of Garuda Mall, one of the largest malls in the city, situated in an upscale neighbourhood close to downtown Bangalore. His purchase of the land on which the erstwhile Ejipura slum in Koramangala existed, the eventual eviction of Ejipura slum dwellers in 2013 as well as Garudachar's stakes in the land around the cluster of slums in Koramangala, where he intends to build a second mall, have been critically represented in the media and resisted by slum dwellers' associations and NGOs. These have been discussed in detail in the next chapter. In the context of the present chapter, it needs to be highlighted that Garudachar's election from the Chickpet constituency, which is home to a large number of slums, would appear to go against the logic of his controversial role with regard to slum land acquisition and eviction of slum residents.

Moving to parliamentary elections, the BJP has held the Lok Sabha seat from this constituency for the last four parliamentary elections. This continuous victory record of the BJP in the Lok Sabha elections from this constituency has not brought any benefits to the slums in this area. This pattern indicates that the relationship between votes, promises and actual action is complex and multilayered. Both the Congress and the BJP have a long history of lack of attention to slum dwellers' demands. On the other hand, political support of slum dwellers for particular candidates is possibly anchored in a structure of exchange, where short-term individual benefits are prioritised over a long-term programme of collective demands.

To summarise briefly, this chapter has highlighted that inner-city slums which have been in existence for more than half a century, and house residents over two or three generations, lack any substantive links to the so-called modern and dynamic sectors of the city's economy. Many households are bound to traditional occupations, which remain low paying and precarious due to lack of state regulation. Those who have transitioned to jobs in the city's growing service sector may receive a monthly salary, but their incomes remain low and service conditions are irregular. Lack of access to institutional credit, skills deficit and absence of social contacts have been highlighted as major factors that prevent slum communities from accessing better-paying jobs and eventually social and economic mobility (Krishna 2013). While these institutional factors are of critical importance, the analysis in this book shifts to a second level of causal factors. Framing the structure of disadvantages under which slum residents seek a livelihood are two features of the city's political economy: first, the absence of jobs in the manufacturing sector and, second, informality, or the absence of state regulation, which provides a precarious framework for work in the occupations the urban underclass is engaged in. The politics of electoral representation at the city, state and national levels draws attention to a consistently similar history of neglect of slum residents and slum-related issues. These points are discussed in the Introduction and again taken up in the concluding chapter.

Appendix 6A   Note on Poverty Line Estimation

The poverty line of rural and urban Karnataka according to Planning Commission using 68th round of NSSO data for the year 2011–12 was identified as follows:

Rural Karnataka – INR 902 (monthly per capita expenditure)

Urban Karnataka – INR 1,089 (monthly per capita expenditure)

Using the consumer price index from the *Economic Survey of Karnataka 2018–19*, the poverty line of Karnataka for the year 2017–18 was estimated. Since monthly per capita income = per capita expenditure for poor (as almost the entire income is typically spent on consumption), it can be used to estimate poverty.

Estimated poverty line for the year 2017–18 using the consumer price index (2017–18):

Rural Karnataka – INR 1,468 (monthly per capita expenditure)

Urban Karnataka – INR 1,654 (monthly per capita expenditure)

The methodology for estimation is explained below:

Table 6A.1 Consumer price index for industrial workers (CPI-IW)

Month	2017–18	2011–12
April	826	531
May	829	537
June	835	540
July	845	545
August	849	546
September	845	554
October	849	558
November	856	566
December	846	563
January	845	567
February	844	575
March	842	580
Average (rounded to nearest tens)	**843**	**555**

Sources: Economic Survey of Karnataka, 2018–19 (GOK 2019); *Economic Survey of Karnataka, 2013–14* (GOK 2014)

Table 6A.2 Consumer price index for agricultural labourers (CPI-AL)

2017–18	2011–12
1,056	649

Sources: Economic Survey of Karnataka, 2018–19 (GOK 2019) *Economic Survey of Karnataka, 2013–14* (GOK 2014)

1. **Estimation of poverty line for rural Karnataka for the year 2017–18 using CPI-AL**

   For estimating the poverty line of rural Karnataka for the year 2017–18, CPI-AL is used. At the CPI-AL of 649 for the year 2011–12, the poverty line for rural Karnataka is INR 902. Hence, at the CPI-AL of 1,056 for the year 2017–18, the poverty line for Karnataka is:

   Rural poverty line of Karnataka for the year 2011–12

   * CPI-AL for the year 2017–18

   CPI-AL for the year 2011–12

   INR 902

   *1,056 = INR 1,468

   649

   Thus, the estimated poverty line for rural Karnataka is INR 1,468.

2. **Estimation of poverty line for urban Karnataka for the year 2017–18 using CPI-IW**

   For estimating the poverty line for urban Karnataka for the year 2017–18, CPI-IW is used. At the CPI-IW of 555 for the year 2011–12, the poverty line for urban Karnataka is INR 1,089. Hence, at the CPI-IW of 843 for the year 2017–18, the poverty line for urban Karnataka is:

   Poverty line of urban Karnataka for the year 2011–12

   * (Avg) CPI-IW for the year 2017–18

   (Avg) CPI-IW for the year 2011–12

   INR 1,089

   *843 = INR 1,654

   555

   The estimated poverty line for urban Karnataka is INR 1,654.

Notes

1. See also Krishna (2013).
2. The six slums studied here were a part of a research on 16 slums where we studied mainly the issue of slum land. See RoyChowdhury (2008). The information on the six slums presented in this chapter has been updated during 2017–19.
3. A flower seller who has an assured market of 50 houses in a large campus or apartment complex charging INR 400 per house for a daily supply of garlands will earn INR 20,000, of which she would spend INR 10,000 on daily transport to the flower market, cost of raw material and hiring a part-time worker to help with stringing flowers. Most street sellers of flowers do not have an assured market.

4. The estimated poverty line for urban Karnataka in 2011–12 was INR 1,089, and in 2017–18, it was INR 1,654. See Appendix 6A.
5. See our report on café workers and security guards, RoyChowdhury and Vani (2016).
6. Information on poverty in Bangalore slums at a macro level is available in Madheswaran and Vani (2017).
7. Of the close to 18,000 BBMP-employed scrap pickers/sweepers in the city, around 3,000 are permanent employees whose monthly wage is INR 21,000. There are 17,700 contract workers employed by a number of contracting agencies whose monthly wage of INR 7,000 was raised to INR 14,000 in 2016. However, contract workers of the BBMP have a long history of not being paid the full salary by contractors and there have been several organised protests in the city on this issue led by different organisations.
8. Some of the waste management companies that had been set up were called Citizen Waste, SRV Waste and Mother Waste.
9. The National Skill Development Policy was enacted by the UPA-led central government in 2009, followed by the formation of the National Skill Development Commission in 2013 and the National Skill Development Agency in the same year. With the coming of the BJP-led NDA government in 2014, the National Policy for Skill Development and Entrepreneurship was enacted, putting the skills imperative on a mission mode with the formation of the National Skill Development Mission in 2015.
10. For discussion on the Skill India policy and programmes and impact on youth in Karnataka, see RoyChowdhury and Upadhya (2020).
11. Chickpet with six wards – Sudhamanagar, Dharmarayaswamy temple, Sunkenahalli, Vishweshwarapuram, Siddapura and Hombegowda Nagar – is a densely populated constituency in the heart of the city.
12. In 2015, the Kalasipaliya police registered a case against the MLA for grabbing land that belonged to the BBMP. In 2018, the Karnataka High Court issued a reprimand to Mr Devraj for repeated recommendations to the BBMP to allot open spaces in the Kalasipalya municipal market to particular individuals. In 2018, again, as Chairman of the Karnataka Slum Development Board, he was accused of taking a commission of 10 per cent when handing out contracts to build houses under the Pradhan Mantri Awas Yojana. See *Citizen Matters* (2018), *New Indian Express* (2018a, 2018b).

References

Citizen Matters. 2018. 'What Has the Chickpet MLA Been up to in the Last Five Years?' 26 April.
Directorate of Census Operations, Karnataka. 2011. Census of India 2011, *Karnataka District Census Handbook*. Bangalore.

Government of Karnataka (GOK). 2014. *Economic Survey of Karnataka, 2013–14.* Bengaluru: Government of Karnataka.

———. 2019. *Economic Survey of Karnataka, 2018–19.* Bengaluru: Government of Karnataka.

Krishna, A. 2010. *Why People Become Poor and How They Escape Poverty.* Oxford: Oxford University Press.

———. 2013. 'Stuck in Place: Investigating Social Mobility in 14 Bangalore Slums'. *Journal of Development Studies* 49 (7): 1010–28.

Madheswaran, S., and B. P. Vani. 2017. 'Slums in Bangalore: A Status Report'. Government of Karnataka and Institute for Social and Economic Change, Bangalore.

New Indian Express. 2018a. 'Congress Pays Price for Ignoring Real Issues in Chickpet'. 13 May.

———. 2018b. 'Karnataka High Court Notice to MLA, BBMP officials for "Disobedience"'. 16 February.

Ramachandran, H., and S. V. Subramanian. 2001. 'Slum Household Characteristics in Bangalore: A Comparative Analysis 1973 and 1992'. In *Living in India's Slums: A Case Study of Bangalore,* edited by H. Schenk, 65–68. New Delhi: Manohar Publishers.

RoyChowdhury, S. 2008. 'Slums and Civil Society: Limits of Urban Activism'. In *Inside the Transforming Urban Asia: Processes, Policies and Public Actions,* edited by Darshini Mahadevia, 601–18. New Delhi: Concept.

RoyChowdhury, S., and B. P. Vani. 2016. 'Work and Workers in the Services Sectors: A Pilot Study in Bangalore.' Unpublished report, Institute for Social and Economic Change, Bangalore.

RoyChowdhury, S., and C. Upadhya. 2020. 'India's Changing City Scapes: Work, Migration and Livelihood'. Unpublished report, ISEC and NIAS, Bangalore.

Schenk, H., ed. 2001. *Living in India's Slums: A Case Study of Bangalore.* Delhi: Manohar Publishers.

7

Impact of Slum Housing Policies

Bangalore's New Ghettoes

This chapter looks at state initiatives to address the issue of poor housing in urban areas. Three major central legislative enactments, the Jawaharlal Nehru National Urban Renewal Mission/Basic Services to Urban Poor (JNNURM/BSUP), Rajiv Awas Yojana (RAY) and the Pradhan Mantri Awas Yojana (PMAY), are outlined. This provides the backdrop to a discussion of the implementation of BSUP and RAY in Bangalore city. It should be noted that both JNNURM/BSUP and RAY have been discussed widely in both policy and academic forums. Much of this discussion has been in the nature of surveys to examine resource allocations, targets and achievements by counting projects and beneficiaries. Some studies have looked at the role of urban local bodies (ULBs), designed to have played a catalytic role in raising finance and in execution of housing projects. The emphasis in this chapter is on understanding the broader politics that surround the process of implementation of housing projects, and, importantly, the impact of projects and processes on the lives of slum dwellers.

The chapter draws on field-based research on housing projects in Bangalore city, looking at three spaces: slum development based on in situ housing; relocation of slums; and slums where housing projects could not be undertaken due to local resistance. The study reveals some important microfeatures of poor housing projects.

First, the state, through housing projects, provides to slum dwellers renewable leases for new apartments, which is meant to ensure protection from soaring rents and eviction. These, however, do not provide a sale deed or property rights. The projects, in this sense, have bypassed long-standing demands of the urban poor for right to land (Benjamin 2008, 2011; RoyChowdhury 2008, 2012). The projects have also ignored slum dwellers' long-expressed demand for 'land-to-sky' rights on land (that is, right to own a piece of land and to build vertically on it) and their resistance to the idea of small apartments in multi-storey buildings which do not address their need to use housing for livelihood as well as for large and expanding families.

Second, the housing projects typically provide small accommodations, without the necessary and promised related infrastructure, thus bringing little change to the generally low quality of life in slums. State-sponsored housing projects were therefore, to a great extent, distanced from the actual needs and demands of slum dwellers for land rights, water, sanitation, stable supply of power, schools, *anganwadi*s and health centres.

Third, the process of implementation, which varied widely, highlighted the many different and conflicting responses of slum dwellers to the idea of slum redevelopment, which stemmed from the diverse and multilayered structure of interests that characterise the urban poor. Recent migrants, typically households with fragile incomes and tenuous claims on land, had little choice but to opt for multi-storey housing projects; others with stronger economic means and longer claims on the land resisted the projects even as they reiterated their claim to 'land-to-sky' rights, that is, right to land and right to build vertically, rather than move into government-given apartments. Particular slum communities, with the occasional political network, managed to get individual plots and build their own houses. Yet others who opted for housing projects continued to suffer serious infrastructural deficits like water and sanitation and lived with the absence of basic amenities. This diverse process created groups of gainers and losers and further divided slum communities.

Finally, in terms of the state's relationship with urban poor groups, two features stood out: on the one hand, the state's ostrich-like position in bringing and insisting on a one-size-fits-all project, ignoring the diversities in the target group; on the other hand, the state's own complicities were seen at multiple levels – many apartments were allotted to households that did not have the necessary legal entitlements, and state alliances with private companies were brought in through the public–private partnership (PPP) channel, ostensibly to contribute to poor housing, but in a context where slum dwellers were being denied long-standing rights to land, the same land was sold to private companies to be used for commercial purposes.

The following section provides a broad outline of recent housing policies, particularly in the context of changing legal and institutional paradigm of slum redevelopment; the next two sections outline housing policies and programmes in Karnataka and Bangalore and present case studies of six slums across west and south Bangalore; the last section concludes the chapter.

Recent housing policies: JNNURM/BSUP/RAY

The need to provide housing to urban poor communities has been a sustained concern through successive five-year plans and legislative enactments at both the central and state levels. As urbanisation expanded, the proliferation of slums and temporary settlements highlighted the inadequacy of policy responses to the need for subsidised poor housing. In 2012, the total number of households without decent housing in cities was pegged at 18.78 million (Ministry of Housing and Urban Poverty Alleviation, GOI, 2012). This reflects the number of those who live in non-liveable, temporary, overcrowded and dilapidated houses as well as the homeless (D'Souza 2019). Successive governments at both federal and state levels enacted several laws addressing slum development and urban poor housing, such as the Indira Awaas Yojana in 1985 and the Valmiki Ambedkar Awas Yojana (VAMBAY) in the early 2000s. The approach typically had been to provide small, one-room apartments in large multiplexes built for the urban poor in the peripheries of cities. Apart from issues of low-quality construction and poor access to infrastructure and services, the removal of the urban workforce from the spaces of employment to peripheral areas attracted much criticism.

Subsequently, three landmark judgments by the Supreme Court changed the face of future legislation on urban poor housing. In *Chameli Singh v. State of UP* (1996) and in *Shantisar Builders v. N. K. Totimane* (1990), the Supreme Court laid down that the right to life is not a mere animal existence, and the right to housing is a fundamental right. Thereafter, in *Sukama Singh v. Government of Delhi* (2010), the Court emphasised in situ rehabilitation, except in extraordinary situations, when relocation may be permitted. In another recent case, *Gainda Ram v. Municipality of Delhi* (2010), the Court reiterated that hawkers must have a fundamental right to hawk and must stay reasonably close to their place of work. These judgments created a moral imperative for governments to change the paradigm framing housing policies. In principle, these judgments present livelihood, as well as subsidised housing, as not merely something that the state may choose to provide for the urban poor; rather, it is among the fundamental claims that the poor can make upon the state. Provision of housing is therefore mandatory for the state. Further, the in situ clause, in a sense, rewrites the urban poor's relationship to land. Previous to this judgment, policy discourse on slum development had perceived the slum dweller typically as a squatter or an illegal encroacher who could be justifiably evicted or forced to relocate. The clause relating to in situ housing, read along with the positive judgment on hawkers, recognises the urban poor's right to the city's land in terms of livelihood as well as habitation.

More specifically, it recognises that slums and squatter settlements do not merely represent illegal encroachments. The history of the urban poor's lack of economic choice that led them to encroachment and squatting and their struggles to seek livelihoods and habitation in poorly provided settlements are built into the in situ clause when it grants that the slum dwellers have a right to the land on which they have lived.

While poor housing in cities has been a sustained policy concern since independence, the UPA's ten-year tenure from 2004 to 2014 marked a watershed in policy thinking on housing- and shelter-related issues. The JNNURM, unveiled by the UPA in 2004, offered a broad vision of urban renewal, with infrastructure development as one of its main pillars. Slum development and provision of housing for the poor were subsumed within this broader mission as Basic Services to the Urban Poor (BSUP). Housing was, in fact, seen as part of the larger goal of providing the urban poor with better access to civic amenities.

Even as slum redevelopment under the BSUP was underway in several states, a second national housing scheme, the RAY was introduced (2013–22) that continued the basic principles of the JNNURM with a more defined and focused attention on the vision of a slum-free India. By 2014, the NDA, led by the BJP, had come to power. That year, the PMAY was launched, which integrated the BSUP and RAY. The PMAY is not qualitatively different from the earlier BSUP and RAY. It seeks to take the mandate of these two earlier policies forward by committing the state to the goal of 'every person must have his own house by the year 2022'. Additionally, 2 million non-slum urban poor households are proposed to be covered under the mission. Hence, the total housing shortage to be addressed through the new mission was estimated to be 20 million.

Each of these policies has been widely discussed in the literature on housing and urban land. Therefore, without going further into the details of the policies, in this section I provide a few highlights that are important for understanding the purpose and practice of the state vis-à-vis the urban poor in the context of housing.

First, underlying each of the three enactments was a clear, albeit unstated, distinction between tenurial security and right to property. Earlier housing projects typically offered a Possession Certificate, which did not provide sale or heritable rights, nor could the property be legally mortgaged. The Possession Certificate itself was frequently offered as a favour or patronage, negotiated between slum communities and local leaders, not as an entitlement. Within the JNNURM/BSUP, the need for revamping the legal framework of slum housing to enhance tenurial security was an important concern. A central objective was to scale up service delivery to the urban poor (for example, water and electricity) by providing security of tenure at affordable prices. However, the definition of security of tenure did not incorporate providing actual property rights on land: under the BSUP, housing units would be non-transferable for a period of 10 years, after which they could be sold back only to the government. The legislation thus provided tenurial security for a period of time, free of rent and, most importantly, freed the slum household from the fear of eviction, but fell short of providing actual saleable property rights or recognising the claim of the slum dweller to significantly expand or improve their allotted dwelling place. In most instances, state provision of poor housing fell back on the old practice of providing a Possession Certificate, which could, in principle, be renewed. Thus, the moral imperative set up by the Supreme Court in favour of recognising slum dwellers' rights on land was largely ignored.

Second, the JNNURM, for the first time, introduced the concept of private sector participation in the provision of housing for the urban poor, thus making the private sector in a sense a partner of the state in this social responsibility, as well as a stakeholder. With JNNURM/BSUP, the centre envisaged a total government cost of INR 50,000 crores, with another INR 50,000 crores to be raised through private sector participation for the reinvigoration of 63 cities as model cities. Urban local bodies (ULBs) and parastatals were envisioned to play a catalytic role by being encouraged to leverage credit and market capital. Prime Minister Manmohan Singh, in his inaugural speech of the JNNURM, proclaimed that the 'functioning of the Mission would do away with those statutes that inhibit the functioning of land and housing markets'.

The Rajiv Awas Yojana (RAY), introduced in 2013, carried forward the JNNURM/BSUP concepts. RAY's singularity was in bringing all existing slums, whether notified or non-notified, within the formal system and making basic amenities accessible to all, thereby creating a framework of equality. Furthering the idea of private participation, RAY brought in the phrase 'Affordable Housing in Partnership' (AHP). Central support was extended at the rate of INR 75,000 for economically weaker sections (EWSs) and lower income group (LIG) dwelling units. For private players to come in, a minimum availability for EWS was made mandatory.

The PMAY (2014) made the role of private capital in slum uplift more explicit. The PMAY underlines the importance of 'slum rehabilitation with the participation of private developers, using land as a resource'. There is a provision of reservation of space for EWS/LIG categories. Through the lure of highly valued urban land, private developers could be roped into sharing the state's responsibility of providing cheap housing to the poor. At the same time, slum dwellers would be provided with credit-linked subsidy (at 5 per cent interest for a loan of INR 5–8 lakhs).

While the impact of housing policies and projects has inevitably varied across states, some common themes of dissatisfaction and criticism have emerged centring around governance. These relate mainly to criteria used for selection of slums and beneficiaries and the provision of houses/apartments without attention to civic amenities. Activists have pointed out that PPP led to easy and increased access to urban land for real estate developers. Additionally, within the broad framework of the scheme's given mission of 'urban renewal', we need to enquire into the ways in which housing projects have made an overall difference to the lives of slum dwellers, including in terms of livelihood, employment and income.

Housing the poor in Karnataka and Bangalore

Academic as well as popular media representations of Karnataka and Bangalore have focused mostly on the high economic growth rates of the state, driven by the growth of IT and ITES primarily in Bangalore. In Chapter 4, I have discussed the unevenness of Karnataka's development, and one of the features of this unevenness is the stubbornness of urban poverty in the state. This is more conspicuous in the case of Bangalore, given its dramatically high economic growth. The population living in urban slums in Karnataka increased from 14.02 lakhs in 2001 to 32.91 lakhs in 2011 – that is, by 18.89 lakhs in a decade. This is a rise from 7.8 per cent to 13.9 per cent of the total urban population. Bangalore district constitutes 21.94 per cent of the total slum population in the state and every fifth person in the BBMP area lives in a slum.[1] It is in that broad context that the present chapter examines the impact of low-cost housing projects on the lives of urban poor households.

While the percentage of slum dwellers to total population is lower in Bangalore as compared to several major Indian cities, the number of slums as well as the number of slum households have been consistently growing. This is discussed in Chapter 6. This disparity between the city's economic growth, represented by the rising prosperity of the educated middle class, on the one hand, and the growth of slums, signalling an emerging exclusivist pattern of growth, on the other, has drawn much attention.[2] An important study on the impact of the JNNURM on slum regeneration is based on surveys that have looked at the number of intended housing projects, amount spent, implementation in terms of construction of houses, and so on (Pani 2017). Other studies have reflected on the weakening of ULBs, the expanding role of parastatals and consultants, and the role of local politicians and NGOs in determining the trajectory of housing projects (Kamath 2012). The analysis below highlights that the housing projects emerging out of the JNNURM/BSUP and RAY were out of tune with slum dwellers' long-standing demand for property rights. Slum communities were deeply divided in their response to the projects, revealing a complex politics of resistance/ acceptance structured by their socio-economic profile. New housing projects rarely provided for an enhanced quality of life in terms of access to basic services, and slum communities in redeveloped settlements remained trapped in a continuing cycle of low access to basic services, education and employment. In other words, housing projects were placed atop the poverty of slum households, bringing relief from rent and eviction but no substantive change in the structure of assets, opportunities and mobility.

Case studies of six slums

The following discussion presents case studies of slums across the city, representing the different and contrasting ways in which housing projects have been proposed by the state, received or rejected by slum communities, the emergence of the concept of PPP, and the impact of projects on the lives of slum households. I draw on studies of six slums mainly in the western and southern parts of the city: four housing projects across in situ and relocation sites, and two slums in which new housing projects did not happen as small but powerful sections of the slum communities resisted the idea of a universalising housing scheme.

Housing project in Lakshmidevi Nagar, Laggare (relocation)

Laggare is a huge housing complex on 95 acres of land located in the western part of Bangalore, surrounded by the Ring Road on the east, Peenya Industrial Area on the west and a residential neighbourhood on the south. The land now belongs to the Karnataka Slum Development Board (KSDB). Around 60 per cent of this total acquired land has so far been used for building purposes under different housing projects. From 1983 to 1999, the Housing and Urban Development Corporation Limited (HUDCO) built around 3,026 houses. Under VAMBAY, BSUP and RAY, 2,109 houses were built, bringing the total number of housing units in the complex to approximately 5,135 in 2018.

Underprivileged communities from different parts of the city have gradually shifted here.[3] The reasons for relocation were varied: in some cases, the slums or settlements had been burnt down, while in others the land had been reclaimed by private owners. Within the umbrella Laggare settlement, there are two large settlements: Lakshmidevi Nagar and Laggare. Most of the households have been given Possession Certificates but not the coveted *hakku patra*. There are two *anganwadi*s and two government schools. The following discussion presents a study of a slum community that relocated to Lakshmidevi Nagar.

The history of this community of migrants from north Karnataka dates back only 20 years, when several migrant households had moved from Gulbarga and Raichur to Bangalore and set up temporary, self-constructed one-room tenements in the Peenya Industrial Area (Second Stage). Of the 155 households, several had found employment in the industries in Peenya. In due course, however, a private owner of the land requested the Karnataka Small Industries Area (KSIA) department to have the land vacated and the site returned to him. The KSIA department in turn requested the KSDB to provide alternative accommodation to these households.

The initial move to allot houses to these families became caught up in the competitive party politics of two electoral constituencies: as part of Rajarajeswari Nagar, Laggare was a Congress Party constituency for the past two assembly elections. On the other hand, Peenya Second Stage, where this community had been earlier located, was a BJP constituency. Therefore, initially, Muniratnam, the Congress MLA from the Rajarajeswari Nagar constituency, was reluctant to offer houses to the community that was supposedly a BJP supporter. Eventually, however, it was seen that most of the households were migrants from Gulbarga where they have traditionally voted for Mallikarjun Kharge, the Congress strongman. Kharge finally convinced Muniratnam to provide the allotments. The process of allotment, therefore, highlighted the slum community's entitlement to housing being decided in terms of their political loyalties in their village of origin, with very little to do with their needs or rights as migrants in the city.

While the negotiation was in progress, the entire slum in Peenya was burnt down in a fire accident, which some interpreted to be a deliberate act by the landowner. The BBMP then provided small amounts to the households to arrange for temporary accommodation until they could be shifted to Laggare, where a housing complex was under construction. By 2015, the 155 households had increased to 179. At the time of allotment, some households were found ineligible, that is, they did not possess the necessary identity documents, and others preferred to remain where they were. Finally, only 80 families were shifted to Lakshmidevi Nagar. The total population in the slum is about 400.

The households were given accommodation in a JNNURM project building. The apartments are of 300 square feet, consisting of one bedroom, a hall, a kitchen, a toilet and a bathroom. The toilets do not have flush tanks. With borewells and tanks, there is regular supply of water. However, sanitary blockages are a perennial problem in the settlement, with no response by the authorities to repair the damages. The households have been given allotment certificates. Before the 2018 assembly elections, the MLA Muniratnam had promised *hakku patra*s, particularly that these will be given after the elections. This remains an unfulfilled promise.

Concrete roads and newly painted houses made of concrete presented a very different and more pleasant profile compared to the dilapidated structures of older city slums, which have been discussed in the previous chapter. However, the key aspects of urban deprivation, the right to property and the right to a decent livelihood, had been completely overlooked. Cramped into small apartments on the upper floors, households were prevented from engaging in the kind of activities that slum dwellers typically use their living space for: putting up a small vegetable shop, a small provision store, using the space outside for a cycle repairing unit or even to keep some livestock. The majority of households in the community were marked by low levels of education, and incomes came only from irregular employment in informal work.

The economic condition of the men in this community reflects the condition of unskilled migrant labour in the city. In case of this particular community, several of the men had earlier been employed as unskilled labour in lathe and machinery factories in Peenya. The decline in Bangalore's SSI sector, which had particularly affected industrial estates like Peenya, has been discussed in Chapter 4. As factories closed down, several households lost work. Some took to working as construction workers and petty shop owners, and women worked mostly in garment factories and domestic service. There has been no intervention from the government or from NGOs to provide job-oriented vocational training. As one participant in a focus group discussion said, 'Sochnewala koi nahi hai' (There is nobody to think about us). In the absence of NGO interventions, many were not aware of social security schemes or how to access these.[4]

The slum community exhibited typical features of vulnerability that characterise the urban poor. In this case, as settlers in Peenya, their survival was threatened thrice over: by the private landowner's decision to reclaim the land, the fire that reduced their small houses to rubble, and the political bargaining that took place before they were actually allotted space in the Lakshmidevi

Nagar housing project. The relocation brought them security of tenure with protection from the threat of evictions. Ironically, however, there was no sign that the relocation had brought in any dynamism into the community. As shown here, dislocated from factory work in Peenya, the men had turned to construction work, many of the women remained without work, and the younger generation had little recourse to the skills that could have pulled them into the growth channels of the city.

Housing project in Koramangala

Koramangala, in southern Bangalore, is known for being an expensive, fashionable neighbourhood, with large corporate offices, swanky shopping areas and restaurants, and luxury residences that primarily house affluent IT personnel. The other side of Koramangala, however, is a dark underbelly that represents the highly unequal trajectory of Bangalore's rapid economic growth. Koramangala consists of six large slum zones: Rajendra Nagar, L. R. Nagar, EWS Quarters, Ambedkar Nagar, Shastri Nagar and Samatha Nagar (PUCL 2013). The total number of households in this huge complex of settlements is around 6,800, covering 50 acres of BBMP-owned land. The movement of different communities into this area and the setting up of temporary shacks began in the mid-1970s and continued into the 1990s. A large number of households came in groups from other parts of Karnataka, from neighbouring states and from slums in other parts of the city as a result of eviction. Yet others moved here when new housing projects were set up, and they were able to utilise contacts with local politicians to have their names registered in the list of claimants.

The trajectory of policy implementation in the Koramangala area highlights that while a set of policies are in principle applicable across slums, there are, in fact, multiple and negotiable levels at which the state may define the urban poor's claim to land and housing: those at the bottom of the pit may be denied any claim to the city and may be relocated; occasionally, a particular slum community may be offered title deeds; others may receive housing (in situ or relocation) but would not be provided with title deeds or even basic infrastructural facilities. These varying offerings by the state bring to light the structural differences in the socio-economic profiles of different slum communities: recent migrants and floating populations, who have neither a claim based on years of stay nor the political and social networks to press their claims, and who may settle for poorly constructed small apartments or even relocation; in contrast, older slum communities may either successfully press for title deeds or successfully resist housing projects. In the following, three cases are presented, the EWS Housing Community, the L. R. Nagar slum and the Samatha Nagar slum, each part of the larger Koramangala slum complex.

The EWS Housing Community (relocation)

In the context of the large influx of slum households into the Koramangala area, the Bangalore City Corporation (predecessor to the BBMP) had constructed a set of EWS quarters in the area in 1993–94, issued letters of allotment and executed lease-cum-sale agreements with the respective allottees. There were 1,512 flats in 42 blocks over 22 acres of land. However, due to poor construction and use of sub-standard material, several blocks collapsed, and over the years a large number of households moved out to different parts of the city. Out of 1,512, just about 230 of the original occupants remained in the blocks until around 2010. All 1,512 households were, however, given biometric cards of identity that would entitle them to future housing. After a large number of the original occupants moved out, new occupants came in either with some kind of legal claim through power of attorney given to them by the original occupant or just began to live in the vacant quarters, often without any paperwork to support their stay. The new occupants as well as the older ones who had stayed on represented extremely poor and vulnerable socio-economic groups that inevitably had no option but to stay in the endangered quarters.

Eventually, the entire complex was demolished, and all households were shifted to tin sheds on the same land. A promise was made that new housing would be built by the BBMP and allotted to all those who were displaced. At the same time, the BBMP entered into negotiations with Maverick Company (owners of Garuda Mall) for a PPP arrangement whereby a part of the land would be used by the company to build low-cost housing for the poor and another part would be used to construct a mall. This proposal came in for intense criticism by several NGOs who eventually filed a case in the High Court challenging the BBMP's decision to collaborate with Maverick. In the process, the proposal to construct housing for the displaced EWS community was massively delayed and the demolished space, in the meantime, came to be occupied by new, mostly migrant households coming into the city. Thus, the number of households in the temporarily occupied tin sheds swelled to almost 1,000, bringing the total number of households with some kind of claim on the to-be-built complex to around 2,500.

Initially, the BBMP had acknowledged that the supposed new occupants also had a claim to be rehabilitated in the complex that was to be constructed. However, older occupants (the original allottees, many of whom had moved away) challenged the new occupants' claim in a writ petition made to the High Court. The BBMP eventually stepped back from its broader, inclusive definition of beneficiaries, and in its new formulation, only the original allottees could claim the upcoming new housing. In response, a writ petition was submitted on behalf of the new occupants, staking their claim to the upcoming complex as well.

In the legal battle that followed, the EWS quarters became a site of intense contestation at two levels: in the first place, the original allottees appeared to have based their claims only on the fact that they were the original occupants; on the other hand, the new occupants' claims invoked the idea that the state has a general obligation to act fairly, and, more importantly, that the new occupants have a set of legitimate expectations of the state. New occupants also asserted that they were part of the community that had been asked to leave the premises prior to its demolition, had been put up in tin sheds on the adjoining street on the promise of the new building construction, and therefore had a claim to being rehabilitated in the same space. The BBMP, in its arguments against this claim, maintained that 'legitimate expectations' were only the expectation of some benefits and they did not amount to rights, and therefore were not enforceable. The idea of 'legitimate expectations' also could not be used to construct a notion of what could be the state's fairness towards its citizens. The BBMP took the decision that the new occupants would be moved to a village in Anekal district where a new housing complex would be built for them. In doing so, the moral imperative laid down in the Supreme Court judgment that in situ housing should be provided wherever possible was clearly being set aside.

The other domain of contestation brought up by the EWS quarters site was the debate over the PPP concept, broadly speaking, and the role of Maverick Company, which owns Garuda Mall, more specifically. Several NGOs criticised the idea of PPP as entirely inappropriate in this context: the space that could be used for housing the poor would be constricted as half of the available land would be used by the company for commercial purposes. NGO leaders underlined that the battle over EWS in Koramangala underlines that 'actually there is no scarcity. It is the rich who have encroached', thus creating the scarcity.

The government has money only to build houses, not to buy land on behalf of the poor. JNNURM has two parts: Infrastructure (for which land is always found) and BSUP (for which land is never found). The idea of ghettoisation is important. Through relocation, large numbers of Dalit communities are being taken and put in the peripheries where housing projects are being executed.[5]

Following the eviction of 900 families from the EWS site, the Housing and Land Rights Network (Delhi) and PUCL (Karnataka) brought forth a fact-finding report. This report highlighted that the number of planned apartments at the site had been reduced from 1,640 to 1,512. In the 15.64 acres of BBMP land available in Ejipura, Maverick was supposed to build EWS quarters on 8 acres and the remaining 7.64 acres of commercial land was to be shared between BBMP and Maverick. According to the agreement, half of the area of the commercial space (3.83 acres) would be transferred to the developer following the completion of the project. While the owner of the Garuda Mall claimed that he would be the owner of the 3.82 acres after the title was transferred to him, BBMP claimed, at least in public, that this was not a transfer of ownership, as the land must be returned to the BBMP after 30 years. The conflicting interpretations are in themselves interesting: the definition of PPP typically is that the asset is returned (by the private partner) to the awardee (state) at the end of the concession period, which is usually 25–30 years. The claims made by the owner of the Garuda Mall of actual ownership of the land in question signalled that specific agreements with developers can in effect move away from the basic principles of PPP.[6]

The contested nature of these claims and counter claims is reflected in the activists' resistance and the ensuing legal case. A group of NGOs, such as the Samatha Sainik Dal, Slum Jagruthu, combined with the Koramangala Development Committee, and with the leadership of a city advocate, Mr Narasimhamurthy, filed a case against the BBMP and Maverick. The case continued from 2010 to 2014 and finally went to the Supreme Court, where it is now pending. Even as a legal verdict is awaited, the PPP project has been negotiated between Maverick Company and the BBMP and the proposed construction has begun and is proceeding.

L. R. Nagar (in situ)

L. R. Nagar slum, part of the Koramangala slum cluster, has gone through multiple phases before the JNNURM redevelopment plan was proposed for the slum. Since the early 1970s, a large number of migrant and floating population in the city had found their way to this sprawling settlement of thatched one-room tenements on a low-lying area in Koramangala. Many had constructed their own thatched rooms. Despite the promise from local leaders that the land would be developed, there has been no work at all for several years.

During the chief ministership of Gundu Rao of the Congress (1980–83), about 250 small two-room apartments were constructed, although there were almost 3,000 households in the slum. In popular memory within the slum, the issue of housing was seemingly caught in a continuous rift between members of the bureaucracy on the one hand, and a political network represented by slum leaders and the local MLA on the other. Members of the bureaucracy appeared to be interested in bringing a housing project to the slum. However, local political leaders emerging from the slum, as well as the then MLA, wanted to maintain a direct relationship with the slum for votes on the basis of continuous promises.[7]

It was in this situation that the KSDB proposed, in 2005, a scheme of redevelopment of the slum under the auspices of the BSUP/JNNURRM. A large multiplex was built on a nearby plot of 6.7 acres of land, which was provided by the BBMP for construction. One side of the road is lined with 900 multi-storey apartments spread over several blocks. This multiplex presents an astonishing story of corruption and mis-governance, hopelessly inadequate infrastructure, and state indifference and neglect. Ironically, out of the 900 newly created apartments, only 400 have been occupied so far. There is no answer to the question of why, amidst acute paucity of decent housing, there should be unoccupied apartments. Slum residents as well as slum leaders uniformly stated that political parties and NGOs play a central role in apartment allocations. Several apartments, according to them, have been given to households who were not original members of the slum. The process of allotment then becomes both complex and contested, thus leading to the ironical situation where apartments are left vacant and locked for long stretches of time.

Those currently occupying these apartments uniformly reported the low quality of construction materials and unavailability of services. Historically, basic service delivery has been deeply flawed in this area. Until 1990, there had been open defecation. After an escalation of popular agitation on the issue of water and sanitation, the government had spent INR 2 crores on laying of pipes across the entire slum area. However, the supply of water remained extremely limited, and the situation did not change after the construction of the new buildings under BSUP. There is no regular water supply as Cauvery water is not available, no pump is provided, and BWSSB is the only source of water. The taps received water only once every alternate day at 2 a.m. Many apartments are not connected to an overhead tank, so water has to be manually pulled up. There are toilets but no doors, and toilets are not connected to any sanitation pipes. Electricity is available only through individual connections which some households have obtained for themselves. The slums are flooded every year and the poorly tarred roads lead to inevitable and continuous waterlogging.

An elderly woman lives in a ground-floor apartment with her aged and ailing father. Despite it being sunlit outside, the single, windowless room was dark. They had no electricity. The old man was on the floor in a half-upright position. The room was bare except for a few old clothes and rags. There was a tiny anteroom – supposedly the bathroom – in which the single tap looked dry. The woman showed us the small bucket in which she collects water from a tube well outside. The kitchen seemed unused and had just a couple of vessels on the floor, along with an old brick and coal stove. She told us that they receive rice free of cost from the fair price shop, which she cooks sometimes. Apart from that, they are dependent entirely on their neighbours who provide them with some food once a day, and the occasional cup of tea.

The other side of the road is occupied by ground-plus-one and sometimes ground-plus-two floor houses. The occupants of these latter types of houses were predictably the more affluent sections of the community. There are 600 individual units built under the RAY scheme. Under RAY, individual cash loan assistance of INR 4.26 lakhs was offered for building small houses. Several slum leaders stated that INR 1.50 lakh, on an average, had to be distributed among officials, contractors and politicians. Typically, a household would be left with INR 2.50 lakhs for the construction. However, they would still have to repay the entire loan of INR 4.26 lakhs. For this, the households frequently took loans or mortgaged the house. The corruption involved in the execution of housing projects thus left the urban poor indebted even though state policies were designed to provide financial assistance for construction of houses.

No one has been given the *hakku patra* or ownership rights as the land belongs to the BBMP. According to a leading city slum activist, who is also a long-term resident of L. R. Nagar slum, the housing projects

> have not been set up for human development or human dignity. It is not designed to change anything – there is the same squalor, dogs, mosquitoes. It is so congested that there is no space even for children to play. Only huts have been replaced by concrete structures.[8]

The slum represents a highly diverse community in terms of economic and social parameters. The largest majority belonged to the SCc. Like most of the slums examined in this study, there were a large number of households where the main earner worked in construction. If the occupational structure could be represented as a pyramid, construction work for men and domestic work for women would form its base. Many were self-employed at low earning levels, as flower sellers, vegetable vendors, push-cart sellers of plastic goods and stationary cart sellers of street food. Younger men who had received a few years of school education typically dropped out at class 10 or even below, and entered jobs as drivers, vehicle repairers and phone repairers, and a few who owned two-wheelers would work as delivery boys for app-based suppliers. At the higher end of the pyramid, however, were men who had somehow managed to scrape together a little capital to start a small business, typically of recycled paper, scrap, and so on. This small section of prosperity within the slum was inevitably represented by the higher castes: a limited number of Gowda and Naidu families have utilised their connections in the BBMP to receive contracts for solid waste management. Their incomes are relatively high, between INR 20,000 and INR 25,000 per month, and several have built three- or four-storeyed houses within the slum. The interest of this relatively prosperous group in staying on in the slum is closely related to the potential market value of the land that they occupy, looking at a possible future when ownership rights might be granted to them by the state.

Samatha Nagar slum (relocation)

Samatha Nagar slum is in Koramangala. A community of around 400 households were originally part of a large slum settlement in Ejipura on the northern side of Koramangala. In the early 2000s, a large fire had affected the entire settlement. Following discussions with the affected households and slum leaders, in which the Koramangala Slum Development Committee played an important role, the BBMP decided to provide 1.5 acres of land for reconstruction of the settlement in an adjoining plot in Koramangala called Samatha Nagar.[9] In the process of selection of households by the Urban Development Department, the claims of 102 households were rejected as they were found to be unstable or floating residents. Of the 294 households whose claims for housing were accepted, about 84 chose to stay back in Ejipura and finally just about 110 households moved to Samatha Nagar. These 110 households were provided small sites; the government provided building material, and houses were built by construction workers who were part of the slum. The houses are typically structured as consisting of a hall, a kitchen, a bathroom and a bedroom. The housing complex is built horizontally as most are one-storeyed houses. The settlement has concrete roads, storm drain and underground drainage. Finally, the *hakku patra* was provided in 2008–09.

A majority of the people in the slum are construction workers or domestic workers. A few youths work as drivers or at gas supply agencies. Members of the slum asserted that they now have the dignity of owning *pukka* houses. There is a sense of 'our house, our project'. After the fire incident, they lived in transit sheds, and 'with their own hands' they built the Samatha Nagar slum. Several infrastructural problems, however, cast a shadow on the slum's quality of life on an everyday basis, foremost of which is shortage of water. The BWSSB is the only supplier. Water is received only on alternate days for about three or four hours, but the supply is frequently disrupted. There is no alternative source of water. Supply of electricity is unstable and fluctuating, and the power supply is often disconnected. Water stagnates on the roads during rains due to their poor condition and quality.

These are, however, less challenging issues for the slum households than the emerging threat of being forced out or persuaded to sell. Over the last two decades, the threat to land has emerged whenever the promoters of any large project, either of the government or of private builders, have perceived the Samatha Nagar settlement as an obstruction to their proposed construction. Thus, in the early 2000s, when the National Games Village was being constructed, the BBMP wanted a part of the land that belongs to the slum. They had proposed shifting some of the households to another location. On that occasion, the slum residents resisted the BBMP successfully. In 2010, again, the residents rejected a proposal by the government to build a multi-storey complex as part of the BSUP as they already had the *hakku patra* and were interested in land-to-sky rights, not in apartments. Currently, for the third time, government officials are making efforts to shift the residents. Residents believe that these efforts are being made on behalf of Maverick Company, which has bought the adjoining land and wishes to extend its domain into the land now occupied by Samatha Nagar. It is in this context that Garuda Mall is now considered a huge threat to themselves by the Samatha Nagar slum residents. The owners of Garuda Mall (see discussion on EWS earlier) are already encroaching upon the locality under the land sharing and PPP concepts. Community leaders in Samatha Nagar slum voiced the fear that the company may succeed in splitting the slum over the issue of land. The fear centred around the possibility that if one person is offered, and he or she accepts, a lucrative amount (which could be between INR 10 and 20 lakhs), they may decide to sell, persuading their friends and associates within the slum into making a similar decision. An alternative strategy is that of slow eviction. There is now a claim being made by government officers that only 40 of the 100 households who shifted were original residents of Ejipura and were affected by the fire. The remaining 60 came from elsewhere and thus have no legitimate claims and can therefore be evicted. If this threat is carried out, the slum community will be reduced to less than half its strength, and it will be easy for the authorities to evict them under 'eminent domain' despite the fact that they have *hakku patra*s. In this context, the community perceives itself as constantly under threat from the government–Garuda Mall combine.

The Samatha Nagar slum focuses our attention on the many contradictions at the heart of the state in its relations with the urban underclass. The reasons why the residents of this slum was able to obtain the *hakku patra*, in a context in which most others fail, had to do primarily with the very small size of the community as compared to other slums within the same Koramangala cluster.[10] This made it possible for slum leaders to put forward the claims in a unified and coherent manner and, at the same time, state officials were prepared to consider and commit to awarding property rights given that the awardees were very few in number. The award of property rights to this small community thus did not threaten the land-based balance of power in the Koramangala neighbourhood, where large tracts of slum land belong to the municipal corporation. However, this balance of power changed with the state's invitation to the large real estate developer, Garuda Mall, through the PPP channel and resulted in increasing pressure on the Samatha Nagar community to surrender their rights to the land.

Ramanna Garden slum

Ramanna Garden slum is one of a cluster of six slums in the inner-city neighbourhood of Lalbagh, discussed in Chapter 6, which looked at livelihood and income of slum households. Here I focus mainly on land and housing issues in the slum. In contrast to the slums discussed here, which are relatively new settlements, Ramanna Garden slum of 450 households has existed for approximately 80 years, located right behind the busy commercial hub in the Lalbagh area. The slum was originally on disputed land, claimed by a private individual. It is currently owned by the KSDB.

Several households in the slum had been given Possession Certificates, issued to them in 2004–05 for a period of 15 years by the then JD(S) MLA Zameer Ahmed. After the period lapsed, there was no initiative by the government to renew the certificates. The households therefore lived in a somewhat undefined domain: their claims to stay could be substantiated both by the number of years they had lived there and by the previously received Possession Certificates; however, the residences could not be sold or even leased as the title deeds had not been transferred to the householders.[11] None of the government housing schemes, such as BSUP, RAY or PMAY, had reached the slum, and there was hardly any awareness regarding these schemes amongst householders. While a few slum dwellers were aware of the state government's willingness to offer INR 3 to 5 lakhs as support for constructing houses, neither NGOs nor local politicians had actually discussed this scheme with slum householders or explained to them the method by which to avail of the loan.

With growing families, the living spaces of each household have shrunk. The houses have a single room and a small kitchen space. Out of 450 houses, only about a 100 have toilets built within their houses. The slum has two public toilets that are not maintained adequately. Most households use the toilets in the nearby Purnima theatre, paying INR 5 per visit. There is now free water supply to the slum. However, taps and connections are damaged and are in a state of disrepair. While many of these houses are brick-and-concrete structures, they lack maintenance and even basic amenities. At the bottom of the housing pyramid in the slum, around 170 tenements are made up of plastic sheets spread on bamboo poles. With regard to the possibility of a loan of INR 5 lakhs from the KSDB to construct in situ, several households said that a new layout would have to be created, and the houses need to be rebuilt, as currently the land on which each house is situated is too constricted for any kind of rebuilding to be possible. The smallest houses were only about 5 × 7 feet or 4 × 8 feet in size and the larger houses would be just about double of this dimension. On the other hand, if a new housing layout comes to the slum, each of the households would be given a total area of 265 square feet. Most households would prefer new houses and the formation of a new layout.

The slum community was, however, deeply fragmented over the idea of a housing project. Those who have larger plots are not interested in the idea of a layout because the KSDB would distribute same-sized apartments, or equal pieces of land, to all. Within the slum, composed largely of single-storeyed, small houses, a few multi-storey houses could be seen. In the local jargon, these are known as 'ground plus 2 or 3'. There are about 75 of those and each is owned by individuals who live on one floor and accommodate or rent out to their own extended families on the other floors. Interestingly, some of these houses were seen along the periphery of the slum, which seemed to have extended the slum's boundaries. This was a process whereby vacant plots of land adjacent to the slum had been encroached upon, and when the original owner of the plot (typically, not a slum insider) showed up to challenge this, and sometimes even went to court, the encroacher negotiated a compensation. Therefore, the original owner lost their land but received a compensation. Typically, such encroachers, relatively moneyed and resourceful, had built vertically on the piece of land which they had gained. In several cases, households within the slum on the brink of some kind of financial crisis (brought on by ill health or death) sold their land and house to an outsider, or even an insider, and were forced to leave the slum (such deals are entirely on the margins of legality as the households do not have a saleable right to the house which they occupy). The new occupiers were seen to have built vertically to improve the living conditions within the house. Such occupiers, whether original residents or new entrants, and whether their houses are inside the slum or on the periphery, do not have the Possession Certificates relating to the plots. Understandably, as a group, they do not support the other residents in their demands for a new layout or for apartment buildings, not only because they would have to give up the larger units that they have built, but also because they are illegally occupying a plot, which they may be asked to surrender.

Finally, from the perspective of the larger house owners who do have Possession Certificates, the formation of a layout and apartments would dislocate their investment in larger units, as well as their more powerful position within the slum as occupiers of larger plots. Their concern, then, is to hold on to the plot of land, given its potentially huge value. Even if they cannot obtain selling rights, the units have considerable rental value. Thus, there has occurred a certain coming together of the larger plot occupiers, whether legitimate slum dwellers or encroachers, in jointly resisting any universalising housing scheme.

It is this smaller but relatively more prosperous group that also has networks with local politicians, police and the lower bureaucracy. In case of conflict between residents on the issue of land, the local police typically act on behalf of the larger owners. Local strongmen also are sometimes deployed to intimidate small householders. Even though the slum occupies land owned by the government (KSDB), the government fails to fulfil, or rather ignores, its responsibility of protecting the land against encroachments by private land holders. Therefore, in an ironic twist, the government-owned land is actually under the control of a handful of private homeowners as they decide the fate of the other households by preventing the formation of a layout.

Cement Huts slum

Cement Huts slum is one of the oldest slum settlements in Bangalore, having existed for about 70 odd years. Cement Huts is located on J. C. Road near the Lalbagh area. The slum consists of 400 households. Composed predominantly of a community of waste collectors, the slum has households that represent extreme poverty, low and irregular income, child labour engaged in scrap collection, and occupational and economic marginalization which appears to replicate itself across two or three generations. Over the years, however, several households have managed to pull themselves up into higher earnings through commercialised and organised scrap collection. The history and socio-economic profile of the slum has already been presented in Chapter 6. In the following, I present a discussion of the housing situation.

Most of the houses in the slum were in the 10 × 20 feet size bracket. About 25 houses were larger, and owners of these larger plots had also built vertically atop their ground floors. Some of the houses had two or three floors above the ground floor. Several owners of the larger houses said that they had built from their savings and own earnings. No external financial help had been available to them.

As in the case of Ramanna Garden, many of the smaller-sized, one-room houses are in a state of extreme disrepair and house large families across two or three generations. Residents in the slum had received Possession Certificates from a JD(S) MLA, Zameer Ahmed, in 2004. Since then, there had been no interventions in the slum in terms of housing projects, either by the government or the state. Neither the BSUP nor the RAY, the two central pieces of poor house legislation of this century, had reached the slum. A sum of INR 5 lakhs is now available to BPL families as interest-free credit for renovating or constructing houses. This scheme too had not reached the slum. The general opinion seemed to be that concerned representatives (elected councillors who are members of the city corporation) have little or no interest in making these loans available to the slum community, as their main interest is in continuing a relationship of dependence. When asked about problems in the slum, the uniform response across households was the word *mane*, which means house.

Slum leaders appeared to be aligned with or were members of the group which had constructed larger houses. They were of the opinion that there was very little interest in the slum in housing projects like RAY, or the formation of a layout, as the allotted space to each household would be extremely small, with no scope for expansion or modification. Additionally, the shared understanding about BSUP and RAY across low-income households in the city was that these schemes provided a single apartment with no saleable rights.

> Therefore, for us, vertical, individually constructed buildings only would be preferable; government should do a survey and find out what is the size of each household and construct houses accordingly. If they give us some money, then we can also add some amount and build the house. (Mr Venkatesh, leader in the slum)

In the community of 400 households, there were 25 such houses that were vertically built and through individual resources, which were a combination of earnings and loans. Mr Nagraj, a slum activist, said, 'The demand in general was for "land to sky", which includes ground plus two floors. They do not want apartments, nor do they want to convert to a layout.'

Households residing in the smaller houses had a somewhat different narrative. In focus group discussions with the women of the slum, it was revealed that each of these women lived in one-room tenements, and the number of people sharing this space could be as many as 10. As residents of a slum that is more than 70 years old, the women had been born and raised within it, married to men of the slum, and their adult children now lived in the same slum with their families. In several cases, it was found that three generations lived in the same one-room tenement.

Radhamma, a 50-year-old widow, lives with her daughter, Lakshmi, 30 years old. Lakshmi's husband is a daily-wage labourer at the nearby lorry stand where he works mainly as a head-load bearer. He sometimes also works as an electrician. He earns INR 200–300 per day. They have four children. This entire family lives with Radhamma in a house that has one room and a kitchen. They use the public toilets in the slum, paying INR 3 for each use.

Sitamma, a 55-year-old elderly woman in the same group, said that she too has a similar accommodation (one room with a small kitchen and no toilet) and 10 of her family members live there, including her four grandchildren. A third woman, 55 years old, in the group said that her home had no space for all the members and so some sleep outside.

Thus, households with large families and small, uncertain incomes did not have access to the resources (earnings and loans) that would enable them to build on the dream of 'land to sky'. While a housing project may be their only hope of improved living conditions, they were not aware that such an option was in principle available to them – through recently enacted laws like BSUP and RAY – nor were they in a position to fight for their claims by using the legal framework.

The households which own larger plots and houses, even though these are only 25 in number, set the discourse in the slum, control the flow of information and also control the channels of communication to the local corporator and the MLA. These households have successfully resisted the coming of housing projects, which they see as threats to their vested interest in slum land as well as their power within the slum. Why and how have they prevailed upon slum residents who live in smaller houses and support the idea of a layout? As more resourceful persons and opinion leaders, the former group have been able to persuade their less fortunate counterparts in the slum that if a housing project appears, the entire slum would be cleared, no transit accommodation would be provided, there would be no guarantee that every household would find housing in the new project, and, most importantly, once a housing project is accepted, the claim to own a piece of land would be in principle given up once and for all. As mentioned earlier, within the framework of housing projects, households are given a 10 to 15 years' renewable lease but not a sale deed. The basis of the power of the smaller group is not only political (links to politicians, which are used to help the slum dwellers in times of trouble, such as a water crisis or a real or imagined threat of eviction) but also economic, as several households have taken loans from these more prosperous members of the slum.

Housing policies and conflicting interests of the urban poor

The discussion above indicates a significant distance between the aspirations of the urban poor relating to housing/land and the responses of the state, both in terms of policy and execution. First, the central-government-enacted policies (across the JNNURM, RAY and PMAY) consistently looked away from slum households' long-standing demand for right to property in slums and provided only renewable leases without the right to sell. This position is echoed at the level of the state government, where, in providing apartment buildings with only tenurial security, the urban poor's demand for right to land was consistently ignored. Second, continuing poor basic infrastructure as well as the failure to provide the amenities which both JNNURM and RAY had stipulated (schools, *anganwadis*, polyclinics) signalled that housing is provided without any serious state commitment to improving slum dwellers' quality of life or opportunities. As an activist described the housing project, 'only huts were replaced by concrete buildings'. Third, successive governments' increasing openness to private builders to participate in slum redevelopment translated to scarce land in upmarket neighbourhoods of the city going to real estate developers who could then use part of the land for commercial purposes.

Chapter 5, on migrant slums, highlighted that migrants frequently lack voting rights in the city and do not feature in the radar of local politicians, thus accounting for their neglect in policymaking. The slums studied in this chapter represent a certain mix of new settlers with older, more entrenched communities. As the Koramangala cases showed, the state demonstrates varying and complex set of engagements with these communities: claims of migrant and floating populations to in situ housing were denied in the EWS community in Koramangala; in other cases, the state adopted a giving-with-one-hand-taking-with-another approach, thus providing housing but denying land rights, failing to provide basic services and other resources to occupants of new housing projects (L. R. Nagar); in yet another case, the state was instrumental in bringing a real estate developer to Koramangala, leading to the threat to the land on which slum residents had constructed their dwellings (Samatha Nagar); finally, in both Ramanna Garden and Cement Huts, which represented older slum communities, larger plot owners and better-off households resisted universalising housing schemes, and the majority of the poor households were either unaware of housing projects or averse to projects which would deny them the *hakku patra*. A common thread that runs through this range of state–urban poor interface is that housing projects, whether in policy or in execution, are not designed to address the real needs of the urban poor.

What explains slum communities' political powerlessness, their failure to get policies they want, or to hold officials accountable in the delivery of services? Chapter 5 has provided a discussion of political representation from these constituencies, highlighting a pattern of indifference to the plight and demands of slum dwellers across party lines. Some scholars have written about land as an emerging focal point that could provide a shared platform of urban underclass activism (Benjamin 2008, 2011; Sanyal and Bhattacharya 2011). This chapter has shown, to the contrary, that the land issue deeply divides slum dwellers, pitting migrants against old settlers, occupiers of small plots versus larger plots, or those who would benefit, even partially, from housing projects versus those who see universalising projects as taking away their power and privilege within the slum. The land question in fact brings to light the slum itself as a highly unequal structure rather than the homogeneous space assumed in state policies. Within this structure, a few households, who have higher incomes, occupy larger plots of land, have built vertically on their land to construct larger houses and enjoy positions of power and privilege (as money lenders, connected to local politicians). Insofar as they see universalising housing projects as a threat to their resources (larger plots and houses) and power, they are able to influence slum households' responses to such projects. The slum as a whole is either given insufficient information and remains indifferent about such projects or can even be made to turn hostile to such proposals. These positions, however, represent a fragile unity criss-crossed by multiple pulls and pressures, and shaped by the many-layered structure of interests that slum communities have in relation to urban land. Unequal access to slum land and the resulting inequities create a fragmented structure, such that even the claim for *hakku patra* – notwithstanding its widely shared demand – does not have a unified platform. This then creates a context where local politicians can play with these divisions within the slum communities to perpetuate the structures of deprivation and marginalisation. I take this theme up again in the conclusion which discusses alternative ways of imagining informal workers' politics.

Notes

1. According to the Karnataka Slum Development Board, the number of slums in Bangalore increased from 473 in 2003 to 597 in 2013. Official figures of the percentage of households living in slums is around 13.45 per cent. Civil society organisations have pegged this to much higher, at 25–35 per cent. See Madheswaran Vani and Kumar (2018).
2. The JNNURM has been implemented in Bangalore for more than a decade now. Between 2005 and 2009, a total of 73 slums (18 BBMP and 55 KSCB, or Karnataka Slum Clearance Board [later changed to Karnataka Slum Development Board, or KSDB]) came under the BSUP; 1,690 dwelling units were built in 18 slums and 14,754 in 55 slums (GOK 2009). In 2011, the total number of dwelling units approved was 19,984.
3. The slum areas are: Rajendra Nagar, with 950 families, shifted mainly from Jakkaraynakare, during 1970–80; L. R. Nagar, a huge settlement, with families who shifted during 1983–84, of 950 individual plots, where houses were built under RAY and 1,650 flats in multi-storey complexes; EWS quarters, with 1,512 households, who shifted during 1986–87; Ambedkarnagar, with 1,400 households that had shifted during 1987–88; Shastrinagar, with 227 families, who shifted in 1988 and Samatha Nagar, with 110 houses, shifted from Ejipura (after the fire) in 1993.

4. Meetings at the Action Aid Office, Bangalore, on 29 March 2018 with Khitish, Mr Issac and Mallar and meeting with Mr Selva of Slum Jagriti, at Koramongala, 17 March 2018.

5. An example cited by several members of the slum was that of S. Ramesh, a slum leader, who took the Possession Certificates from dwellers in order to pledge these to a bank to get INR 500,000 for building flats. However, the slum dwellers themselves were not sure as to which bank their Possession Certificates had been pledged to. A few unfinished houses were constructed and given to the slum dwellers.

6. Meeting with Mr Selva at Slum Jagruti office, 17 March 2018.

7. Between storm drain and the plot of land now being used for construction.

8. Discussions with members of the slum and particularly with Mr Sampath, slum leader, and Mr Nagraj, member of the erstwhile Koramangala Slum Development Committee, on 19 September 2018 and 25 September 2018 respectively.

9. Many of the householders themselves lacked clarity as to the nature of the document that they had received. Some considered it *hakku patra* (granting title deed) even though it was only for a limited period: 'We have received the *hakku patra* but it is specifically for a particular duration.' Thus, there was little awareness that a title deed confers a permanent and heritable right to ownership, which cannot be granted for a limited time frame.

10. In one case, the house had collapsed due to rains, and the household was living in a neighbour's house. The MLA and corporator had been approached for help, but no financial help had been offered.

11. Interestingly, over several visits to the slum, we were told by the slum leaders not to speak about the housing schemes during our discussions with the slum residents.

References

Benjamin, S. 2008. 'Occupancy Urbanism: Radicalizing Politics and Economy beyond Policy and Programs'. *International Journal of Urban and Regional Research* 32 (3): 719–29.

Benjamin, S. and B. Raman. 2011. 'Illegal Claims, Legal Titles and the Worlding of Bangalore'. *Revue Tiers-Monde* 2: 37–54.

Government of Karnataka (GOK). 2009. 'Status Report of the Karnataka Urban Infrastructure Development Finance Corporation (KUIDFC)'. Bangalore.

Kamath, L. 2012. 'New Policy Paradigms and Actual Practices in Slum Housing'. *Review of Urban Affairs* 47 (47–48): 76–86.

Madheswaran, S., B. P. Vani and Sanjiv Kumar. 2018. 'Slum Governance in Karnataka: Trends, Issues and Road Map'. Monograph No. 54, Institute for Social and Economic Change, Bangalore.

Pani, N., and C. G. Iyer. 2013. 'Evaluation of the Processes in the Implementation of JNNURM in Karnataka'. Karnataka Evaluation Authority, Planning Program Monitoring and Statistics Department, Government of Karnataka, and National Institute of Advanced Studies, Bangalore.

Peoples Union for Civil Liberties (PUCL). 2013. 'Governance by Denial'. Fact Finding Report by PUCL, 21–23 February.

RoyChowdhury, S. 2008. 'Slums and Civil Society: The Limits of Urban Activism'. In *Inside the Transforming Urban Asia: Processes, Policies and Public Actions*, edited by Darshini Mahadevia, 601–18. Delhi: Concept.

———. 2012. 'Civil Society and the Urban Poor'. In *Reframing Democracy and Agency in India: Interrogating Political Society*, edited by Ajay Gudavarthy, 73–92. London: Anthem Press.

Sanyal, K., and R. Bhattacharya. 2011. 'Bypassing the Squalor: New Towns, Immaterial Labour and Exclusion in Post-colonial Urbanization'. *Economic and Political Weekly* 46 (31): 41–48.

8

Women Workers in Bangalore's Garment Export Companies

The debate on employment has been outlined in Chapter 3, and I briefly highlight here that while the increasing share of services in GDP has made this sector central to the current phase of growth, there remain concerns that the share of services in creating employment has been relatively lacklustre. In this context, the drying up of manufacturing sector employment has drawn much attention. As manufacturing industries turn increasingly towards globally competitive, capital-intensive, and high-technology production, the question that has been asked is whether this trajectory is appropriate in a country where the majority of the workforce is still unskilled and therefore unemployable in technology-embodying domains, whether in manufacturing or in services.

In this context, the emergence of apparel exports as a labour-intensive, growing industry rings a very optimistic tone. Apparel production was an exclusive domain of the industrially developed countries until the 1970s or 1980s, when the relocation of the industry to less-developed countries and China began primarily in search of cheaper labour costs in a predominantly labour-intensive industry. The significant contribution of the ready-made garment (RMG) sector in terms of development of exports as well as generation of employment notwithstanding, the use of a largely female workforce in highly irregular and insecure wage and working conditions has cast a long shadow on the RMG sector. A critical discourse emerging from researchers, NGOs and trade unions has increasingly framed this industry, forcing, to some extent, the attention of international brands on the unfair conditions in factories across the Global South which produce for global apparel retail. However, ground-level conditions, in terms of wages and working conditions, remain poor and particularly so in the absence of collective bargaining mechanisms, aided by the indifference of governments and political parties (Mezzadiri 2016).

My earlier work on garment workers in Bangalore provided ethnographic accounts of the lives of women workers, touching on socio-economic backgrounds, worker households, aspirations and mobility (RoyChowdhury 2010, 2015). This chapter draws upon recent field research, conducted in 2016 and in 2018. Garment factories in Bangalore are spread across the city, with some concentration in older industrial areas like Peenya and Yeshwantpur in north Bangalore and Mysore Road in the west of the city. The research in 2016 was on women workers in garment industries who live and work mainly in the Mysore Road area of Bangalore. A small study was conducted in 2018 of single, young migrant women who come into the city from backward states like Bihar and Orissa to work in the garment sector. As researchers are typically not allowed entry into factories, meetings with workers were conducted at their homes and in the local offices of the Garment and Textile Workers Union (GATWU). The chapter provides a broad overview of Bangalore's RMG women, focusing on wages, migration, shop floor coercion, labour shortage in the industry and organisational avenues available to women workers. Interstate migrant workers' movement to Bangalore is facilitated by skill centres in their home states which, in alliance with garment factories in Bangalore, provide information about Bangalore's garment industry to rural young women and their families, provide free skill development as well as board and lodging in Bhubaneswar and Patna, and then arrange for their travel to Bangalore where they are employed in garment factories. The chapter reflects on the conditions of work, alienation at the workplace and their lack of choice, as new and very young women migrants, in terms of looking for alternative employment.

Main features of RMG industry in India

The RMG industry is a rapidly growing sector. World garment exports jumped from USD 412 billion in 2011 to USD 708 billion in 2014. Currently, Asia dominates garment production. The top garment-exporting countries are China, Bangladesh, India, Turkey and Vietnam, while top garment-importing countries are the European Union, USA, Japan and Canada. The RMG industry is predominantly labour intensive. Evolving, particularly, at a point in time (late 1980s) when blue-collar manufacturing sector jobs were rapidly drying up, the RMG sector offers a large and potentially growing domain of factory-based employment to an expanding urban workforce. Important features of the industry include a large percentage of female employees and a globally integrated production and distribution system.

Of the 15 top world exporters of RMG, India (3 per cent) and Bangladesh (5 per cent) are third and second, respectively, behind China (38 per cent).

India's exports of RMG increased exponentially from USD 8.5 million in 2005–06 to USD 40 million in 2014. In 2016, RMG exports constituted 3.5 per cent of total exports from India. The apparel industry contributes significantly to the economic development of many developing countries. Between 1974 and 2004, the Multifibre Arrangement (MFA) heavily regulated this industry. Since the total abolition of the MFA in 2005, competition in apparel trade has increased manifold.[1] While textiles contribute over 15 per cent of exports from India, the RMG sector contributes over 40 per cent to textile exports, employing over 12 million people.[2] The industry operates mainly in the informal sector, with varying degrees of regulation of wages and working hours. While the textile industry is one of the oldest in India, production of ready-made apparels for export is a relatively recent phenomenon, dating to the mid-1980s. There are around 30,000 garment manufacturing companies in India producing just for export. Of these, about 5,000 are in the medium to large range. About 96.57 per cent of women workers and 86.39 per cent of the men are in the unorganised sector in this industry. Estimates from government labour department sources and from trade unions place the employment in the garment export factories at around 5 lakh workers each in Karnataka, Tamil Nadu and the NCR. Thus, given the total employment in the sector in India is around 20 lakh workers, about three-fourths of the export production is concentrated in these three regions (Deshpande 2015; Stotz and Kane 2015).

The dynamics of the RMG industry in India are closely related to the issue of migration. The majority of workers in the industry are recent migrants (GATWU 2012b; Mani 2018). The character of the migrant workforce in this sector appears to vary from region to region in the country. In north India, particularly in the NCR – a major hub of the RMG sector – the workforce is predominantly male, while in the south, particularly in Karnataka, close to 90 per cent of RMG workers are female. The pattern of migration is expectedly different in these two regions. In Karnataka, women migrant workers in RMG most typically have migrated with family from different parts of Karnataka. For most, the immediate destination or purpose of migration might not have been the RMG sector, but, as part of a low-income, unskilled workforce moving from rural areas to Bangalore, frequently with only 10 years or less of school education, many of the women eventually found work in RMG factories. This has been the typical trajectory of women who are employed in the RMG industry in Bangalore.

Recently, a new trend is seen (discussed in greater detail later) whereby women from other states are employed in Bangalore's RMG industry, and while some have come with their families, there is also an emerging pattern of young unmarried women from Orissa, Bihar, Chhattisgarh and Jharkhand coming here with the specific purpose of working in the RMG sector, and who live in hostels set up by the companies themselves. In the NCR, in contrast, the trajectory of migrants appears to be different, as predominantly single men travel from different parts of north India (UP, Bihar) to find work in RMG, put in long hours at work and live in spaces shared by men similarly employed. Many remain in this situation for several years, unable to bring their families to the city because of inadequate wages and high costs of living.

The RMG sector is therefore clearly one which interstate as well as intrastate migrants use to gain a foothold in cities. It is well known that the large majority of unskilled migrant workers are pushed into the construction sector, where wages are low, working conditions are unregulated and access to social security is minimal. Migrant workers are also found in highly vulnerable occupations such as scrap collection, street selling, service work in low-end eateries, street cleaning, and so on. In that context, does the RMG sector – insofar as it fills a vacuum in the rapidly declining scenario of manufacturing sector employment – provide a viable livelihood for the typical rural-to-urban unskilled worker, particularly women?

The RMG industry in Bangalore

The garment and apparel manufacturing industry in India is spread across several states, with the principal centres being Gurgaon (Haryana), Mumbai (Maharashtra), Bangalore and surrounding districts (Karnataka) and Tirupur (Tamil Nadu). Karnataka – Bangalore in particular – has been a central player in the growth of garment exports in India. In the last three to four decades, IT and garment exports have been at the forefront of Bangalore's economic growth. The RMG industry, which has an annual business turnover of thousands of crores, is composed of small, medium and large garment export units, employing workers as many in number as 500 to 50,000. The garment units are spread across locations along the outlying areas to the north and west of the city. In recent times, with increasing business and rising costs of running units within Bangalore city, the industry has spread to districts and towns around the city such as Ramnagaram, Doddaballapur, Nelamangala, Tumkur, Maddur, Mandya, Shivamogga, Hasan and even as far as Mysore. According to government estimates, there are 900 recognised garment manufacturing units in the city of Bangalore alone, with a total workforce of 355,000. According to trade union and NGO estimates, there are over 1,500 units, small and big, employing more than 500,000 people, of which over 85 per cent are women, with an overwhelming number working at the shop floor level.

In Delhi and Mumbai, which are two important hubs of the apparel industry, large segments of the industry had begun predominantly as home-based production units. In these cities, the transition to factory-based production is relatively new, and the industry still remains tied to outsourcing to home-based production units. In Bangalore, on the other hand, the specific character of the industry is that it has been factory-based from the beginning and there is a process underway whereby larger units are emerging on the basis of acquisitions and mergers and, at the same time, the industry remains essentially diverse in terms of structure, with a large number of firms employing as few as 50–100 employees.

Inserted into the global supply chain of apparel production, the RMG industry in Bangalore demonstrates that globalised production processes, while providing employment to unskilled labour, also produce deep pockets of poverty and deprivation. Regulated, in principle, through a Minimum Wage Board and formal wage revisions, the RMG industry nevertheless employs a workforce that is, largely, non-unionised and footloose. This is also a predominantly female workforce, comprising young and first-generation migrants to the city. The dynamics of this industry highlight the deep structural conflicts between this workforce on the one hand, and local producers and global retailers on the other.

The tailoring industry was brought into the ambit of the Minimum Wages Act (1948) in 1979. Accordingly, in Karnataka, the minimum wages in this sector are fixed and revised by a Minimum Wage Board. In principle, a Minimum Wage Board is responsible for the revision of fixation of wages every three years in this sector. However, after the Wage Notification of 2001, there were no revisions until a Minimum Wage Notification appeared in 2009. While it brought a few much-awaited revisions, the industry failed to implement these for over a year. In response to legal proceedings initiated by GATWU, the labour department issued a new notification in March 2010, diluting the provisions of the 2009 notification. The claim put forward by the labour department was that there had been a 'clerical error' in the 2009 notification. GATWU moved the High Court on the 2010 notification and obtained a judgment quashing the notification. According to GATWU members, by not complying with the 2009 notification, without even a challenge in court against the notification, the industry had clearly violated the Minimum Wages Act.[3]

Since 2010, minimum wages have been regularly revised in the RMG sector (Table 8.1). However, the implementation of minimum wages in this sector has remained faulty, and the stipulated minimum wage itself remains

Table 8.1 Minimum wages (in rupees)

Year	Skilled per day	Skilled per month	Unskilled per day	Unskilled per month
2010	166	4,240	156	4,056
2013	282	7,072	272	7,332
2015–16	307	7,982	287	7,462

Source: PUCL et al. (2016).

below that of other categories of scheduled employments. In 2010, the minimum wage for skilled workers was INR 4,240. A survey conducted by GATWU in 2012 revealed that amongst skilled workers the average salary drawn was INR 4,502, thus indicating that many were getting much more than the minimum wage. For unskilled workers, the minimum wage in 2010 was INR 4,056. However, as many as 45 per cent were receiving less than INR 4,056 (GATWU 2012b).

The Karnataka government had issued a preliminary Minimum Wage Notification for the garment sector on 22 February 2018. This had brought the minimum wage in the garment sector up to INR 15,000 per month. However, in the first week of April 2018, the government withdrew the notification. The reason cited was that in their representations to the government, factory owners had stated that the increased minimum wage would make garment manufacturing uncompetitive in Karnataka. This recent case of withdrawal, as well as similar instances earlier (mentioned before), clearly indicate the state's closeness to and compliance with the industry and signals a clear pattern of state indifference to the plight of RMG workers.

What needs to be highlighted is that the minimum wage itself is a deeply contested construct. A recent report, 'Critiquing the Statutory Minimum Wage: A Case of the Export Garment Sector in India', provides a discussion of the ways in which the statutory minimum wage fails to take account of certain realities of the lives of garment workers in Bangalore (Mani 2018). For example, in the computation of the minimum wage, house rent is considered as INR 600 per month, whereas, in fact, the rent for a one-bedroom accommodation, even in the EWS neighbourhoods is nothing less than INR 3,500 and can easily cost about INR 6,500. Similarly, in order to define the minimum wage, the family size is assumed to be composed of one earning adult, one dependent adult and two dependent children. The study highlights that a significant number (19 out of 85 respondents) reported that they had five–seven members.

Often, the RMG worker is the sole wage earner of the household. While the average wage earned was INR 8,000 per month, 14 respondents from a sample of 85 (in the study mentioned earlier) reported that they were the sole wage earners in their family. In this group, 11 of the women had dependent children, 8 were the sole adult member of the household, 10 were in the age group of 40–50 and one was as young as 28. Most of them, the study reports, inherited the responsibility of bringing up their families on their own at a relatively young age. Apart from single-women-headed households, it needs to be highlighted that RMG women workers, even when they are part of a household in which ostensibly there are two incomes, in reality are often single earners or are often called upon to be the sole providers in situations where their husbands do not have a regular income or, as is frequently the case, may have an income which they do not bring home as the men may have some kind of addiction or the other. Thus, in successive surveys, RMG women have reported that they need to augment their income from the factory with extra income which they get through other work, such as stringing and selling garlands, taking in additional tailoring work at home, and so on (Murayama and RoyChowdhury 2006; GATWU 2012a). These considerations, drawn from systematic observations of workers over a period of time, indicate that the minimum wage is not designed to meet the real needs of workers.

Wages, work and lives of garment workers in Bangalore

Wages

Garment factories in Bangalore are spread across the city, although there is some concentration in old industrial areas like Peenya, Yeshwantpur and Mysore Road. This section draws from a study of 117 workers that was carried out in the Bomanahhali and Mysore Road areas where it is possible to find neighbourhoods with a concentration of garment workers. The age group of the women was 25–50, with most in the 30–35 range. Each woman who participated in the study was married and had migrated to Bangalore 10–15 years ago with their families, either before or after marriage. Information on wages received, drawn from the survey of 117 workers, is presented in Table 8.2.[4]

This survey does not provide the break-up between skilled and unskilled workers. However, one can assume that those in the bottom-most categories were unskilled (in 2016, INR 7,462 was the minimum wage for unskilled workers and INR 7,982 was the minimum wage for skilled workers), wherein 21.4 per cent were receiving amounts below INR 7,000, which is well below

Table 8.2 Wages received (in rupees)

Wage	Frequency	Percentage
Up to 7,000	25	21.4
7,000–500	28	23.9
7,500–8,000	29	24.8
8,000–500	18	15.4
8,500–9,000	12	10.3
9,000 and above	5	4.3
Total	117	100

Source: Survey of 117 RMG women workers conducted by the author through GATWU, August 2016.

the minimum wage, and 23.9 per cent were receiving wages in the range below to just above the minimum wage (INR 7,000–7,500). Twenty five per cent were receiving wages just above the minimum in both skilled and unskilled categories, while 30 per cent were receiving wages above the minimum for skilled workers. These findings confirm our earlier studies where it was found that about 28 per cent workers received below the stipulated minimum wage (RoyChowdhury 2010, 2015). The 2016 study also found that about 45 per cent workers do not get paid for overtime work. A more recent survey conducted in Bangalore and surrounding areas found that the average wage for RMG workers is INR 8,000 per month. Interestingly, the same study found the average wage currently in the RMG sector in the NCR to be around INR 11,000 per month. In the NCR, the workforce in RMG is predominantly male and working hours are much longer. While the working hours in Bangalore are in the range of 48 to 60 hours per week, in the NCR it is 68 to 80 hours per week, according to the survey (Mani 2018).

A footloose workforce?

Earlier research has recorded that the garment industry is marked by a high rate of turnover, quick movement from one factory to another as well as movement from RMG to other jobs in the informal sector, often even less paid, but work which is less strenuous and stressful (typically domestic service). My recent research confirmed these trends. It was found that only 22 per cent had worked in their present factory of employment for more than seven years, whereas 77.8 per cent had worked in present factory of employment for less than seven years (Table 8.3). Almost 60 per cent had worked in other garment factories before they came to their present employment (Table 8.4). The industry as a whole is marked by quick turnovers. The reasons for movement were varied. However, as Table 8.5 shows, for close to 15 per cent of the women, harassment, low salary and lack of promotions were reasons for shifting factories or leaving the industry, while for 7.7 per cent, the company's closure was responsible for their exit. Thus, together, for 22.2 per cent, factors related to the structure of the industry were responsible for the workers moving out of their employment in a particular factory or in the industry. Notably, 41 per cent of the women did not wish to give a reason for their exit, which may be related to not wanting to talk about harassment in the workplace and its specific forms. Coercive supervisors, a highly regimented work environment where the worker's every moment is under surveillance, and sexual harassment are widely recorded features of the RMG sector. In a recent interview, a member of the GATWU described the experience of women workers in RMG factories as 'production torture'.

Table 8.3 Frequency distribution of number of years working in current garment factory

	Frequency	Percentage
Up to 1 year	14	12
1–3 years	24	20.5
3–5 years	29	24.8
5–7 years	24	20.5
7–10 years	14	12.0
10–15 years	8	6.8
Above 15 years	4	3.4

Source: Author's survey, 2016.

Table 8.4 Worked in another garment company

	Frequency	Percentage
Yes	69	59.0
No	48	41.0
Total	117	100

Source: Author's survey, 2016.

Table 8.5 Reasons for shifting to other factories or out of the industry

	Frequency	Percentage
Marriage and childcare	15	12.8
Health	3	2.6
Distance	11	9.4
Family and personal problems	7	6.0
Harassment	4	3.4
Less salary	9	7.7
No promotion	4	3.4
Closure of company	9	7.7
Others	7	6.0
No answer	48	41
Total	117	100

Source: Author's survey, 2016.

Health, hygiene, shop floor coercion and 'fear'

A repeated complaint from workers, reported in several studies, has been about the lack of basic physical amenities in the workplace. Many women reported not only the lack of proper toilets but also the time constraint in being allowed to use the toilet, that their time spent in the toilet was monitored by the shop floor security guard who noted the timings and ensured they returned soon. If she did not, the matter was reported to the management and a warning was issued. Further, the manager and supervisor's offices were located opposite the washroom so that they could keep a check on the amount of time spent on a toilet break (Mani 2018).

Garment workers are vulnerable to several occupational health hazards: backache, headache, knee pain, asthma and menstrual problems, several of these caused by the hazardous nature of work performed by them. This requires them to receive regular medical treatment. Although it is mandatory for any factory employing more than 500 workers to ensure the provision of a nurse, doctor and an ambulance, these are not provided. Workers from Shahi Exports in Mysore Road reported that although a nurse was present at the factory, very few medicines were available with her and for any ailment, only pain killers were provided. No ambulance, doctor or other emergency health assistance was available. Despite the availability of a resting room, the nurse discourages the workers from using it for more than 10 minutes.

Workers from Gokuldas Exports (Triangle Apparels) at Gorguntepalya, Tumkur Road, reported that the nursing room in the factory had no medicines; on several occasions, workers collapsing from exhaustion and fever were given no medical treatment but were sent back home, losing their day's wages. Further, workers also spoke about the difficulties faced by them in accessing treatment under the Employees' State Insurance Scheme (ESI). Most women garment workers reported that the ESI hospitals did not function properly, as a result of which they were forced to seek medical assistance from private hospitals and bear the expenses of the same (Mani 2018).

Framing these very obvious gaps in the physical infrastructure of what is available to garment workers is a broader environment of coercion, fear and force that plagues the work life of a woman in a garment factory. On an everyday basis, stiff and non-negotiable production targets set the tone for the day. It is this target – determining the time allowed to them at the toilet and for lunch – which, if the worker fails to reach, brings on the floor supervisor's relentless fury.

Closely interwoven with this 'production torture' (PUCL et al. 2016), as the workers call it, is the issue of gender, wherein, in every factory, women workers face a hierarchy of male managers – the in-charge, the floor supervisor, the unit HR (Human Resource), the HR general manager and, finally, the top-level directors and general managers. The enforcement of production targets that happens through this hierarchy very often involves gendered aggression by male supervisors through the use of objectionable verbal language, aggressive body language, physical punishment such as making a woman stand for hours without giving her work, or pushing a table or instrument at her in anger, sexually suggestive comments and behaviour, and even demands for sexual favours. This combination of tough production targets (enforced through shouting, intimidation, humiliation and punishment) and a gendered atmosphere facilitating sexual harassment in both overt and indirect forms creates a situation where few women survive in the same company for more than a few years.

Being first-generation, rural or semi-rural young women workers, women in RMG lack the history and language of resistance to the management. A culture of subservience generally prevails; resentment and bitterness rarely get expressed as resistance or complaints to management and do not reach visiting inspectors from brands or from the government, who typically receive uncritical testimonies by compliant worker representatives.

Out-of-state migrants in the RMG industry

Migrant women workers in RMG from other parts of Karnataka typically come to Bangalore as part of families or accompanying their husbands; the garment industry is not necessarily their only or specific destination, and they may look for employment anywhere else (as unskilled women workers, their typical occupational options are domestic service, home-based tailoring, *bidi* rolling, and so on) before choosing to work in garments, or may quit the industry to do other work.

In contrast, a new pattern is now seen of young, out-of-state women brought in to Bangalore with the specific purpose of providing them with employment in the garment sector. Several garment export factories have adopted the practice of hiring women workers from other states.[5] Bihar, Orissa, West Bengal and Chhattisgarh appear to be the states from which garment workers are being recruited. Out-of-state women workers thus come into the city with the specific purpose of working in the RMG industry. As young migrants who have come to Bangalore unaccompanied by family members and with the factory as their only link to the city (the factory provides work as well as accommodation in hostels), the women have little resources in terms of occupational or social networks and remain tied to the employer in multiple dependencies.

Research conducted in 2018 studied a group of 25 women from Bihar and Orissa aged between 18 and 23 who have migrated alone (that is, not with families). They lived in rented flats or in hostels in Bomenhalli in the Mysore Road area in west Bangalore. The accommodation had been rented by the company that they worked for, and the women had to pay INR 500 each towards rent. Interestingly, each of the young women had more or less the same story to relate. Mostly hailing from a village in Orissa called Noapara, and from Rohtas, a village in Bihar, the women were educated up to class 10 or 12. Their families had been approached by the Deen Dayal Upadhyaya Grameen Kaushalya Yojana (DDU-GKY) with the promise of free skilling, followed by employment in good export companies in Bangalore. After agreeing to enrol, they had moved to Bhubaneswar and Patna, had been provided free board and accommodation and had received two months of free training from the DDU-GKY outlets in these cities. Upon completion of the training, they were met by an HR official of the company in Bangalore which eventually employed them. Formally recruited by this official, the women were then given train tickets, were received at Bangalore station and were put up in accommodation provided by the company. The shared accommodation ranged from three to ten women per room, depending upon the size of the room. While the rent was subsidised by the company, the women were responsible for making arrangements for food, for which a kitchen was provided.

The socio-economic position of these young women leaves many questions unanswered for development scholars and practitioners. Each woman belonged either to a Scheduled Caste or Tribe. In terms of education, most had studied up to class 10, some up to class 12 and only one was a graduate. Almost uniformly, their parents were landless agricultural labourers, unable to make ends meet. Several of the young women described their families as being on the brink of an economic crisis, mostly brought on by events like unmanageable debts, being unable to bear the costs of their children's education beyond a few years of schooling, or a family member's medical treatment. Their encounter with officials of the DDU-GKY at such junctures in their lives led them to take the decision to send their daughters to an unknown city to earn a living and support their families.

The two-month training that the young women received culminated in their current job. After completion of six months of work, they would be entitled to a certificate. With this certificate, in principle, they could move elsewhere or back to their home states. However, the garment industry is confined to a few cities in the north and the south, and is not found in the eastern states the women come from. In terms of remuneration, as they had all started at the factory at the same time, their pay was more or less the same, ranging from INR 7,000 to INR 9,000 every month. They were not aware of schemes like provident fund or ESI. Each of them sent a large portion of their salary to their families in Bihar and Orissa.

Although young and working, the women had little time or money to spare for any kind of entertainment or enjoyment. Their weekly off days were confined to doing household chores, shopping for vegetables and provisions, and washing clothes. They were aware that the city had attractions like malls and movies, but low earnings did not permit them to be a part of urban leisure, consumption and entertainment.

Within the framework of the workplace, their work was limited to their given functions without any opportunity to learn more and improve their occupational standing. The young women lacked any understanding of the concept of mobility within the workplace. As one of them put it: 'ek-hi kaam karna hai' (we have to do only one kind of work). Thus, within a very short time, they had imbibed a certain dullness associated with work, as day after day they repeated the same functions (stitching buttons, cutting threads) which did not involve them in the actual shaping or creation of a garment. Thus, monotony and lack of mobility were the important features of the work environment, and each of these features was replicated in their lives beyond work as described here.

The women's sense of alienation in a strange city was compounded in the workplace, where language was an important element in their feelings of fear and threat from the supervisor. Lack of communication and the inability to understand instructions often led to supervisors shouting at them; the strangeness of the language made this aggression even worse. The young workers reported that they would not mind being hit instead of being subjected to foul language. Within the shop floor, a linguistic and age-related divide had emerged naturally, as older women workers were Kannadiga-speaking locals while the younger cohort were primarily drawn from out-of-state migrants. The older women, although employed as unskilled workers, had the advantage of experience in the workplace; more importantly, they were part of families and households belonging to a local community. These connections provided important networks of information about vacancies in other garment factories, or other jobs, which opened up a space of options for these women. In contrast, the younger Hindi-speaking women were isolated as a group within the shop floor, with little access to information about other factories, alternative sectors of employment, and so on. This generated feelings of being trapped in the place of work.

While reticent about expressing any criticism of the employer, several of the young women said that as they were not educated ('we did not study well', 'we did not study in college'), they had to continue working in the same place to meet the needs of their families. A frequently shared regret was that there was no work in the village where they had lived, or even in the nearby towns, and that if there were similar opportunities in their village, they would not have considered migrating to another place for earning. In a group of 25 women, 10 had lived in Bangalore for over one year. Whatever the length of stay, none of the women had any wish to settle in Bangalore or even to continue staying there beyond a limited period, which they saw as just one or two more years. The reason cited for wanting to go back was uniformly that their family was at their village. They all cherished dreams of 'going back home and living in peace'. However, what was remarkable was that the city had not in any way struck the imagination of these young women. Their migration and urbanisation were confined to a single road, where they lived and worked; the lights of the city did not feature in, or even reach, their aspirations.

This story of migration is distinct from other channels through which temporary or even circular migration happens, for example, that of construction workers. Migrant construction workers move from site to site, as well as maintain a regular cycle of movement to their villages of origin – during harvests, festivals and to take care of families left behind. This facility of movement, between projects and temporarily quitting to return to the village, makes for an inevitable set of instabilities, but at the same time provides a certain space to negotiate their lives within the framework of urban informal work and habitation. Additionally, migrants in construction are typically part of large communities of such workers hailing from particular regions or villages. In contrast, young migrant garment workers in Bangalore, hailing from the eastern states, are a small and isolated ethnic community; more importantly, they are pinned down for the first six months of employment until they receive their training certificate; beyond the first six months, too, they find their work and lives tied to a single employer with little scope of movement.

There are two points to highlight here. First, from the supply side, the economic vulnerabilities of rural households in backward states like Bihar and Orissa provide the context whereby a large and continuous supply of unskilled labour is made available by means of minimal intervention of two months of skill development. It was clear from the discussions with the women workers that they had come to work in Bangalore only because there were no opportunities of work in their home states. Therefore, given the conditions described earlier (low wages and coercive working conditions), it is not surprising that many would eventually leave.

Second, in terms of demand, it was clear that this pattern of migration was the result of a coordinated set of activities between the government agency (the DDU-GKY) and the garment companies in Bangalore who are keen to recruit labour from rural areas of backward states. The coordinated activities of officials of the DDU-GKY began with planned visits to the most backward districts, followed by consultations with the *gram panchayat*, which help them to identify families in distress in the village; from then on, engaging with the families to provide information and encouragement to send their daughters to skilling centres in Bhubaneswar and Patna, holding out the promise of a job in Bangalore. What comes thereafter – the short skilling programme, followed by the visit of the Bangalore companies' HR personnel and the eventual placement of the young women in garment factories in Bangalore – can be seen as part of a design not only to provide skilling and employment, but also to meet the needs of the industry for low-cost labour. Post skilling and placement, the certificate of training was given to the young workers only after completion of six months of employment. This ensured that a trained workforce would be available at least for six months; if and when some left, as they inevitably did, they would be replaced by a fresh group of trained workers. Thus, through this pattern of planned migration, the industry's continuous needs of a workforce were being met.

Labour shortage

Labour shortage is a perennially reported problem as far as industry managers are concerned, given the high turnover and a footloose workforce. Additionally, recent studies have found that the average age of women RMG workers in Karnataka is around 35, and a significant number of the workforce are women in the older age group of 40–50 years. This conforms to the views of trade unions and company management that the garment sector in Bangalore finds it difficult to attract younger workers in the city. Younger women prefer employment in the service sector where work and supervisor pressure is less and wages are slightly higher. In the context of the RMG industry, the planned supply of a young, female, out-of-state migrant workforce also ensured to factory managers a relatively compliant set of workers, thus allowing the industry to continue with the kind of wage and working condition practices that are detrimental to worker interests, as described here.

In any discussion of labour shortage in the RMG sector, it should be remembered that this is still an industry where 25–28 per cent of the workers do not receive the minimum wage, and most studies show that even the minimum wage, when translated into household per capita income (assuming single earners), would itself represent just a subsistence income (Mani 2012, 2018; RoyChowdhury 2010, 2015). Additionally, one would expect that with genuine shortage of labour, the workforce as well as trade unions in the industry would be empowered to press for higher wages. In this particular context, we find that neither the market (that is, the economics of supply and demand) nor activism has helped the workforce to bargain for higher wages or for adequate implementation of the minimum wage.

Therefore, where the labour shortage is clearly not translating itself into higher returns to labour, it highlights the need to take a closer look at the actual nature of labour shortage in this sector. In the first place, labour attrition is taking place more in the categories of unskilled labour than in skilled tailor categories. We find that wages earned by skilled tailors are frequently higher than the minimum wage in this category (GATWU 2012b).

Therefore, higher level of skills and wages are clearly making a difference in terms of a more stable workforce in the tailor categories. In the unskilled categories, pull factors – increasing opportunities in retail, ITES, receptionist and clerk jobs – have attracted young women away from the RMG sector. However, the expansion of such opportunities has happened significantly in south and central Bangalore, whereas in the northern and eastern parts of the city, Yeshwantpur and Peenya, RMG still remains only one of the two work options for unskilled women, the other being domestic service. Therefore, there is in fact a large actual and potential workforce still available for unskilled work in this sector, and the increasing availability of out-of-state young migrant women reinforces this availability. This explains continuing low wages and non-compliance with minimum wages. The instability of labour in this sector then is better described as frequent labour turnover than as labour shortage, that is, while many leave the industry, they are continuously replaced by the available labour force outside. The reasons for leaving the industry are largely internal to the industry itself, that is, low wages, harsh production targets, underpaid overtime work and coercive supervisors. These characteristic features of the industry have been discussed many times in the literature on RMG. The point to be underlined here is that, typically, labour shortage pushes wages up, both as a function of the market and as a result of workers' increased bargaining leverage, which has not happened in the case of RMG workers. In this case, then, a high turnover needs to be seen in terms of the exploitative nature of this global supply chain (GSR: Joint Fact Finding 2013). What describes the situation is workforce instability rather than labour shortage.

Collective action in the garment sector

The Garment and Textile Workers Union, Bangalore (GATWU), affiliated to a national-level organisation of the same name and to the New Trade Union Initiatives (NTUI), is the largest trade union in the RMG sector in Bangalore. The other two trade unions in this sector are the Garment Labour Union (GLU) and the Karnataka Garments Workers Union. Each of these trade unions has a history of originating from NGOs. It is important to highlight that in the early years of RMG exports in Bangalore, workers' issues in the sector were primarily addressed by NGOs. Foremost among these was Civil Initiatives for Development (CIVIDEP). Foundation for Educational Innovation in India (FEDINA), another city-based NGO, has also been active in this sector. CIVIDEP, which combines leaders drawn from middle-class activists with former RMG workers, provided significant leadership in the initial years, that is, from the late 1980s onwards. The primary concern of this NGO was to organise RMG women workers, focusing on their residential neighbourhoods. The organisation deliberately kept away from the factories, did not directly address wage-related issues and focused instead on activities pertaining to credit, basic amenities, awareness raising, and so on. Subsequently, there was a perceived need for imparting a more unionised character to workers' issues, leading to the formation of the GATWU in the mid-1990s.

GATWU has a national-level presence and is affiliated to the NTUI, which is a national umbrella organisation for unions working with informal sector workers. In Bangalore, GATWU works mainly on wage- and work-related issues. As union presence is not allowed within factories, most women workers are reluctant to engage in union-like activities. Collective bargaining is unknown in this sector. GATWU is the largest union in Bangalore in this sector; GATWU's membership currently stands at around 6,000 only, which is a miniscule proportion of the total number of women employed in Bangalore's RMG industry.[6] GATWU's functioning must be seen within the framework of these constraints.

As indicated earlier, 21 per cent of the RMG workforce continue to receive wages below the stipulated minimum. The RMG industry thus could be characterised as one where a framework of government regulations has been put in place, through the Minimum Wage Act and the Minimum Wage Board, but the implementation of this is hugely flawed. The efforts of GATWU have been towards establishing a space for collective bargaining. These efforts, however, are confined to negotiations with the Labour Department, being part of the Wage Board or taking up these issues in court. An important achievement for GATWU in recent years has been the securing of dearness allowance (DA) for workers who are paid above the minimum wage. Over the years, GATWU's most significant contribution has been to maintain a steady pressure for the upward revision of the minimum wage. In this, it has been successful as the minimum wages have been raised in both skilled and unskilled categories. The implementation of minimum wages, however, remains incomplete as 21 per cent in our sample were receiving less than the minimum wage, and 23 per cent were receiving wages in the range of INR 7,000–7,500, which is also low considering that INR 7,462 was the minimum wage (in this context it is relevant to mention that in Karnataka, the minimum wage has already been raised to INR 10,000 in 23 scheduled employments). However, as trade unions are not allowed to function from within factories, the union is handicapped in having no recourse to traditional collective bargaining mechanisms.

The constraints to collective bargaining are given in the broader politics of trade unionism as well as in the structure of the industry. Mainstream left trade unions such as the Centre of Indian Trade Unions (CITU) have not engaged in a sustained manner with grassroots issues in the RMG sector. For GATWU, the principal protagonist for RMG women, local-level struggles are centred around specific, sector or unit-level issues, such as implementation of minimum wage in a particular factory or protesting sudden dismissals or termination of individual workers. Such struggles are not linked to larger political mobilisations. Local struggles, then, are defined more in terms of advocacy at the level of government departments. In the absence of alliances with other unions and political parties, such struggles do not translate into an imagination of a moment of political resistance. In 2016, garment workers in Bangalore held a massive rally to protest a proposed change in the Employees' Provident Funds and Miscellaneous Provisions Act, 1952, which would prevent workers from withdrawing their provident fund before the age of 58. While the government withdrew the proposal, the movement did not extend to other issues, nor was the moment of struggle repeated in subsequent years.

In terms of the structure, the industry demonstrates conflicting tendencies. On the one hand, as has been mentioned earlier, there are signs of growth of mega companies, and a certain degree of centralisation and concentration is taking place.[7] Along with these features, in response to the industrial recession in the west and reduction of orders, the industry has moved towards 'just in time' production, smaller orders and shorter, more flexible delivery times. In this situation, it makes sense for the industry to move increasingly towards a flexible labour force, using home-based, piece-rated workers – in other words, adopting outsourcing as an employment practice. As such, even the largest companies hire up to 10–15 per cent piece-rate workers for short durations (Mani 2012).

Thus, the structure of the industry is marked by a predominantly non-unionised factory-based workforce, and additionally a workforce that is invisible due to its location outside of the factory, primarily in homes. Given the political as well as the structural constraints to collective action, the future of activism in this sector possibly lies in the small, albeit valuable, steps taken by GATWU so far.

GATWU's strategy of organising has, over the years, been impacted by the constituency that it handles. One of the biggest hurdles for the union has in fact been the small number of workers who are ready to be unionised. Of the close to 4 lakh workers in Bangalore, as few as 6,000–7,000 are actually unionised. For many years, GATWU had pursued a strategy of active efforts at unionisation. This involved both efforts to talk to women workers outside the factory gates and to locate them in their homes in order to enlist their membership. Primarily in response to the low record of unionisation, GATWU has now changed its strategy and no longer engages in direct efforts at unionisation. Instead, the strategy is to locate women workers who may play leadership roles on the shop floor, and to train them in ways in which they can communicate the value of unionisation to their fellow workers and thus increase the scope of unionisation. GATWU has in that sense stepped back from direct involvement with women workers and instead is relying upon a core set of leader-workers in each factory to spread the message of unionisation. It should be mentioned that low level of unionisation is at least partially a consequence of the fact that union activities are not permitted inside the factory gates. The only way to approach the women workers was to talk to them outside the factory gates or to meet them in their homes. Women workers are typically in a rush to get home, and, once at home, they are caught up in multiple commitments in terms of house work and family members. As such, the biggest challenge to the union, given the predominantly female constituency, is to set up the time and the space in which the women can be engaged in conversations about workers' issues, membership of the unions, and so on.

A second reason why the strategy has been changed – from direct dialogue with workers to reliance on worker-leaders – is that GATWU no longer has any full-time activists. In 2010, a serious internal conflict situation within CIVIDEP led to the splitting of GATWU away from the NGO. Thereafter, a second trade union, the GLU, came into being with the support of CIVIDEP. GATWU, now delinked from sources of funding which came from the NGO sector, has considerably diminished resources, both in terms of finances and manpower, as indicated earlier. But more importantly, given the existing constraints to unionisation, the emergence of two rival trade unions resulted in further fragmentation and weakening of the unionisation endeavour. It was also mentioned by GATWU leaders that a workforce which is already shy of union activities is rendered further confused when they are approached by two rival unions for membership and loyalties.[8]

RMG women workers in the shadows of the city

The plight of workers, particularly women workers, in the RMG sector has been widely reported, both in popular media and in scholarly work. The industry as well as the workforce raise several questions regarding the trajectory of industrial growth in developing countries, which have emerged as major hosts of this global supply chain industry. First, low wages, non-compliance with minimum wages, harsh working conditions and insecure tenures have characterised this industry for a long time. At the same time, it must be acknowledged that garment export plays a very useful role in providing employment to a large number of unskilled women with low levels of education, particularly in a context where factory employment is drying up. In this sense, the RMG sector typifies the situation which Kaushik Basu (2008) had posed as the dilemma between poverty and inequality: in other words, whether we should support an industrial sector which provides employment (and therefore addresses the issue of poverty) but at terms and conditions that are highly disadvantageous to the workforce (and therefore generates or escalates inequality). The RMG sector clearly typifies the horns of this dilemma, thrown up by the broader context of globalisation that made possible the emergence of this global supply chain in developing countries.

The second important dimension of this industry is its close connection with the issue of female labour force participation rate (FLFPR), an important indicator of development. In India, over the preceding two decades, the FLFPR has fallen from 34 per cent in 2006 to 27 per cent in 2018, and is higher than only Pakistan and Saudi Arabia.[9] In terms of the rural–urban divide, in 2016, the labour force participation rate for urban women was 14.2 and for rural women 14.7 per 100 women. In 2018, these numbers had fallen to 10.4 and 11.4 for urban and rural women respectively (Menon 2019). In Karnataka, the FLFPR, at 32 per cent (in 2018), is higher than the national average. However, there had occurred a notable decline in FLFPR in Karnataka after 2005. This was particularly sharp in rural areas, from 62 per cent in 1993–95 to 38 per cent in 2011–12. In urban areas in Karnataka, the decline in FLFPR was from 28 per cent in 1993–94 to 26 per cent in 2004–05 to 23 per cent in 2011–12. In the context of this decline, it is interesting to note that 53 per cent women in urban Karnataka held salaried jobs in 2011, whereas 43 per cent of urban men had salaried jobs (World Bank 2017). In Bangalore, the FLFPR in 2011 was 24.01 per cent, the lowest among other urban areas, for example, Shimoga (28 per cent), Dharwad (26 per cent) and Mysore (26 per cent) (Statista 2020). Declining FLFPR in India has generated a huge debate, and typically factors such as rising participation of women in education, rising household prosperity, and so on, are seen to lead women to withdraw from the labour force. This debate is beyond the scope of this chapter. However, the decline in female employment in urban areas in Karnataka can be seen in the context of the RMG industry, which is the largest employer of urban women in the state. A large number of women workers in the RMG sector can be described as footloose, that is, many quit the factory they work in, go into part-time domestic work or begin tailoring work at home. Or they may spend a year or even more without any work and ultimately join another RMG company. There is a great deal of horizontal movement between factories, interspersed with workers being without work or in part-time or home-based work. Successive surveys that have recorded this instability of the RMG workforce have also recorded the reasons for it, related predominantly to the nature of the industry, where working conditions are perceived by workers to be highly coercive, and they face a lot of gendered aggression on the shop floor. The point therefore is that the withdrawal of women from the workforce, in this particular sector, is clearly related to the structure and dynamics of the industry more than to other factors.

This chapter has provided a broad outline of the socio-economic and occupational situation of women employees in the RMG industry, drawing from field research conducted in Bangalore. The RMG industry provides much-needed employment to unskilled women, particularly those migrating to cities in search of work and income. However, the unregulated nature of the industry creates conditions wherein low wages and coercive working conditions continue to plague the industry. There are three important points that need to be highlighted here.

First, the limits to union impact stem from the structure and dynamics of the industry (unionisation is not permitted, the workforce is fragmented through outsourcing). The union therefore seems to be caught in a situation where it is attempting to wage what could be termed a classical or traditional workers' struggle, while the essential conditions necessary to construct this struggle are denied.

Second, the profitability of the industry clearly is tied to multiple ways in which management is able to squeeze the workforce for additional productivity and profits, through unpaid overtime, shop floor coercion, denial of termination benefits, and so on. However, if the union is limited in its scope to battle these issues, it is also constrained by the fact that the fundamental conflicts of capital and labour are never articulated as part of its discourses and actions. The union, therefore, is possibly walking a tight rope, where the structural features available to traditional trade unions (collective bargaining) are unavailable to it, and neither is the discursive space of a broader, political and ideological critique.

Finally, in Bangalore the industry occupies a shadowy space, which represents as well as contributes to its political marginalisation. This space is seen not only in terms of the location of the industry in what has been called the graveyard of a failed engineering sector, the Peenya Industrial Area (Mani 2012), but also in its very marginal representation in the city's public discourse. In Bangalore, IT and RMG can be said to have emerged around the same time, in the mid-1980s, as part of the changing developmental profile of the state, from the public to the private sector, from small-scale industries to large corporations, and to a definitive turn towards export as the catalyst of the city's growth. While IT supports the growth of a technically skilled middle class, the RMG sector offered employment to a large number of unskilled rural and semi-rural women. Both sectors, to a certain extent, have anchored the city's growth in the last four decades. However, the difference between these two domains in terms of visibility is indeed striking. IT and ITES are part of the public imagination of Bangalore as Silicon Valley, or Bangalore as the next Singapore, with iconic leaders of IT straddling the regional and national political spaces, and IT workers as the symbol of the face of India's future. The city's newest, most globally networked, business and luxury spaces are identified with IT. On the other hand, the RMG sector has rarely, if ever, stepped out of the shadows of the failed engineering sector. Industry leaders have no visibility or presence in the public domain, their reticence as least partially explained by the critical shadows that have from time to time publicly fallen on the industry's employment practices. A huge and powerless female workforce provides the silent and invisible backbone of a sector that is closely connected to the global apparel industry.

Notes

1. On the impact of the withdrawal of the MFA on the garment industry in India and other South Asian countries, see Murayama (2008), Hashim (2009) and Alam et al. (2018).
2. After the introduction of demonetisation and GST, domestically produced products became costlier and exports declined. The RMG sector's share in world trade in garment declined from 6 per cent in 2013 to 3.5 per cent in 2016. See RoyChowdhury (2018) and Narasimhan (2019).
3. Interviews with Mohan Mani, member of New Trade Union Initiative of India, and Shri Jayram, General Secretary, GATWU, Bangalore. August–December 2016, April–May 2018.
4. This survey was conducted in August 2016 by the author, with the help of GATWU, Bangalore. Respondents were selected from members of GATWU

who were then employed in the RMG industry in Bangalore. Respondents were drawn mainly from Shahi Exports as well as smaller companies in the Mysore Road area.

5. The information and analysis in this section draws on discussions held at the GATWU offices in April–May 2018 with Mr Mohan Mani, Mr Jayram and Ms Pratibha of the GATWU and in two focus group discussions with migrant women workers from Bihar and Orissa at Bomanhalli and Rajarajeswarinagar on 30 April 2018 and 18 May 2018.

6. The other two unions, GLU and the Karnataka Garments Workers Union, have around 2,000 members each.

7. Six of the largest RMG companies, Bombay Rayons, Gokaldas Exports, Gokaldas Images, Texport Garments, Shahi Exports and Sonal Garments, together employ one-third of the total strength of RMG workers in Bangalore. Bombay Rayons and Gokuldas Exports together employ 50,000 workers, with an annual combined turnover of INR 3,500 crores.

8. Trade unions in this sector increasingly rely on retailers' pressure and global NGO-led movements to ensure compliance. See de Neve (2009).

9. Among developing countries, FLFPR in Sri Lanka is 35 per cent and in Bangladesh 57 per cent. In the developed world, in the US, it is 56 per cent and in China 63 per cent, which makes the Indian situation starkly weak in contrast.

References

Alam, M. S., E. A. Selvanathan, S. Selvanathan and M. Hossain. 2018. 'The Apparels Industry in the Post Multi Fibre Arrangement Environment: A Review'. *Review of Development Economics* 23 (1): 454–74.

Basu, K. 2008. 'India's Dilemmas: The Political Economy of Policy Making in a Globalised World'. *Economic and Political Weekly* 43 (5): 53–62.

De Neve, G. 2009. 'Power, Inequality and Corporate Social Responsibility: The Politics of Ethical Compliance in the South Indian Garments Industry'. *Economic and Political Weekly* 44 (22): 63–71.

Deshpande, P. 2015. 'Garment Export Industry in India: A Comparison of Pre and Post-liberalization Performance'. *Arts and Social Sciences Journal* 6 (2).

Garments and Textile Workers Union (GATWU). 2012a. 'Survey of Women Workers in Bangalore's Garment Sector'. Mimeo.

———. 2012b. 'Wage Survey of Garments Workers'. Unpublished report, Bangalore.

Garments Sector Round-Table (GSR): Joint Fact Finding. 2013. 'A Write Up on the Qualitative Research on Various Stakeholders Groups of the Indian Garments Industry'. Unpublished report, Meta Culture, Bangalore.

Hashim, S. R. 2009. 'Economic Development and Urban Poverty'. In *Urban Poverty Report 2009*, by Ministry of Housing and Urban Poverty Alleviation, Government of India. New Delhi: Oxford University Press.

Mani, Mohan. 2012. 'Issues of Garment Sector Labour and the Global Supply Chain: Some Lessons from Bangalore'. Unpublished paper.

———. 2018. 'Critiquing the Statutory Minimum Wage: A Case of the Export Garments Sector in India'. ILO and the National Centre for Labour, National Law School of India University, Bangalore.

Menon, Rahul. 2019. 'Never Done, Poorly Paid and Vanishing: Female Employment and Labour Force Participation in India'. *Economic and Political Weekly Engage* 54 (19): 2349–8846.

Mezzadiri, A. 2016. *The Sweatshop Regime: Labouring Bodies, Exploitation and Garments Made in India*. London: Cambridge University Press.

Murayama, Mayumi. 2008. 'Female Garment Workers in India and Bangladesh in the Post MFA Era'. In *Globalization, Employment and Mobility: The South Asian Experience*, IDE-JETRO Series, edited by M. Murayama and H. Sato, 62–93. Basingstoke: Palgrave-Macmillan.

Murayama, Mayumi and Supriya RoyChowdhury. 2006. 'Survey of 200 Women Garment Workers in Bangalore'. Institute for Social and Economic Change, Bangalore, and Institute of Developing Economies, Tokyo, mimeo.

Narasimhan, T. E. 2019. 'Garments Exports Show Early Signs of Revival after Two Years of Decline'. *Business Standard*, 25 June.

Peoples Union for Civil Liberties (PUCL), National Law School of India University, Vimochana, Alternative Law Forum, Concern IISC, Manthan Law and Munnade. 2016. *Production of Torture: A Study of Working Conditions of Women Garment Workers in Bangalore and Other Districts*. Bangalore: PUCL Karnataka.

Ray, S. 2019. 'What Explains India's Poor Performance in Garments Exports: Evidence from Five Clusters'. Working Paper 376, ICRIER.

RoyChowdhury, S. 2010. 'Women in the Unorganized Sector'. In *Social Movements II, Concerns of Equity and Security*, Oxford in India Readings in Sociology and Social Anthropology, edited by T. K. Oommen, 161–74. Delhi: Oxford University Press.

———. 2015. 'Bringing Class Back in: Women Workers in Bangalore'. *Socialist Register 2015* 51 (*Transforming Classes*): 73–92.

———. 2018. 'Migration and Women Workers in the Export Apparels Industry'. Working Paper No. 12, International Labour Organization, New Delhi, and Centre for Women's Development Studies, New Delhi.

Sen, K., and D. K. Das. 2015. 'Where Have All the Workers Gone: Puzzle of Declining Labour Intensity in Organized Indian Manufacturing'. *Economic and Political Weekly* 50 (23): 108–15.

Statista. 2020. 'Work Participation Rate of Females across Karnataka in India 2011 by District'. 19 May.

Stotz, L., and G. Kane. 2015. 'Facts on the Global Garments Industry'. Clean Clothes Campaign, Amsterdam.

World Bank. 2017. 'Karnataka, Gender'. 20 June.

9

Conclusion

The dualities in the developmental trajectories of cities of the Global South have drawn much attention. Critical debates have been generated on processes which had earlier been assumed to be part of the normal stages in development. I highlight two themes here briefly: migration and technology. The positive links between migration, urbanisation and development shaped modernisation theory in the 1950s, advocating the replication of the western industrialisation/urbanisation model to developing countries. Modernisation theory, hegemonic for a long time, has perhaps been officially discarded in the social sciences. Nevertheless, the image of industrially advanced nations, which are predominantly urban societies in which the erstwhile rural communities became fully integrated into the structure of cities, continues to fuel the imagination of policymakers as well as development scholars and practitioners, located both in the west and in developing countries like India. On the other hand, continuing processes of cyclical movement of migrant labour have been seen to challenge the classical approaches linking migration and development. Patterns of circular migration suggest that points of rural origin left behind continue to provide, at least partially, not only the sustenance of those who stay back but also the security of those who migrate (discussed in Chapter 3), thus disrupting the universality/uniformity message of migration/urbanisation theories. Nothing has illustrated this more than the massive exodus of migrant labour from cities in India back to their villages during the recent pandemic of 2020.

The issue of migration is closely linked to changing technologies of production and shifts in the structure of urban labour markets. Saskia Sassen, in her landmark work on global cities, underlined the proliferation of sweatshops in exploiting undocumented immigrant workers. Her broader point was that 'even the most dynamic and technologically developed sectors of the economy generate jobs that can conceivably be held by unskilled foreign language workers' (Sassen 2005). She highlighted the massive arrival of immigrants from low-wage countries to global cities of the west. Cities in the Global South too have recreated that space of exploitation, as a middle and upper class of professionals greatly benefit from the technologically driven wealth generation of globally connected cities like Bangalore and New Delhi while simultaneously a low-paid class of service providers, most often migrants from rural areas, appear as housekeepers and nannies, watchmen and waiters, drivers and app-based delivery boys.

All of this does not take away from the fact that for millions, migration, temporary or otherwise, has been and will continue to be a way to earn a better livelihood, or a higher level of subsistence, than what is available in the rural areas. Nor is it contested that new technologies of production and services have created spill-over opportunities of earnings for unskilled and semi-skilled urban youth, which did not exist perhaps three decades back. Emerging critical perspectives on these processes, however, highlight that cities generate the vulnerabilities of unskilled labour, both migrant and non-migrant, which are sustained over several generations and which cast many shadows on the purpose and practice of urbanisation within existing policy paradigms.

The present work locates the city of Bangalore at the intersection of many of the dilemmas and contradictions that current developmental trajectories have posed. The study highlighted Karnataka's sustained high growth rates even as the state fell back on human development indicators; regional imbalances between an industrially developed south and a backward, predominantly agrarian north; and Bangalore's hyper growth as technology city, even as small cities and towns declined or stagnated and large numbers of the rural population remained tied to an increasingly unproductive agricultural sector.

The study of slum households in Bangalore (Chapters 5 and 6) showed that recently arrived, often cyclical migrants in new, fragile settlements in the city's peripheries were crowded into the construction industry, where wages were low, and living conditions and lack of access to health and education spoke of stark state neglect. In old, inner-city slums, we saw a more complex picture. Bangalore's so-called modern economy and its benefits had reached a limited number of households who worked in sales, at cash counters of malls and super markets, as receptionists in small offices, drivers, or app-based delivery boys. Salaries were low and unregulated, but there was a certain prestige to these service jobs. In contrast, large numbers remained confined to traditional low-paying, low-status occupations, such as head-load bearers, unskilled construction workers, street cleaners and waste pickers, flower sellers and domestic workers. We found that the passage to the modern service sector jobs were the result of fortunate circumstances in the lives of individuals or particular households, and of social contacts and networks, not of systematic state intervention in slums by provision of education and skills.

While infrastructure and civic services remained minimal, sometimes abysmal, the question of slum redevelopment through state-sponsored proposals of new housing projects had become locked in issues of slum resistance to redevelopment projects, multiple and competing layers of interests in slum land, structured by households of differential and hierarchical resources, as well as the increasing presence of private builders in PPP arrangements with governments. Where housing projects had happened, these were marked by the absence of civic services and other facilities like schools and clinics (Chapter 7). Finally, large numbers of unskilled rural and semi-rural women had found jobs in the global supply chain of RMG export industry, but were in informal, unregulated employment (Chapter 8). Overall, the study showed that the impact of globalisation on the city's working classes was complex and multi-layered. While many remained outside the ambit of the modern dynamic growth channels of the city's economy, others were inserted in it under disadvantageous terms and conditions, whether in manufacturing, as in the garment industry, or in the lower rungs of the service sector.

In an important recent work on Bangalore slums, Anirudh Krishna, studying occupations of slum households over three or four generations, found that sons were inclined to follow fathers and uncles into similar low-skilled informal jobs.

> Three generations in a city, accompanied by rapid economic growth, buoyed in the case of Bangalore by the software boom, have resulted in slum men and women working no longer primarily as carpenters or vegetable sellers but, instead, as salespersons, drivers, security guards, shop assistants, and secretaries. Further inquiries revealed that the majority of these new occupations are informal in nature and not highly paid.

Krishna concluded: 'Slum dwellers have been unable to connect with better opportunities' (Krishna 2013).

In analysing the causes of this malaise, Krishna mentions three main institutional obstacles to mobility in slums: the absence of adequate finance and credit, inadequacy of avenues to obtain job-related skills and lack of access to information. The absence of institutional support in the lives of slum residents, leading to serious deficits in information, skills and opportunities, as pointed out by Krishna, has been endorsed in the present study. Chapter 6 narrates the absence of intergenerational mobility in inner-city slums, linked to lack of access to education, skills and jobs.

Solomon Benjamin's work on Bangalore slums (discussed in Chapter 1) has underlined that poor groups and slum communities manage to make livelihoods out of robust local economies. They also negotiate on obtaining civic services and limited material benefits through their contacts with and the mediation of local councillors and corporators. While the idea of informal work has been widely deployed to describe urban poor livelihoods, Benjamin argues against viewing slums within a ghettoised economic perspective, or the poor in the informal sector as outside the larger processes of economic development. On this view, such a perspective misses out on understanding the role of the local in enabling the poor to shape their economies. Local governance structures, the lower bureaucracy as well as councillors and corporators facilitate these enabling processes. Thus, governance – or rather local governance – is central in this analytical framework (Benjamin 2000).

Local governance can indeed in principle make a difference to slum dwellers' lives. Beyond specific instances, how generalisable this thesis might be, or whether local governance can make a substantive difference to opportunities and entitlements of large and growing poor households, is not known. Entrenched economic inequalities frequently intermesh with lack of access to political power holders, even at grassroots and local levels, as the empirical chapters have shown in this book. Finally, while the informal sector is complex, rather than homogeneous and uniform, the connections between petty self-employment, casual/contract wage earners and poverty have been well established in the literature (as discussed in Chapter 3). The empirical material presented in this book (Chapters 5 through 8) narrate the story of that deprivation in multiple sectors and levels.

The present study has looked closely at the structure of the political economy and at informal work which frames the lives and livelihoods of the urban poor. Bangalore's growth from the mid-1980s onwards was predicated on the rise of IT, framed by the growing presence of private capital, the appearance of a large number of multinational companies and a galloping service sector. As a capital- and knowledge-intensive, globally competitive model of growth, and one that was dominated by the presence of IT, took hold of the city, organised employment in traditional manufacturing declined. The question of employment of unskilled and semi-skilled labour became the blind spot of policy, even as the state went all out in its support of these new technology-driven and private-capital-led domains of growth, in the backdrop of a withdrawing state sector, a fading SSI sector and declining labour-intensive industries such as textiles.

Framing these processes are the broader political economy features of the national economy and of Karnataka state (Chapters 3 and 4). The analysis highlighted disquieting features of Karnataka's political economy – large numbers of people remained attached to agriculture even as agriculture's share in GDP rapidly diminished. This is a feature of the national economy as well, drawing attention to the fact that the overall pattern of industrial and urban growth in India has been such that the expected scale of movement from agriculture to the cities has not happened. Despite the hype about cities, India's rate of urbanisation remains low compared to other countries at similar stages of development. In the case of Karnataka, although the rate of urbanisation has remained higher than the national average, the analysis draws attention to the narrowness of both the process of urbanisation – confined to large metropolitan cities, while smaller cities and towns stagnate – and of the nature of urban growth, which have made cities like Bangalore exclusivist epicentres of technology and consumption. Bangalore's growth as an IT hub has brought it an iconic status as India's Silicon Valley, attracting a technical/professional class of globally consumerist citizens. On the other hand, there is a clearly discernible wasteland outside, perhaps which can be imagined in terms of three ribbons: those who work in low incomes and poor working conditions in the city, somehow eking out a living from wages in low-end services, self-employment as petty traders, and so on; migrant labour in the peripheries whose only connection to the city is their daily journey to construction sites; and, in the background, a vast army of rural dwellers who remain tied to low incomes in agriculture, but who would not find a foothold in the city.

Overall, the material presented indicated that the trajectory of Bangalore's development since the mid-1980s has followed a path of wealth generation along channels that have been by and large unavailable to the city's underclass, as seen in a range of low-income occupations and low-quality settlements. That path is one where global competitiveness increasingly defined the purpose of industrialisation, while private capital, both domestic and foreign, and technology became the drivers of this model. In this process, factory jobs, historically where unskilled and semi-skilled labour have found a foothold, steadily disappeared. Work available to the city's underclass, in construction, garment factories and lower rungs of services, is marked by precarity and lack of regulation.

These features are of course closely linked to the political economy development in India in the present century, triggered by major policy shifts towards globalisation/liberalisation which occurred in the early 1990s. The absence of a broad base to globalisation-led growth is now increasingly acknowledged. At the same time, public policies remain by and large indifferent to the rough edges of urban deprivations. There is an emerging contradiction in state policies oriented to so-called welfare even as work and income issues are largely ignored. It is in this broad context that this book has presented the specific nuances of lower-class lives and livelihoods in Bangalore.

Political representation, agency and community

The trajectory, outlined here, of sustained deprivations and inequalities in a context of democracy raises the question of the urban poor's political agency. Woven through the chapters is a consistent theme that representative political structures at the city, state and federal/central levels have been inattentive to demands and needs of slum residents (Chapters 5, 6 and 7). Where new, peripheral settlements are concerned, recent and transient/circular migrants frequently do not vote in the city; they return to their villages at election time. As such, there is understandably very little interest of local politicians in these communities. In the inner-city slums, the two largest national parties, the BJP and the Congress, are represented at different levels. Political parties are tied to slum-based committees and associations in a structure of reciprocal support. However, local functionaries and slum leaders have confined themselves to events and issue-based support to households in times of need and have mediated between households and local corporators or even the MLA. No programme or discourse of slum renewal has emerged from grassroots leaders. On the other hand, while corporators and MLAs have been attentive to occasionally raised slum problems (water, toilets, sanitation), their direct interactions with slums remain confined to election times and do not translate to substantive programmes. The latter's interest in slum communities vary according to the size of the slum, whether the community is a significant political constituency, and whether the households are voters in the city or in their native villages or towns. The discussion in Chapters 5 and 6 also revealed that as political representation gets split along party lines at different levels (council, assembly and parliament), the engagement of politicians with slum-level issues lacks coherence. Apart from election times, and if at all then, slums have so far failed to generate the sustained interest or accountability of politicians.

There are multiple ways in which the agency of the urban underclass/slum residents has been imagined. Mainstream development discourse has used the word 'community' as an anchor in this context. Low-quality physical habitat and exclusion from basic services provide an intuitive basis for talking about a community, even though cleavages such as religion, ethnicity and caste divide such 'communities'. Within this discourse, the local community in slums and poor urban neighbourhoods has emerged as the principal organisation of the urban poor which can engage with NGOs and government agencies to create and maintain access to better civic amenities. Thus, according to the UK-based Department of International Development, best practices in development involve pilot projects in savings and housing programmes (building or improving homes, running credit schemes, setting up and maintaining public toilets, organising community-determined re-allotment, and so on) with local community management, supported by governments and international donors (Loughhead, Mittal and Wood 2001). In a review of case studies across Latin America, South Africa and South Asia, there is a clear indication that locally driven activities may not impact upon employment or income-poverty, but, at the same time, local infrastructural and civic deficits can be substantively addressed by local communities, their political representatives and state agencies (Satterthwaite 2002). The community discourse continues to be central in the development sector, and is echoed in the functioning of grassroots-level NGOs who work with slum committees and associations over specific projects.

How effective are community organisations in management of local projects in terms of sustained urban development? As is well known to development scholars and practitioners, much of the welfare work in urban slums happens through the organisational and fund-raising activities of NGOs in multiple sectors such as primary education, women's SHGs, health checks, literacy programmes, and so on. In energising and organising local slum communities in project-related welfare work, the NGO sector fills the great vacuum created by state inaction at multiple levels. On the other hand, there are countless instances of civic facilities (toilets, drainage and sanitation) and other services (*anganwadi*s, poly clinics and mobile clinics) being constructed in slums through civil society and NGO initiatives but which quickly degenerate and become dysfunctional due to lack of management, absence of attention of local governments and shrinking NGO funds. Community-level initiatives and management of civic projects often flounder on inadequate finances and lack of other kinds of support.

Perhaps more important than these operational failures of community management (and indeed there are success cases as well), what emerges from this approach is a partial profile of the urban underclass, seen as consumers of specific items, whether it is for housing, schools, water, sanitation or micro credit. Slum committees or local NGOS, conditioned by the discourses and project-oriented approach of government/donor/civil society, are tuned to claim specific items of consumption. The nature of such activism and organisation is fragmented, issue-based, limited in time and space and lack a sustained and consistent profile. In the paradigm of basic services/community management, as well as in the dynamics of the poor's claim making, the question of 'who is the urban poor' or why they are poor is almost entirely lost sight of, as the livelihood question – wages, employment, hours and conditions of work – never figures in this community/welfare discourse. Thus, the profile of the worker does not appear as a significant element in the identity of the urban poor. This is puzzling, insofar as much of urban deprivation remains predominantly a matter of low and insecure income, as has been shown in the empirical chapters in this book.

Land and urban activism

The task of imagining a collective platform for the representation of informal workers is of course hugely challenging. Given their dispersion and fragmentation across the economy, there is little by way of a unified set of issues, ideologies or politics that provides a framework of action to this sector of the workforce. In the absence of the workplace and a workforce potentially available for unified action on the classical issue of wages, working hours and conditions, informal sector theories have highlighted that petty producers, home-based workers, street sellers, and so on, continuously defend their rights to life and livelihood by staking a claim to urban land.[1] Land can be seen then, in this view, to have replaced wages as the most keenly contested urban resource. To what extent does such theorisation provide us with conceptual tools for thinking about organised political action of the urban underclass? What kind of representational and discursive politics would make this possible?

First, the nature as well as the scope of activism in the domain of land contestations are highly circumscribed in time, space and scope of activities. The urban poor's claim to city land remains tied to isolated efforts at claim staking, organised by NGOs and civil society associations, very occasionally supported by local politicians. Such claims frequently confront the hugely powerful government–real estate vested interest in urban land. Real estate developers gradually encroach on prime urban land which slum residents have claimed, as also insert themselves into the state machinery through seats in the state assembly or city corporation. These processes have been traced in Chapters 6 and 7.

Second, the dynamics of slum land contestation is frequently framed in the discourse of legality/illegality, wherein slum dwellers are often presented by the state as illegal encroachers. The demand for slum land, represented by NGOs and slum associations, typically rests on length-of-stay arguments, rarely challenging the legality/illegality paradigm by posing an alternative and specific vision of land redistribution (comparable to, for example, rural land reform). In other words, an alternative vision of urban planning based on lower-class claims to urban land has never emerged. Finally, it has to be noted that urban land is a finite resource, which cannot be reproduced. There are thus natural/physical limits to the redistribution of a finite resource.

The trajectory of new housing projects in selected slums (Chapter 7) showed that the state has differential responses to slum communities' demand for land, determined by relative strength of their political networks and resources, the history of their stay and claim on a particular piece of land, their fragile status as recent migrants to the city, and so on. Depending on these factors, the state may grant the elusive *hakku patra*, or property rights, may provide a set of apartments or houses on lease, or may relocate a slum community to a suburban locality. The chapter also revealed that in the case of older slums, resourceful occupants of larger houses and pieces of land may successfully resist the implementation of a layout and housing project which would take away their present access to larger plots. These dynamics surrounding new housing projects highlighted that the complex structure of interests in urban land deeply divided slum communities and precluded a unified stand on the issue of urban poor's right to land. At the same time, the civil society organisations engaged with these issues (the Koramangala Development Committee) had little impact and soon ceased to exist.

Slum communities do not represent a homogeneous collective, and competing and conflicting agendas and politics most frequently attend the ways in which slum communities engage with the state. The dynamics of civil society groups and NGOs which seek to represent and protect the interests of slum dwellers are deeply affected by these divisions within slum communities. Therefore, while urban land is indeed the most contentious issue in urban politics today, much more so than work and wages, it is still relevant to ask: can land replace work and wages as an issue that unites the urban poor?

Informality: the many faces of wage work

To turn our attention to the domain of informality is challenging. Informality, or the informal sector of work, provides the basic conceptual lens through which this book has viewed the world of urban work. Spread widely across a large number of informal occupations, ranging from pushcart or pavement selling, daily-wage work in construction sites to contract work in road cleaning, the world of informal work eludes theorisation, and does not offer an easy framework of activism. To what extent can we bring back the fragmented world of urban work within an overarching conceptual framework that might provide a clue to understanding the structure of urban poverty? Does the domain of urban livelihoods, in all its variedness, hold the possibility of such theorisation and a possible politics?

There is now an emerging convergence of opinion towards a matter-of-fact acceptance of informal work as a part of modern capitalism, and an inclination to conceptualise new models of organisations, essentially those which work with the state to bring some welfare to the urban poor. In Chapter 2, I have reviewed this dominant paradigm, wherein workers must no longer look to private employers for social security, but to the state, and the state is in fact responsible for bringing welfare to large numbers of workers who are outside the ambit of employment-related claims for social security or minimum wages. The anchoring principle in these arguments seems to be that democracy facilitates such negotiations – between the poor, their representative associations and the state. Representative associations have been seen variously as NGOs (Kanbur 2009), political society (Chatterjee 2008) or new unions (Agarwala 2013). A key theme that runs through this literature is that through supportive state policies and the facilitative role of NGOs, a significant element of inclusion of informal workers is possible. A critical literature on the weak impact of these mechanisms of political representation has emerged in this context, and discussed in Chapters 2 and 3. I note in passing here that the main points of criticism have been that despite a plethora of recent welfare legislation, the democratic state's commitment to the poor cannot be assumed in a context where the asset distribution remains deeply skewed, governance of welfare highly flawed and the political leverage of civil society representations of the poor severely constricted.[2]

On the other side of the scholarly divide, the classical capital–labour relationship is seen to structure informality. Scholars have stressed on the process of informalisation of the formal sector (contractualisation, outsourcing, home-based work), pinned to the changing institutional structure of industrial capitalism in the globalisation context, where global as well as domestic capital can take advantage of unregulated employment practices. In this scholarly genre, the work of Kalyan Sanyal has significantly furthered our understanding of informality. Sanyal (2007) distinguishes between two domains of the informal sector. The first are informalised employment practices, which are taking place within the circuit of capital as a result of globalisation, increased competition, and so on. Second, and Sanyal's point of departure from other works on the informal sector, is that given the declining rate of growth of jobs in the manufacturing sector, even informal wage employment in industrial manufacturing has declined. Thus, it is that huge numbers, displaced from agriculture and other traditional occupations, become self-employed; given the nature of their operations, minimum capital investment, use of self and/ or family labour, and meagre earnings at subsistence levels, their singular characteristic feature is that they are, for the most part, disconnected from the mainstream capitalist economy. On this view, proletarianisation, even in the sense of the existence of a reserve army, is not occurring. Sanyal, therefore, viewed the informal sector as not only disparate and diverse, but also in terms of a structured and permanent exclusion. By implication, the question of activism or representation of this class is deeply problematic.

Sanyal's arguments have been widely engaged with, and I mention here only two, written from the viewpoint of intermeshing of classes which has a bearing on the understanding of both the structure of informality and the potential for informal workers' activism in the current context. Bardhan (2018) pointed out that it is hardly true that proletarianisation is not happening in late development, giving the example of China's post-Mao decades of labour-intensive industrialisation as well as supply chain export sectors, which are also labour intensive, in many developing countries. In the Indian context, he points out that there are clear links between formal and informal manufacturing, through out-sourcing, subcontracting, and so on. Similarly, Gidwani and Wainwright (2014) point out that substantive links between the accumulation and need economies preclude a theory of exclusion. These links are not only economic; gender, race, caste and religion inform each of the sectors. Their more important point emerges from their discussion of the concept of abstract labour: 'Marx's argument that the emergence of abstract labour is specific to capitalism, because capitalism creates a social mechanism which takes the dispersed, disparate labouring activities of producers and forces them into the common metric of labour time.' On this formulation, they argue that those with labour power sometimes sell it within the accumulation economy, sometimes outside it, and as such there is no absolute expulsion as given in Sanyal's formulation of the formal–informal, inclusion–exclusion binary thesis.

The fluidity between the accumulation and need economies, between capital and non-capital, as pointed out by Gidwani and Wainwright (2014), provide a nuanced understanding of the reality in which urban working classes find themselves. More recently, the binary thesis has been further challenged: thus, formal and organised labour is seen as a transitory product of the post-war welfare state and social-democracy-inspired industrial relations. The self-employed become central to these theories, as petty commodity producers (Roy 2017), as a category of workers within contemporary capitalism. In an interesting intervention, Mezzadiri and Lulu (2018) point to the highly diverse and complex structure of non-factory labour in global supply chains, producing in small workshops or as individual home workers or as family units. Highlighting these diversities within informal work, Mezzadiri and Lulu deployed the concept of 'classes of labour' wherein the intermeshing of petty commodity production and wage labour appear in varying forms.

There is indeed constant flux in the lives of informal workers, as they move from wage labour to self-employment (for example, from garment factories to home-based tailoring work producing for garment factories), and the latter genre of self-employment remains crucially dependent on the accumulation economy represented by garment factories. The same person may decide to withdraw from her links to the garment factories and engage in part-time tailoring at home, working for neighbourhood customers. As these trajectories unfold in the life of one and the same person, her direct link – as factory labourer or home-based supplier – to the capitalist economy is important to understand, as is the tenuousness of those links, as she withdraws from wage work to engage in petty production.

Therefore, whether we look at workers who flit between self-employment and wage work, those who work for a daily wage, or those who receive a monthly salary, an element of incorporation-exclusion possibly provides a more nuanced understanding of the situation of informal workers compared to the almost formal concept of exclusion that Sanyal had given us. Informality or the lack of regulation is the element of commonality that may heighten our understanding of these livelihoods. Sanyal's most powerful contribution was to highlight the structured nature of exclusion of those who are in the category of petty self-employment. It may be possible, however, to broaden the notion of structured exclusion as we look closer at the reality of urban wage work through the lens of informality.

Indeed, to understand exclusion further, one might draw on the distinction between workers, linked to the modern economy through salaried wage (drivers, security guards, organised scrap collection, retail sale, garments exports, and so on) and others who remain tied to casual daily- wage work (head-load bearing, construction work, contract sanitation, or road- cleaning work, and so on). First, in the former, while a monthly salary may be available, there is hardly any regulation of the minimum wage in large swathes of the services sector, as in different levels of retail, hospitality, security work, and so on. And as Chapter 8 has shown, in the RMG sector, even though a Minimum Wage Board is in place, the process of arriving at the minimum wage, as well as its implementation, may be faulty and contested. In the second category, for construction workers, a daily minimum wage is state-stipulated, but is unavailable to large numbers of construction workers. Second, while salaried wage earners lack any kind of security of tenure and frequently work without a written contract, this precarity matches the vulnerabilities of daily wagers who may get work only two to three days a week. Finally, for unskilled or semi-skilled monthly wage earners, the availability of social insurance depends entirely on the employer, and is not mandated or enforced. On the other side, only a small percentage of construction workers are registered, and can avail of the benefits of the Building and Other Construction Workers Welfare Boards. The similarities across salaried and casual wage work, highlight that what marks these work arrangements is the broad framework of informality, where the wage is unregulated, regular work, security of tenure and social insurance are unavailable.

Scholars have therefore understandably moved beyond Sanyal's conception of pure exclusion, towards a more fluid understanding of the relationship between capital and non-capital, the need and accumulation economies. While greatly adding to our understanding of the complexity of informality in contemporary times, it is when these conceptualisations of labour turn on the question of the sites of exploitation in concrete instances and in the imagination of agency, that certain blind spots emerge. Even as petty production and its multiple vulnerabilities are a function of the broader capitalist system in which they operated, the fault lines of the conflict often remain concealed and difficult to work upon. The push cart vendor or the pavement seller's structural position vis-à-vis vis a vis global capital, the national and local state, remain in the abstract. Secondly, the idea of bringing the hugely varied world of petty production under unifying umbrellas of activism provide a formidable challenge. It could possibly be argued, in the light of the discussion earlier ('Land and Urban Activism'), that locating the petty producer – and land as his/her major resource – at the centre of the urban question to some extent weakens the possibility of imagining a political subject in the context of urban poverty, inequalities and deprivation.

At the same time, in these theorisations, the so-called proletariat recedes further into the shadows. What is being overlooked is the large and ever-expanding world of wage labour, now in the domain of the informal and unregulated. While petty production is central to the domain of the urban informal sector, ever larger numbers of the urban poor are wage earners in an increasing variety of employment relations which are informal and unregulated, varying from daily wage, contract work and apprenticeships to casual work in a variety of industries and services across the public and private sectors. This is certainly true of Bangalore where, as shown in Chapter 4, the share of regular salaried workers is much higher than the self-employed or casual wage earners. It is in fact the unregulated nature of salaried employment that constitutes the rough edge of urban vulnerabilities. It may then be necessary to trace the multiple and diverse ways in which the wage relationship manifests itself outside the formal economy. The insertion of this workforce, often at highly disadvantageous terms and conditions, in the evolving structure of manufacture and services in an increasingly globalised setting calls attention to the economic structures that anchor these inequities.

Re-imagining class[3]

Through the 19th and 20th centuries, the growing political salience of the industrial working class, via trade unions and social democratic parties, provided the ideological/political anchoring for redistributive justice and welfare in advanced industrial countries. The decline of that class began in the west towards the last quarter of the 20th century and its eclipse has continued through the early part of the 21st century. In part due to the structural changes in the nature of industrial capitalism, and in part the result of the rise of neoliberal, pro-market ideologies, the weakening of the industrial working class qua class, that is, its numerical decline, fragmentation and economic and political marginalisation, are by now established themes.

If an important dimension of post–World War II working-class politics in Europe and the UK had been its contribution to the carving out of the welfare state, in the current context welfare itself has become more broadly defined than workers' rights. Thus, we have new conceptualisations of welfare as citizens' rather than workers' rights (Castells and Portes 1989) or welfare as a whole range of claims of the disadvantaged, broadly defined (handicapped, elderly, women, children) (Pierson 1995). These kinds of theorisations, which reflect the reality of western welfare state dynamics, have moved the issue of welfare away from the working class or its politics.

Developing countries like India present a somewhat more complex picture for our understanding. One could say, the industrial workforce here has rapidly changed its profile in the last two decades without giving itself the benefit of the kind of sustained growth and empowerment that the working classes in the west underwent in the last two centuries. The industrial proletariat in India showed early signs of maturity and organised political involvement from the 1920s onwards in the nationalist movement. The role of the Congress Party in harnessing and co-opting this emerging workforce within the framework of the nationalist movement, and the subsequent possible loss of the movement's radical edge as it became incorporated within the larger Congress political project of national integration, has been widely written about. Similarly, the leadership provided by the left, and the subsequent splintering of this as the left itself became divided into multiple political formations, has been part of the explanation of the loss of unity and coherence in the working-class movement. In the period following independence, the organised sector of the industrial workforce became incorporated into the state system through a large public sector. Although tuned to collective bargaining and other structured negotiations, this workforce was nevertheless inward- looking and less interested in broader debates relating to policy than in economic gains and middle-class aspirations. The organised workforce in the large private sector could be similarly characterised.

Constituting only a small fraction of the country's workforce, organised industrial workers were weakly positioned to provide the political face to demands for justice and welfare, which, in any case, were subject to multiple interpretations by many and competing groups defined by cross-cutting social identities. The enlargement of the industrial working class as an expected consequence of economic and industrial development, along the western model, did not take place in India. In fact, as the era of economic reforms and globalisation took off, the decline of the organised industrial workforce began before its substantive expansion and empowerment could take place. The decline of organised manufacturing and the decimation of trade unions, on the one hand, and the growth of employment practices such as outsourcing, home-work and contractualisation, on the other, have created a workforce that is dispersed, being diversely located in varied activities that do not offer a ready or easy framework for collective action.

The space for welfare demands is now predominantly occupied by social (rather than economic) identity based organised groups; erstwhile class-based radical Marxist parties, such as the CPI-ML, now speak almost exclusively as advocates of social groups such as tribals while espousing economic demands such as land or livelihood. Trade unions, for the most part, see themselves as negotiators between labour and management in specific situations, rather than as espousers of workers' rights within the definitional framework of capital–labour conflict.

Chapter 8 provided a discussion of a faltering trade union movement in the RMG sector. Union activism in this sector is beset with low membership, a divisive internal politics, indifference of larger trade unions and a hostile state. In this situation, the main trade union in this sector, GATWU, nevertheless plays a pivotal role in the lives of workers through its sustained struggles around the wage issue. Union activism in other salaried informal sectors, such as construction, waste collection, hospitality and domestic work, battle similar issues at different scales of organisation and mobilisation. Trade union activism in these sectors remains isolated from the federal trade unions, as also unaffiliated to any political party, and these could be points of weakness or strength, depending upon the context or the perspective. While the present of such movements looks bleak, given the twin dynamics of right-wing politics and economics, the broader and expanding context of informal work makes it imperative to bring back a focus on wage-related activism as the starting point of a politics of informal sector workers.

It is widely recognised that the decline of organised industrial manufacturing led to the numerical and organisational weakening of the industrial workforce. In the context of India's employment crisis, well-known labour scholar Ajit Ghosh (2016) articulated a critique of the current developmental model. Drawing attention to the limits of service-led growth and underlining the potential of the manufacturing sector, he wrote: 'In history, remote and recent, countries at India's level of development experienced manufacturing-led and not services-led growth. For India, too, the time is ripe for a transition to manufacturing-led growth.' Whether this genre of critique can be absorbed and articulated through a broad-based labour movement at this time is an unknown.

For the immediate present, labour activism must remain focussed on the everyday issues of wages and livelihoods. Globally, informal work has emerged as the most common and most preferred work arrangement. The structure of informal work and the issues of informal workers' rights and of organisation have proved to be serious challenges for advocates of workers' rights across the world. According to a recent International Labour Organization report (2018), more than half of Latin American informal workers, which is 130 million workers, are not covered by social protection. These numbers are of course much higher in other parts of the developing world, and increasingly visible in the Global North as well. An international consortium of scholars, reporting on trade unions in the informal sector across the world, underlined that there is a strong correlation between globalisation and informal work as a survival strategy. Studying informal worker organisations across the globe, the report stated that even as traditional trade unions have moved beyond the boundaries of their older, established constituencies to fashion new approaches for non-standard, informal workers, collective bargaining remains the most important instrument in their lexicon. In this context, the report drew attention to the fact that issues relating to small-scale entrepreneurs possibly push trade unions beyond their comfort zones, even as they struggle with the issue of how best to work with the NGO sector, which had taken the lead in organising informal workers (Schurman and Eaton 2012).

These struggles are in a sense inevitable. Even as union and NGO activism with informal workers across the globe link local issues with national and global networks, the most intransigent problem of organising informal workers lies in the domain of imagining agency across diverse sets of employments, as this book has traced. And it is in this context that the analysis of informal work indicates that the task of developing a common language and grammar of worker activism could perhaps start at the level of informal wage earners, spread across sectors, employed under different terms and conditions, spanning salaried and casual earnings, but with the commonality offered by a wage relationship that provides an anchor for imagining new forms of state regulation and collective organising around bargaining, negotiations and resistance. What underlies this is the understanding that the commonality of issues around wage, contract, paid leave, working hours, pension, medical and other social insurance may provide bridges between, say, a retail worker in a city mall, a worker in an apparel export factory, a construction worker and a contract cleaner who works for the city corporation. These shared features of precarious work and related urban vulnerabilities could provide the initial steps towards conceptualising worker issues and organisation. Given the fluidity of lines between wage earners and self-employed workers, across economic and social identities, the eventual task of addressing the issues of self-employed workers would perhaps be defined by the dynamics of organisation of informal wage earners and the gains thereof.

Notes

1. See, particularly, Sanyal and Bhattacharyya (2009) and Chatterjee (2008). See also Benjamin (2000).
2. See John and Deshpande (2008), Baviskar and Sundar (2009) and RoyChowdhury (2017).
3. This section partially draws on my paper RoyChowdhury (2015).

References

Agarwala, Rina. 2013. *Informal Labor, Formal Politics and Dignified Discontent in India*. New York: Cambridge University Press.

Bardhan, P. 2018. 'Reflections on Kalyan Sanyal's Rethinking Capitalist Development'. *Economic and Political Weekly* 53 (21): 19–22.

Baviskar, A. and N. Sundar. 2008. 'Democracy versus Economic Transformation?' *Economic and Political Weekly* 43 (46): 87–89.

Benjamin, S. 2000. 'Governance, Economic Settings and Poverty in Bangalore'. *Environment and Urbanization* 12 (1): 35–56.

Castells, M. and A. Portes. 1989. 'World Underneath: The Origins, Dynamics and Effects of the Informal Economy'. In *Informal Economy: Studies in Advanced and Less Developed Countries*, edited by A. Portes, M. Castells and L. A. Benton, 11–37. Baltimore: The Johns Hopkins University Press.

Chatterjee, P. 2008. 'Democracy and Economic Transformation in India'. *Economic and Political Weekly* 43 (16): 53–62.

Ghose, Ajit. 2016. *India Employment Report*. New Delhi: Institute for Human Development and Oxford University Press.

Gidwani, V. and J. Wainwright. 2014. 'On Capital, Not-capital and Development: After Kalyan Sanyal'. *Economic and Political Weekly* 49 (34): 40–47.

International Labour Organization. 2018. 'Labour Outlook: Present and Future of Social Protection in Latin America and the Carribbean'. Geneva.

John, M. and S. Deshpande. 2008. 'Theorising the Present: Problems and Possibilities'. *Economic and Political Weekly* 43 (460): 83–86.

Kanbur, R. 2009. 'Conceptualizing Informality: Regulation and Enforcement'. IZA Discussion Paper No 4186, Institute for the Study of Labour, Bonn.

Kanbur, R., Martha A. Chen and N. Bali, eds. 2012. 'The CORNELL-SEWA-WEIGO Exposure and Dialogue Programmes: An Overview of the Process and Main Outcomes'. Working Paper 128865, Cornell University, Department of Applied Economics and Management.

Krishna, A. 2013. 'Stuck in Place: Investigating Social Mobility in 14 Bangalore Slums'. *Journal of Development Studies* 49 (7): 1010–28.

Loughhead, S., O. Mittal and G. Wood. 2001. 'Urban Poverty and Vulnerability in India'. Department for International Development, New Delhi.

Mezzadiri, A., and Fan Lulu. 2018. 'Classes of Labour at the Margins of Global Commodity Chains in India and China'. *Development and Change* 49 (4): 1036–63.

Pierson, P. 1995. 'The New Politics of the Welfare State: Reagan, Thatcher and the Politics of Retrenchment'. Cambridge: Cambridge University Press.

Roy, S. 2017. 'Informality and New Liberalism: Changing Norms and Capital's Control'. In *Labour and Development: Essays in Honour of T.S. Papola*, edited by K. P. Kannan, R. P. Mamgain and P. Rustogi, 215–34. New Delhi: Acedemic Foundation.

RoyChowdhury, S. 2015. 'Bringing Class Back In: Informality in Bangalore'. *Socialist Register* 51 (*Transforming Classes*): 73–92.

———. 2017. 'New Paradigms of Labour Relations: How Much Do They Explain'. In *Political Economy of Contemporary India*, edited by R. Nagraj and S. Motiram, 172–202. New Delhi: Cambridge University Press.

Sanyal, K. 2007. *Rethinking Capitalist Development: Primitive Accumulation, Governmentality and Post-colonial Capitalism*. New Delhi: Routledge India.

Sanyal, K., and R. Bhattacharyya. 2009. 'Beyond the Factory: Globalization, Informalization of Production and the New Locations of Labour'. *Economic and Political weekly* 44 (22): 35–44.

Sassen, Saskia. 2005. 'The Rise of Global Cities and the New Labor Demand'. In *The Mobility of Labor and Capital*, edited by S. Sassen, 126–70 Cambridge: Cambridge University Press.

Satterthwaite, David. 2002. 'Local Funds and their Potential to Allow Donor Agencies to Support Community Development and Poverty Reduction'. *Environment & Urbanization* 14 (1): 179–88.

Schurman S., and A. E. Eaton. 2012. 'Trade Union Organizing in the Informal Economy: A Review of Literature on Organizing in Africa, Asia, Latin America, North America and Western, Central and Eastern Europe'. Report to the American Centre for International Labour Solidarity, Transformation of Work Series, Rutgers University.

Index